DISCOVERING
the ENNEAGRAM

DISCOVERING
the ENNEAGRAM

An Ancient Tool for
a New Spiritual Journey

RICHARD ROHR
and
ANDREAS EBERT

Translated by Peter Heinegg

CROSSROAD • NEW YORK

This printing: 1998

The Crossroad Publishing Company
370 Lexington Avenue, New York, NY 10017

Originally published under the title *Das Enneagram: Die 9 Gesichter der Seele*
Copyright © Claudius Verlag, Munich 1989

English translation copyright © 1990 by The Crossroad Publishing Company

Printed in the United States of America
Typesetting output: TEXSource, Houston

Library of Congress Cataloging-in-Publication Data

Rohr, Richard.
    [Enneagram. English]
    Discovering the enneagram : an ancient tool for a new spiritual
journey / Richard Rohr and Andreas Ebert.
       p.   cm.
    Translation of: Das Enneagram.
    Includes bibliographical references and index.
    ISBN 0-8245-1017-8; 0-8245-1185-9 (pbk.)
    1. Spiritual life—Catholic authors. 2. Enneagram. I. Ebert,
Andreas. II. Title.
BX2350.2.R6413   1990
248.2—dc20   90-37110
                                        CIP

Illustration Credits: Collages on chapter opening pages by Reiner Schaufler; *The Dancing Dervishes* (p. 6), courtesy of New York Public Library Picture Collection; *"Noli me tangere"* (p. 60), with permission of Archiv für Kunst und Geschichte, Berlin; *Dorothy Day* (p. 80), *Milwaukee Journal* photo, courtesy of Marquette University Archives; *James Dean* (p. 91), © 1988 The James Dean Foundation, with permission of Curtis Licensing Corporation, Inc., Indianapolis; *Marilyn Monroe* (p. 91), with permission of The Kobal Collection, USA; *Doubt of Thomas* (p. 112), courtesy of New York Library Picture Collection; *Oscar Romero* (p. 129), with permission of KNA-Bild, Frankfurt/Main; *Deborah's Song of Victory* (p. 158), with permission of Archiv für Kunst und Geschichte, Berlin; *Jonah and the Whale* (p. 174), from *The Whale* © 1968 by Tre Tryckare; *Christ, the Lord of the World* (p. 225), detail from the High Altar by Friedrich Herlin (1466) in St. Jakobuskirche, Rothenburg/Tauber, with permission of Martin Lagois, Nürnberg.

For our mothers

Eleanore Dreiling-Rohr
Renate Apfelgrün-Mayr

The angels of darkness must disguise themselves as angels of light.
— *2 Corinthians 11:14*

I am afraid to drive the demons from my life lest the angels also flee.
— *R. M. Rilke*

Contents

Part III
INNER DIMENSIONS

Preface
A Mirror of the Soul

This book has an usual prehistory. Some years ago when I visited Richard Rohr, he was still the leader of the New Jerusalem family community in Cincinnati. At that time he introduced me to the Enneagram, an aid for self-knowledge and spiritual guidance of others that is quite ancient (though the West has discovered it only in our time). He was using it within the framework of pastoral care for his community.[1] At that point scarcely any literature had been published on the Enneagram.

In the summer of 1988 I had the opportunity of visiting Richard Rohr's new place, the Center for Action and Contemplation in Albuquerque, and to take part in a workshop on the Enneagram lasting several days. In the meantime the situation in the Unites States had completely changed. Since the mid-1980s a whole series of books on the Enneagram has appeared; many psychologists and theologians believe that the Enneagram is an excellent tool for helping people on their way to intellectual *and* spiritual growth.

After my return from the U.S. I hesitated whether I should translate one of the books that had already come out or instead work up Richard Rohr's unrehearsed workshop that I had taped. For various reasons I opted for the second approach: His style of lecturing, not always systematic but for that reason all the more lively (and sometimes scattered), may be a more appropriate way for communicating the Enneagram — which for a long time was passed down exclusively in oral form — than a strictly scholarly presentation.

In addition I have tried to integrate into the text the previously published literature on the subject, especially in the first and third parts of this book. Beyond that I managed to put together a series of my own personal experiences with the Enneagram. They too found their way into the book, turning it into a rather mixed affair (although the "I" in the description of the types, unless otherwise indicated, always refers to Richard Rohr). I adjusted some of the additions, changes, and completions by writing or calling Richard Rohr — an expensive but exciting proposition. Thus this book also, quite incidentally, testifies to ecumeni-

cal cooperation between an American Franciscan priest and a Bavarian
Lutheran minister.

While working on this book, I discovered that for some years work
with the Enneagram had also been going on in the German-speaking
world. A number of Jesuits and the order's lay organization, the Community of Christian Life (GCL) use the Enneagram with the Spiritual
Exercises and in the formation of retreat masters and "spiritual advisors." The final product is particularly indebted for its essential impulses
to my meeting with Hildegard Ehrtmann, who played a leading role in
this work.

Finally the book has been influenced by the feedback from the first
Enneagram conference that took place from March 31 to April 2, 1989,
in Schloss Craheim in Lower Franconia. Almost seventy participants,
including a number of pastors and therapists, subjected the whole concept to scrutiny. I wish to thank all those who offered extensive written
feedback that I was able to review in drawing up the final version of
this book. A young artist and theology student, Reiner Schaufler, did
collages for all nine types of the Enneagram that we have placed before
each of the descriptions.

I hope this book prepares readers to go on a suspenseful but also
laborious path of self-knowledge and conversion. I clearly see the danger
that a typological model as exciting as the Enneagram could be misused
for fitting oneself and others, in a cheap, flat fashion, into a scheme,
so as precisely *not* to grow, but to petrify. Real self-knowledge means
interior work that is strenuous and painful. Real change occurs amid
birth pangs. It takes courage to walk this path.

Many people fear the way of self-knowledge because they are afraid
of being swallowed up in their abysses. Christians know — if often only
theoretically — that Christ has gone through all the abysses of human
life, and that he goes with us when we risk an honest confrontation with
ourselves. Because God loves us unconditionally — with all our abysses
and dark sides — we do not need to dodge ourselves. In the light of this
love the pain of self-knowledge can be at the same time the start of our
healing and becoming whole. God loves us even when we don't take this
path; but then we are depriving ourselves of many fruits of God's love.

The masters and soul guides of all spiritual traditions of the West
and East have known that true self-knowledge is the presupposition of
the "inner journey." Teresa of Avila, the great Christian mystic, writes
in her masterpiece *The Interior Castle:*

Not a little misery and confusion arise from the fact that through
our own guilt we do not understand ourselves and do not know

who we are. Would it not seem a terrible ignorance if one had no answer to give to the question, who one was, who his parents were, and from what country he came? If this were a sign of bestial incomprehension, an incomparably worse stupidity would prevail in us, if we did not take care to learn what we are, but contented ourselves with these bodies, and consequently knew only superficially, from hearsay, because faith teaches us, that we had a soul. But what treasures this soul may harbor within it, who dwells in it, and what great value it has, these are things we seldom consider, and hence people are so little concerned with preserving their beauty with all care.[2]

The Enneagram is a mysterious model of the psyche that is not originally Christian, but probably derives from the Eastern tradition of Sufi wisdom. Nowadays in the Christian churches people are discussing how to meet the spiritual currents from the East that are having an increasingly powerful influence on the consciousness of the Western world. There are no formulas telling us which components of extra-Christian experience and knowledge can be integrated into the faith and which must be rejected. The "discernment of spirits" (1 John 4:1) is necessary, but not always simple: "Test everything; hold fast what is good" (1 Thess. 5:21). Paul at any rate trusts that his community is capable of deciding for itself what it can and cannot critically adopt. In principle Christians have at their disposal the whole world and everything in it that is good, true, and beautiful: "All things are yours...and you are Christ's" (1 Cor. 3:21, 23).

In their writings Paul and John the Evangelist took over and "baptized" without misgivings ideas and images from the current Greek philosophy of religion.[3] Thus John describes Christ as the *incarnate Logos* (John 1). The notion of Logos implies that there was a kind of world reason lying behind everything visible and ruling in it. Logos designates rather exactly what esoterics today call "highest consciousness." John did not hesitate to borrow this esoterically "encumbered" concept. He took fresh possession of it and used it to explain the Gospel to his contemporaries *in their language*.

It is striking how similar the analysis of human "interior life" reads among mystics of all the great religions, be the individual Jewish, Zen-Buddhist, Sufi, or Christian. We construct our "empirical self " above all in the first half of our life. This self can also be understood as the sum of our attitudes and behavioral mechanisms. The over-identification with such roles, habits, and character traits is the chief obstacle in our search for our (true) "self."

All mystical ways offer methods for unmasking this illusionary self —
whether through knowledge, asceticism, good works, or meditation. A
text from the German mystic Johannes Tauler brings the point at issue
into focus:

> When a person continually practices self-communion, the human
> ego has nothing for itself. The ego would be glad to have some-
> thing, and would be glad to know something and to will something.
> Until this threefold "something" dies in us, we have a wretched
> time of it. This does not happen in a day nor in a short time. Rather
> one must force ourselves to it, must become used to it with keen
> industry. We must hold out until it finally becomes easy and plea-
> surable.

In Christianity redemption from the false self is understood as a gift
of God's grace. What is disputed is the extent to which we ourselves can
prepare ourselves, dispose and open ourselves, or accommodate ourselves to this grace. The problem is generally resolved by saying that
we should pray as if it all depended on God and act as though everything depended upon ourselves. Paul already formulates this insoluble
paradox of the human struggle and God's grace in this way: "Work out
your own salvation with fear and trembling. It is God, for his own loving
purpose, who puts both the will and the action into you" (Phil. 2:12–13).

In the Eastern religions the participation of the person in redemption
is more strongly emphasized, although the aspect of grace — for example
in Buddhism — is definitely present. The flat assertion one hears from
many Christians that the Eastern ways are nothing but self-redemption
is untenable as such. It is true that there is more agreement among the
religions on their *analysis* of the question than on the answer. But Tauler's
text shows that even mystical practice — despite different concepts of
grace — is very similar.

We Christians are inclined to speak in glorious terms of how grace is
"alone efficacious," but we have no answers when people ask how they
can experience this redeeming, life-changing grace. Nowadays many
people report that the ways of the East have helped them to rediscover
their blocked-up faith or to deepen their prayer life. The dispute over
whether this is "legitimate" cannot be settled here. I myself, however,
am convinced that the ways God takes with people do not always match
the norms and laws of God's "ground crew."

In our century it was primarily the findings of the human sciences that
were "baptized" by Christian spiritual advisors, because they proved
useful for the understanding of psychic (and social) events. As early as

1927 the conservative Norwegian theologian Ole Hallesby borrowed the idea of the four temperaments from the Greek physician and philosopher Hippocrates and made it fruitful for Christian pastoral care.[4] In the last few decades Fritz Riemann's idea of the "basic forms of anxiety" has been accepted by Christian counsellors, even though Riemann developed his four types from his astrological speculation. Despite their "non-Christian" origin such models have proved useful instruments of pastoral care. I hope for the same results from the Enneagram.

At the end of the Bible the visionary John paints the picture of the new Jerusalem, the future City of God. In this context he describes how the peoples of the earth bring their gifts into this city (Rev. 21:26). This image implies that everything valuable in the thoughts and experiences of nations and religions belongs to the one God. We can gratefully lay claim to these gifts. Seeing others' gifts preserves us from absolutizing our own Christian experiences and turning them against others. There is much to be learned from the sages of the East. If we listen to their wisdom in modesty and humility, instead of knowing everything better in advance, they themselves will perhaps be ready to take our Christian testimony more seriously.

I believe that the Enneagram can help us to find a deeper and more authentic relationship with God — even though it was not discovered by Christians. Any of us with eyes can discover in it our own face, the face of God, and — as in an icon — the face of Christ. Paul writes: "Now the Lord is the Spirit, and where the Spirit of the Lord is, there is freedom. And we all, with unveiled face, beholding the glory of the Lord, are being changed into his likeness from one degree of glory to another; for this comes from the Lord, who is the Spirit" (2 Cor. 3:17–18).

As a mirror of the soul the Enneagram remains a tool that can be laid aside at any time. The Enneagram is not *the* answer, but one signpost among many. Signposts show the way, but we have to take the way ourselves. So I hope that no one will turn the Enneagram into a new absolute doctrine of salvation. Every form of self-knowledge, be it "only" psychological or "also" spiritual, like the Enneagram, belongs to the realm that Dietrich Bonhoeffer in his ethics called the "penultimate." Our knowledge, as Paul says, remains "partial." But until God perfects us and the world, it is better to recognize and do the partial work than to remain wholly blind.

ANDREAS EBERT

The following books on the Enneagram are cited in the text by the author's last name only.

Beesing, Maria, Robert Nogosek, Patrick O'Leary. *The Enneagram: A Journey of Self-Discovery*. Denville, N.J.: Dimension Books, 1984.

Bennett, J.G. *Enneagram Studies*. York Beach, Maine: Samuel Weiser, 1983.

Frings Keyes, Margaret. *Emotions and the Enneagram: Working Through Your Shadow Life Script*. Muir Beach, Calif.: Molysdatur Publications, 1990.

Metz, Barbara, and John Burchill. *The Enneagram and Prayer*. Denville, N.J.: Dimension Books, 1987.

Myers, Diana. *Using the Enneagram: Paths to Self-Knowledge*. Denville, N.J.: Dimension Books, 1982.

Nogosek, Robert. *Nine Portraits of Jesus: Discovering Jesus Through the Enneagram*. Denville, N.J.: Dimension Books, 1987.

Palmer, Helen. *The Enneagram: Understanding Yourself and the Others in Your Life*. San Francisco: Harper & Row, 1988.

Riso, Don Richard. *Personality Types: Using the Enneagram for Self-Discovery*. Boston: Houghton Mifflin, 1987.

Wagner, Jerome P. "A Descriptive, Reliability, and Validity Study of the Enneagram Personality Typology." Doctoral dissertation, Loyola University of Chicago, 1981.

Part I

The Sleeping Giant

A DYNAMIC TYPOLOGY

The Enneagram is a very old typology that describes nine different characters. It shares with many other typologies the crude reduction of human behavior to a limited number of character types.

Astrology connects its twelve types of human being to the particular constellation "under which" one is born. The Greek physician Hippocrates (d. 377 B.C.) traced his four temperaments (sanguinary, melancholic, choleric, phlegmatic) back to various "bodily fluids" (blood, black bile, bile, mucus). In our century Ernst Kretschmer (1888–1964) investigated the links between body build and the inclination to certain psychological troubles. He distinguished (1) pyknic (stocky), (2) leptosomatic (thin), and (3) athletic body types, and coordinated them with (1) cyclothymic (inclination to manic depressive illness), (2) schizothymic (inclination to schizophrenia), and (3) viscous (inclination to epilepsy) character features.

Carl Gustav Jung (1875–1961) starts from the assumption that there are three pairs of functions that are expressed differently in each person: extroversion-introversion; perception-intuition; thinking-feeling. In each case everyone prefers one of the two possibilities; this results in eight possible combinations or types, e.g., the extroverted-intuitive thinker or the introverted-perceptive feeler.

The American Isabel Briggs Myers discovered a further pair of functions (judging-perceiving; the inclination to quick, clear judgments and decisions as opposed to receptivity to many influences and kinds of information). Following Jung she developed the Myers-Briggs Type Indicator, a test that distinguishes among the sixteen types and is widely used in the U.S., both in industry and the churches.

Karen Horney (1885–1952) originally named three different ways that people try to overcome their fear of life: submission (turning to other persons); hostility (aggression against others); withdrawal (isolation from others). Later she developed a model pointing up four main ways by which people try to protect themselves from their fundamental anxiety: love, submissiveness, power, and distancing.

This last model matches to some extent the scheme worked out by the psychoanalyst Fritz Riemann (1902–1979), who was influenced by astrology. He assumes four basic human fears: (1) fear of nearness, (2) fear of distance, (3) fear of change, (4) fear of permanence. This results in the four basic types: schizoid, depressive, compulsive, and hysterical.[1]

All these models try — under different presuppositions — to account for the experience that people are different, but that some individuals are surprisingly similar to one another. Each one of these typologies can be compared to a map, which has the purpose of facilitating the overview of the realm of the human soul. Just as there are topographical, political, and street maps, so each of the typologies mentioned pursues a particular interest, and hence has its special strengths and weaknesses. None of them is all-inclusive. None of them is the thing itself. In the most popular of all typologies — the astrological — we have seriously to ask whether its presupposition, that there is a correspondence between the courses of the stars and the patterns of human destiny, is at all tenable. In any case, the study of a map never replaces the "experience" of the country itself.

All typologies have the disadvantage of necessarily neglecting the uniqueness, originality, and peculiar nature of the individual. There is no overlooking the danger of forcing oneself and others, for example, into the pigeonhole of a specific "sign" and in that way freezing the individual in place once and for all. The discovery of regular patterns in human behavior has meaning only when at the same time the possibility of change and liberation from the pressure of determinacy comes into view. This possibility, I believe, is opened up by the Enneagram.

The Enneagram is a very old map. Like other typologies, it describes different character types. But that is only the beginning. Beyond the description of conditions, the Enneagram contains an inner dynamic that aims at change. It demands a lot and is exhausting, at least when it is taught and carried out as originally intended. The Enneagram is more than an entertaining game for learning about oneself. It is concerned with change and making a turn-around, with what the religious traditions call conversion or repentance. It confronts us with compulsions and laws under which we live — usually without being aware of it — and it aims to invite us to go beyond them, to take steps into the domain of freedom.

The starting point of the Enneagram is the blind alleys into which we men and women stumble in our attempt to protect our life from internal and external threats. The person, as created by God, is according to the Bible very good (Gen. 2:31). This human essence (one's "true self") is exposed to the assault of threatening forces even during pregnancy and at the latest from the moment of birth. The Christian doctrine of original sin points to this psychological fact by emphasizing that there actually is no undamaged, free, and "very good" person at any point of an individual's existence. We are from the outset exposed to destructive powers and hence in need of redemption. Even the genetic material of which we are composed already contains programming that helps to shape our way of being from the moment of conception.

The external world meets the child first of all in the form of parents and siblings, later though comrades, teachers, the values and norms of one's group and religion, and whatever the general situation of society may be. Many different factors come together, stamp our inner life, and solidify into what in this book we call "voices." These voices can usually be summarized in short and pregnant sentences. They accompany us — often unconsciously — all through our lives and have a definitive effect on our behavior and character. Sometimes these voices have been verbally communicated to us ("Always be nice and say thank you!"). Sometimes they have taken shape as a reaction to the nonverbal overall behavior of the environment ("Don't come too close to me!")

The growing person reacts to these voices by internalizing certain ideals ("I am good, if I . . . "), developing avoidance strategies to escape punishment or other unpleasant consequences of "misbehavior," and by building up specific defense mechanisms. Guilt feelings always appear when one's own ideal is not arrived at or fulfilled. By contrast, real misconduct, which is manifested in the Enneagram in the nine "root sins," remains mostly hidden. Our "sins," in fact, are the other side of our gift. *They are the way we get our energy.* They "work" for us. The Enneagram uncovers this false energy and enables us to look our real dilemma in the eye.

We start from the assumption that we are stamped at once by our inherited structures and by influences from our environment. More important than exploration of the causes (the question of "whence?") is the question of the goal of our life ("whither?"). When Jesus and his disciples met the man born blind, they asked him: "Rabbi, who sinned, this man or his parents, that he was born blind?" Jesus answered: "It was not that this man sinned, or his parents, but that the works of God might be made manifest in him" (John 9:1–3).)

ANCIENT WISDOM REDISCOVERED

Don Richard Riso calls the Enneagram the "sleeping giant." The history of the genesis of the Enneagram is unknown, and hence invites speculation. It was probably used for centuries by spiritual masters and guides. The earliest roots go back, some think, over two thousand years. It is often suggested that it was further developed in the late Middle Ages by Sufi brotherhoods, but this itself cannot be proven.

The Dancing Dervishes

As far back as several hundred years after Muhammad's death there were pious Muslims — influenced by, among other things, Christian monasticism — who wished to lead a simple life. They often renounced all possessions and wore as a sign of asceticism coarse wool garments (*suf* in Arabic). Some of them set out as wandering preachers; others lived in spiritual brotherhoods and communities. Much in their way of life is reminiscent of the later Franciscans, who may themselves have been influenced by the Sufis.[2] As in the Christian mysticism of the Middle Ages there were also a strikingly large number of women involved in the Sufi movement.

Through prayer and meditation the Sufis wished to become deepened in God's love. The love of God was a central theme of the movement, as the prayer of the woman Sufi master, Rabia al-Adawiyya, shows: "O God, if I adore you from fear of hell, then burn me in hell, and if I adore you in hopes of Paradise, then do not give it to me. Yet if I adore you for yourself, do not withhold your eternal beauty from me!"[3]

The Sufis met vehement resistance from official Islam. Among the simple folk, however, they were soon revered as saints. Many of them had miraculous powers ascribed to them. Legends sprang up around the life and works of the great Sufi masters.

The Sufi brotherhoods included the orders of the dervishes and the movement of the fakirs (*faqir* = poor). Many of them still exist today, above all in North Africa.[4]

Among the Sufis there was a tradition of spiritual guidance that pursued the goal of helping people on the way to God. Over the many years in which the Sufi masters developed their methods, they discovered nine constant models for why certain men and women never find God, but always run up against themselves and their inner barriers and blockages.

In the fifteenth century Muslim mathematicians discovered the meaning of the number zero and developed the decimal system. In addition they discovered that a new kind of number comes into existence when one is divided by three or seven (periodic decimal fractions). These discoveries and the experiential knowledge of the dynamics of the human soul ultimately flowed together into the Sufi symbol of the Enneagram. They called it the "face of God," because in the nine points of energy that the Enneagram describes they saw nine refractions of the one divine love. The word "Enneagram" itself is a later invention, compounded from the Greek word *ennea* (nine) and *gramma* (letter, point.

The Enneagram consists of a circle, whose circumference is broken up by nine points, numbered clockwise from 1 to 9. Points 3, 6, and 9 are bound together by an equilateral triangle, while a hexagon of arrows

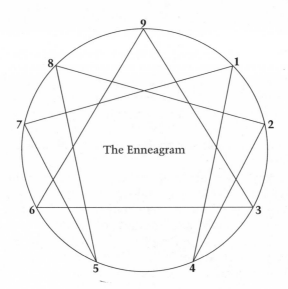

Figure 1: The Enneagram

runs through points 1, 4, 2, 8, 5, and 7, that periodic sequence that always comes up when any cardinal number (except 7) is divided by seven.

The wisdom of the Enneagram was evidently a strictly oral tradition that over the centuries was passed down from master to disciple. Echoes of the mathematic constructions of the Jewish Kabbala and the Kabbalistic doctrine of the tree of life are hardly mere coincidences. Clearly the Christian teaching of the seven deadly sins or "vices" (fourth century) has also left traces behind: All seven classic "capital" sins of church tradition can be found among the nine root sins of the Enneagram. The Enneagram's nine fruits of the spirit are almost identical to the nine "fruits of the spirit" cited by Paul in Gal. 5:22.

The Russian George Ivanovich Gurdjieff (ca. 1870–1949) as an adventurer and seeker in his early years had studied Tibetan, Sufi, Indian, and Christian mysticism; later he was active in the West as a (highly controversial) guru and spiritual guide. According to his own testimony he became familiar with the Enneagram in Afghanistan; he described it as a *perpetuum mobile*. Some of the dance and movement forms that he developed were based on the dynamics of the Enneagram. Gurdjieff compared the Enneagram to the legendary "philosopher's stone" and stressed that in occult literature it was "nowhere to be found. . . . So great an importance was assigned it by the enlightened that they considered it necessary to keep knowledge of it a secret."[5] As a psychological typology the Enneagram played a subordinate role in Gurdjieff's work. He never worked out a description of the nine personality types.

What is today the best known form of the Enneagram as a "mirror of the soul" is mainly derived from Oscar Ichazo. Ichazo claims to have learnt this system from Sufi masters in Pamir (Afghanistan), *before* coming upon Gurdjieff's writings. In the 1950s and 1960s he taught in La Paz (Bolivia) and Arica (Chile). In 1971 he came to the United States.[6] Psychiatrist Claudio Naranjo from the Esalen Institute in Big Sur, California, took over Ichazo's model and developed it further. A series of American Jesuits, above all Fr. Robert Ochs, ran into the model in Naranjo. After years of testing and theological scrutiny many Jesuits decided to take over the Enneagram as a means of spiritual direction and as a model for the work of the Exercises. I first learned it in the early 1970s from a Jesuit spiritual director.

Since the mid-1980s a series of books have appeared about the Enneagram, partly growing out of the work of American religious orders with the Enneagram and partly stemming from psychoanalysis or humanistic psychology.

It has been shown that the Enneagram can be harmonized with the religious (and Christian) tradition of spiritual guidance and human counseling. At the same time it seems that the Enneagram is also compatible with many of the findings and experiences of the modern social sciences. Hence it could build bridges between spirituality and psychology. In its current stage, however, the Enneagram does not claim to have become "hard science." Clinical investigations, it is true, are under way in America, but they are only just beginning. So long as no statistical material is available, supported by recognized investigative methods, we prefer to content ourselves with understanding the Enneagram as a "wisdom" access to the inner world. The form in which we pass it on at present represents a synthesis of very different insights and findings. It works with subjective associations and adopts a series of symbolic elements that may in fact "add up," but this cannot be proved by scientific methods and can be tested only in practical experience. Most of what I say here is based on my many years of teaching and spiritually directing people through the Enneagram. Once I "knew" because a Jesuit taught me; now I know by experience and confirmation.

The combination of psychology, spirituality, and theology may disturb those who insist on a "methodically clean" separation of these apparently so different approaches to reality. On the other hand, the traditions of Eastern and Western wisdom and spiritual guidance, to whom this book is indebted, have always stressed the solidarity of psychological or character-related maturity and religious-spiritual maturity.

In these traditions a phenomenon that we take for granted would be unthinkable, that is, individuals who are analytically experienced and psychologically "integrated," but spiritually atrophied; or religious persons whose character defects and psychic instability are palpably clear.[7] Truth is one. Science and spirituality will confirm one another.

BREAKTHROUGH TO THE TOTALLY OTHER

If you get rid of the pain before you have answered its questions, you get rid of the self along with it.

— Carl Jung

With the Enneagram, the question is: Why in our encounter with life do we human beings so often keep running up against ourselves, instead of making a breakthrough to God, to the Totally Other? In our present-day egocentric society we are especially inclined to remain stuck in our own thoughts or feelings. For this reason God today is for many Westerners, unless they have dismissed God completely, nothing more than a projected image of themselves: a God that we desire, fear, or culturally need. The encounter with the Totally Other, with the Not-I, does not take place for most people.

The old masters and spiritual guides wanted people to acknowledge their blockages and prejudices, or their mode of perception, that is, their habitual way of viewing and shaping life from an egocentric viewpoint. In the Middle Ages such compulsions were called passions. Unrecognized "passions" allow me to take my limited perspective for the whole. The task is to recognize these passions and to learn how to perceive the larger reality, to a certain extent, objectively. We have to press through to God, the Totally Objective, who for Christians is at the same time the Wholly Subjective, since Christ has committed himself to our world and become part of it. We must be capable of meeting someone other than ourselves.

I have been working for years with many different movements within the Church, and I am convinced that we urgently need such an encounter. Many people in the Church speak readily in the name of God. In most cases one can recognize that there isn't much more coming forth from them than their own temperament, their prejudices, or their "politics." This is one of the reasons why the Christian religion has lost so much credibility. Many contemporaries can no longer take it seriously. They meet religious men and women who are not integrated and who even leave the impression of being egocentric, pursuing their own goals, while speaking gloriously of God as their source and center.

The Enneagram can help us to purify our self-perception, to become unsparingly honest toward ourselves, and to discern better and better when we are hearing only our own inner voices and impressions and are prisoners of our prejudices — and when we are capable of being open to what is new.

Ignatius Loyola (1491–1556), the founder of the Jesuits, developed a method for spiritual direction that is highly sensitive, both intellectually and psychologically. His Exercises lead to a way of practice. They discover the cases in which the soul is trapped and instruct the exercitant in the "discernment of spirits," of those inner and outer voices and impulses that continually influence us. The discernment is carried out in three steps: One has (1) "to sense the various stirrings that occur in the soul"; (2) "to recognize them," that is, to understand their origin and goal, and to make a judgment on them whether they lead constructively to the meaning-goal of my life, or destructively lead away from it; and (3) to take a position toward these stirrings, that is, to accept them or reject them.[8] The goal of the Exercises is to find ways to Christian freedom. This is made possible through a personal relationship with Jesus in which we are able to hear Christ's call to our life and are ready to enter his service.

The Enneagram is a related tool, and in some ways a still more precise tool, for reaching this goal. That is one of the reasons why a series of retreat masters have begun to introduce the Enneagram alongside the traditional Ignatian Exercises.

A CARDINAL WAKES UP

When I was first "initiated" into this system, we were enjoined not to pass it on in writing nor to reveal the method behind our "insight." I have to confess that later I felt somewhat dishonest because of this. It has happened on several occasions that someone would come to pastoral counselling with me, and that after a while — thanks to the Enneagram — I would be able to comprehend the energy or the "mode of perception" of this person rather precisely. While I put my "secret knowledge" to work, my interlocutor would think: "Richard Rohr is reading my soul like an open book, and focussing exactly on my problem. Just where did he learn that?" Thus I seemed almost clairvoyant to this person, as if I had the gift of "seeing the heart" attributed to a number of saints in the Church.

This is how the Enneagram was originally used. It was a form of esoteric knowledge that spiritual guides could pass on orally and personally.
I am still convinced that the Enneagram is best taught orally and personally. For some reason, the nine energies and styles are better picked up
through human voices and encounters than through the written word.
Even this book is a concession to demand and merely a complement to
an Enneagram workshop or a set of tapes. When we Americans got hold
of it, what had to happen did happen: a few years ago we began to write
it down. Now one book after another appears. Particularly in the Catholic sphere the method became a triumphal procession of books, tapes,
and retreats. Perhaps this is because we Catholic religious have the time
and the retreat houses to deal intensively with such things. From this
source it has been passed on to interested people from the most varied
levels of society who are searching for answers. Now that the secret is
no longer a secret, I would like to contribute to presenting it as authentically and helpfully as possible. Perhaps the time is ripe for this "sleeping
giant" (Richard Riso) to awake and make its ancient wisdom accessible
to those seeking it. This knowledge was obviously not "invented" by
anyone, but was intuitively grasped and "discovered" by seekers and
admirers of the truth in the course of millennia. Presently Oscar Ichazo
is trying to claim that the nine points are original to him and were taught
him "by an Archangel while he was on mescaline." This has been hard
for the Arica Institute to substantiate in court.

To this date I have never passed on the Enneagram to a group that did
not — for one reason or another — find it fascinating. This is astonishing
because its approach is negative. The Enneagram does not have the
intention of flattering or stroking the "empirical ego." Rather it aims to
support efforts to let go of or render unnecessary what Thomas Merton
calls the "false self." I know no other means of achieving this more
directly than the Enneagram.

Recently I gave a retreat for twenty bishops. On the first day I lectured
on contemplative prayer. The bishops sat there and listened — after all,
they were bishops and had to pay attention when the subject was prayer.
You could see that they were there, but not really "into" the subject. I
don't recall what I told them on the second day, but in any case they were
a little more involved. On the third day two bishops took me aside and
said: "You have to teach the group the Enneagram." I really didn't have
that in mind, but both the bishops insisted, "Why not?!" So I started on it
the next morning. Some participants, including two cardinals, suddenly
woke up and became all ears. From this point on until the end of the
retreat they were both personally touched and fascinated by the many
pastoral implications of the Enneagram.

The Enneagram brings into focus an essential truth of our soul. It does this in a way that most people have seldom or never experienced. I have presented it to many groups of priests and leaders throughout the country and the world, among whom there were some very tradition-conscious and conservative pastors. But I haven't found a single priest who thought there was no truth to the Enneagram: its wisdom is compelling. That is why I don't need to push it or try to sell it. It's truth is its own best authority.

A SOBERING AHA-EXPERIENCE

When I first learned about the Enneagram, it was one of the three great conversion experiences of my life. I felt that a veil had fallen away and it became clear what I had previously been up to: I had always done the right thing (that's a key concern for us ONEs) — but for false motives. It's embarrassing to recognize and admit this. That is why the rule of thumb holds: Whoever is not humiliated has not yet found his or her "number." The more humiliating it is, the more one is looking the matter right in the eye. Anyone who says, "It's wonderful that I'm a THREE" is either not a THREE or hasn't really understood what I'm saying about type THREE. I remind the reader once again that my intention is to unmask the ego and to point to its dark places: the Enneagram uncovers the games we find ourselves tangled in. It will initially be experienced as embarrassing and perhaps shameful. For a time there will even be a loss of energy and motivation until we relearn how to operate from truth.

I believe that this tool and the insights it makes possible allow me to proceed with directness while not appearing direct or confrontative. If for example I had stood up at that bishops' retreat and said to one of the bishops, "You are opinionated and dogmatic," the man would have probably hit the ceiling. Nobody likes to be called "opinionated and dogmatic." But if I say, "ONEs — like me — are often opinionated and dogmatic," I am putting the shoe on my foot first of all, and then I can invite my audience to do the same. Things go a lot more easily this way.

I teach the Enneagram because it's effective, and I hope that it will awaken the soul and lead us to greater spiritual freedom. In the Enneagram God is calling us all to let go of our false self because we don't need it any more. I hope that all who look their "dark side" or "root sin" in the eye will experience something of the freedom that I tasted when I began to face the fact that I am a ONE. Even though I will never finish this job, I still sense that my life has become much more serene. Because

I am confronting the lie of *my* life, my absurdity, my ridiculousness, I can also call others to do the same.

If others can put up with me, then I really have no reason not to be patient with them. I have my dark side, as we like to call it nowadays, and others have theirs. I know that since I recognized my compulsion I don't make so many snap judgments about others. And when I do, I only half believe them!

Many people are afraid that such systems lead people to pigeonhole one another. To be honest this is exactly what *will* happen with the Enneagram in the beginning. That's the only way to learn it. Anyone who has appropriated it will spend some time going around and seeing everything under the aspect of ONE, TWO, THREE, FOUR, FIVE, SIX, SEVEN, EIGHT, NINE. In most cases, however, people at first make many mistakes, because only certain external features of a type catch the eye. You have to live and deal for a while with the Enneagram until you press past these external traits to the energy behind them. Humor will help here. To be able to laugh at yourself can be just as liberating as to cry over yourself. I've done both while working with the Enneagram. Once we have reached this depth of self-knowledge we can confidently put aside the tool.

More than anything I hope the Enneagram will help us to become more loving. If this happens, the goal for which we were made will have been reached. I hope it will make us more capable of loving other people, loving ourselves — and loving God. To realize this was at the time both a sobering and a very beautiful experience: God has known all this all along. God knew that I am a ONE. God knew that I keep on doing the right things for false or at least very mixed motives. God knew that it was for very mixed motives that I became a priest, committed myself to celibacy, founded the New Jerusalem community, went to Albuquerque — but this is normal. It's humiliating and at the same time liberating to know that God knows and that God even uses our sins for God's own purposes! That is truly good news.

Anyone who discovers the power and truth of the Enneagram inevitably comes to a baffling conclusion: God makes use of our sins. (I deliberately use the word "sin," although I know that to many readers it sounds moralizing and religious. I'll come back to that later.) The realization is at once a source of shame and freedom. For it is an experience of unconditional love, as we have probably never known it before. It is, above all for perfectionist ONEs like myself, an upsetting experience when it becomes clear to us that God loves something imperfect — namely me! If God is capable of loving and using something imperfect — and God, so to speak, never gets anything else, because there's nothing perfect in this world — then this opens up an enormous area of freedom and gratitude. God becomes very desirable and loveable.

With the Enneagram it's a matter of inner work that can lend authenticity to our spiritual path. At the same time the Enneagram creates new difficulties. Many of our unquestioned assumptions and subliminal solutions can no longer function as they used to. For the Enneagram shows us, among other things, the dark side of our gifts.

GIFTED SINNERS

The Sufis thought — although this doesn't sound very enlightening at first — that people are destroyed by their gifts, because we identify ourselves too much with what we can do well. Earlier it was made clear to us that we were destroyed by our sins. That makes sense, but the problem is a little more subtle. In the religious language of my novitiate days they would have said: we're fixated on our gifts. We're too fixated on what naturally has come our way. We have a natural prejudice and natural models of behavior, a natural standpoint, a natural passion. We develop all these especially during the first thirty years of our life. We enjoy them and take credit for them whenever possible. We all "do our own thing" whether we admit it or not.

That is why it's not very meaningful to deal with the Enneagram at an early stage of life. In our younger years we join in the game. This is probably right and necessary. Used too soon the Enneagram takes away our energy before we have really grasped it or seen its destructive potential. Jesus once said to Peter — without intending any reproach: "When you were young, you girded yourself and walked where you would" (John 21:18). In the younger years the ego has to be built up and strengthened, but the false self that we build is also the false self that will have to die. It's a "catch 22."

At some point in our thirties, or at the latest at forty, this game gets increasingly dull. Up till now everything has worked so well; we can give people the impression that we are "cool" or "witty" or "the serious, reflective student." Up till now we have fixated on this self-image and led others to fixate on it. It was a help in demarcating our own ego from the environment. But the more such ego boundaries harden and the more anyone identifies with this sort of self-image and tries to maintain it at any price, the more clearly we also see the other side of the coin. If someone has kept busy up to the age of forty cultivating this image, it will be very difficult to change. At the same time it becomes increasingly clearer that the whole thing no longer adds up. What was pleasure becomes a burden. That is why this moment in the middle of life harbors the great opportunity — as difficult as it is — to reflect critically on what has previously been achieved, to change, to become more mature, wiser, and more integrated. Now the following words of Jesus take on a here-and-now flavor: "But when you are old, you will stretch out your hands, and another will gird you and carry you where you do not wish to go" (John 21:18.)

After many years in pastoral counseling I am convinced that there is nothing on which people are so fixated on as on their self-image. We are literally prepared to go through hell just so we don't have to give it up. Ernest Becker rightly calls it "character armor." It determines most of what we do or don't do, say or don't say, what we occupy ourselves with and what we don't. We're all affected by it. The question is: Do I have the freedom to be anything else than this role and this image?

My experiences in pastoral care and counselling have shown that the Enneagram can help people break loose from their attachment to their self-image: "Let go! You don't need that! You mustn't lock yourself up in the limited image you have of yourself. It's not important whether you're this or that. You are God's beloved son, God's dear daughter — that's the crucial point." Our identity is created primarily through a relation; it's not something that we have to encapsulate, protect, define, and defend.[9] The Enneagram can help us to disarm internally, to give up the defense of the self-image that we ourselves have created.[10]

In this sense it's precisely our gifts that can be our undoing. We identify ourselves excessively with what we're good at. Two years ago I took a contemplative sabbatical. It was clear to me that I had to stop giving talks — at least for a year. Some of my friends used to tease me that there wasn't a single idea of mine that hadn't been taped. And it was true. Even now as I say this, the cassette recorder is running again. I told myself: "This is simply too much. You're not a speaker and a preacher. You're Richard. Do you even know who this Richard really is? Do you know this son of God, this person, this man Richard — without these public masks and images that you assume? People confirm them and you dance around with them. Can you live without them?" This is true for all of us: Can we live without the names we have made for ourselves? Can we let God name us and let that suffice? The more public they become, the more dangerous it is for us. But we all play these roles: we can defend them as feverishly at home in our little world as on the public stage.

Thus every gift that we get excessively fixated on paradoxically becomes our sin. Our gift and our sin are two sides of the same coin. To meet your gift, you must, so to speak, chew, eat, and digest your sin. *Eat it, taste it, feel it, let yourself be humiliated by it!* This is very traditional church teaching. Every Mass begins with sins being called by their name. In the liturgy this is called the Confiteor (confession of sins) or penitential rite, and is often performed in a rather antiseptic fashion. I promise that in dealing with the Enneagram we won't proceed antiseptically. We want to feel, acknowledge, and see how exaggerated, excessive, and absurd our false energy really is. If we own and take responsibility for our darkness, if we feel how it has wounded ourselves and others, how it has allowed us not to love and not to be loved — if we do that, I promise that we will become alert to the other side, to our greatest gift, or rather, the actual depth of our gift. Our gift is our sin sublimated and transformed by grace.

For that to be possible, we have to be cleansed and purified. Our old self, our old Adam, our old Eve, must die. This really feels like death. Since there are no romantic trimmings here, it's no fun. It hurts. You will feel as though everybody else is laughing at you. You'll get the feeling that you have loused up and ruined many relationships, once you realize how many people you have used exclusively to build up and maintain your own self-image (the ones who didn't play along we generally banned from our circle of friends).

This is the reason why in the spiritual life our enemies are our best friends. That is why Jesus' command "Love your enemies" is so important. When we keep the enemy outside the door, when we don't allow the not-I to enter our world, we'll never be able to look our sin or our dark side in the face. Men and women who get on my nerves, who threaten me and cause me anxiety, need not become my bosom friends, but they have an important message for me. I hope that the Enneagram will help us to become more receptive to this message. We shall see that there are certain types who are by nature threatening to us because they discover our game — or because they don't need our game. They don't need anyone who's always as right as I am. There are people who understandably don't like my cassettes because there are already too many moral voices at work within them, pointing an accusatory finger at them. And then along comes Richard Rohr and tells them how they can become better and more perfect. There are people who say, "My mother kept doing that with me. I don't want any more of it." They probably need someone else to lead them through their pain. Fortunately, the Church is the "Body of Christ." There are many members with differing gifts (see 1 Corinthians 12). There are people who in their present situation find my way of doing things downright poisonous, and others will find it exactly what their soul needs. I hope you are the latter!

THE TRUTH IS SIMPLE AND BEAUTIFUL

Recently I saw a video cassette about the origins of the universe. It said that Einstein was continually searching for a universal theory of energy. He was convinced that the explanation of the world and its causes ultimately had to be simple and beautiful. He was also of the opinion that a "world formula" that wasn't simple and beautiful couldn't be true either. This is, as it were, the credo of a great scientist. It can be carried over to the Enneagram: the Enneagram imparts an experience that terrifies and challenges us, but that at the same time is simple and beautiful. The Enneagram is beautiful because it shows us as small, partial, and broken people. It is simple because finally we no longer need to act as if we were more than that — and we see that we're all in the same boat. We all play our games, cultivate our prejudices and our unredeemed vision of the world. There is nothing complex or gimmicky here. It is clear and compelling once the insight comes.

That is why we must accept our gift in order to see our sin — and we must accept our sin in order to recognize how gifted we are. We have to limit our gift, otherwise our sin becomes a trap — while we call it "virtue." This too is traditional church teaching. Thomas Aquinas and many Scholastics said that all people choose something that appears good. No one willingly does evil. Each of us has put together a construct by which we explain why what we do is necessary and good. That is why it is so necessary to "discern the spirits," as it says in 1 Corinthians 12:10. We need support in unmasking our false self and in distancing ourselves from our illusions. For this it is necessary to install a kind of "inner observer." Some people talk about a "fair witness." At first that sounds impossible, but after a while it becomes quite natural. Basically we're dealing with a part of ourselves that's honest — not only in the negative sense, but in the positive too. It tells us, for example,"You really love God and long for God. You are good. Stop butchering yourself so brutally. You are a daughter or son of God. You can feel compassion." This helps us to distinguish moralizing from real morality, guilty feelings from real guilt, false pride from genuine strength. With the self-knowledge that the Enneagram gives us, we are not dealing only with the acknowledgment of sin. We are also, and in the end, primarily letting go of what only seems good in order to discover what in us is much better, what is really good. We remember the awesome line from St. Paul: "The angels of darkness must disguise themselves as angels of light" (2 Cor. 11:14).

Particularly those of us who have grown up in a religious environment will find it usually takes a while before we can hear these positive voices. We have all the negative voices inside us, continually passing judgment: "Good, better, best, right, false, holy, mortal sin, venial sin, meritorious, unworthy, damnable" — and the steps in between. In some ways there is nothing more difficult than working with religious people! We have such a moralizing bent that we're incapable of accepting reality and directly confronting it. That is why we can learn so much from creation spirituality, from native American Indian spirituality, and from Franciscan spirituality (at its best moments). Here creation, nature, the earth — in other words everything that *is* — has the word! We religious people, on the other hand, are inclined to come along with our prefabricated conclusions, Bible quotations, and dogmas so that we don't even have a need of perceiving "what is" and the present moment. I hope that the Enneagram can help us to accept what is. It helps us to get rid of moralistic value judgments, because it shows us how exaggerated and even self-serving they are. The Enneagram shows us our compulsive styles of attention, which prevent us from experiencing reality holistically and honestly.

PEOPLE ARE CREATURES OF HABIT

> Sometimes you have to go miles out of your way to go a very short distance correctly.
>
> — Edward Albee

Our sin and our unredeemed perception of the world is also, paradoxically, the method that helps us to get to our driving force. When we commit our "favorite sin," we are "fully there." That is why we can't simply "give it up": it belongs to the specific way that we give our life a goal and a direction. It belongs to the survival strategy that we adopted as children. We're all creatures of habit. We keep retreating back to where we feel at home. That is why we will find our gift where our sin is, while fully aware of the danger and nature of addiction.[11]

Once again I take myself as the starting point. We ONEs are idealists and perfectionists. We want the world to be perfect. We get irritated — most of the time in secret — because the world isn't perfect. At the same time we are geniuses at our own form of perception: more clearly than others we see what is not in order. But it can be hell to live with this. When we are left to our own devices, we become hypercritical faultfinders, people whose presence eventually gets on others' nerves. Too much of a good thing is a bad thing. This is true of all nine types: excess turns all gifts into curses. That's why we have to ask, how can we set all our energies free so that they serve life and truth? As a ONE I get to my own energy by seeing how stupid and absurd this world is. Through anger (my capital sin) I actually tap my best source of energy. But right away I have to have enough freedom to tell myself, "That's enough, Richard!" I have to be able to break away from myself: "Yes — but ... Yes, all that makes sense, but you're exaggerating. You're right, but you're also wrong!" This is the function of the "objective observer." I can perceive something, but I can also detach myself from it. In this way responsibility and freedom work constructively together. The English poet put it well:

> Spirit of the fountain, spirit of the garden,
> Suffer us not to mock ourselves with falsehood
> Teach us to care and not to care
> Teach us to sit still
> Even among these rocks
> Our peace in His will
> — T. S. Eliot, "Ash Wednesday"

I believe that there are few people who have this freedom. I frequently meet ideologues, above all in religious circles: right, left, liberals, conservatives. They are all determining life from their own control tower within. Sometimes this gets tiring to themselves and others. You wonder whether community is possible with people if they all wear their own character armor so much and thus identify with their preconceived ideas and feelings. Their feelings in the meantime have become dogma, particularly among "progressives": "I have an absolute right to my feelings!" they say. But as Etty Hillesum notes:

> Life and human relationships are full of subtleties. I know that there is nothing completely absolute or objectively valid, that knowledge must seep into your blood, into your self, not just into your head, that you must live it. And there I come back to what one should strive after with all one's might: one must marry one's feeling to one's beliefs and ideas. That is probably the only way to achieve a measure of harmony in one's life. [12]

The Enneagram says: "No! Your feelings are too numerous and too dominant. You have to get to the point where you can break free from your feelings. Otherwise in the end you won't have any feelings; they'll have you." I find this in many of the religious groups with whom I work: monastic communities, bishops, religious, lay people, parish councils, charismatics — all people who think they have the truth all to themselves. If you look more closely, you notice that with all of them there's too much ego, no capacity for self-divestiture, no freedom to relativize their own selves (and their own "thing"). But sometimes you meet people who do have this inner free space, who are free from themselves. They express what moves them — and then they can, so to speak, take a step backward. They throw themselves into things, but you notice that they don't think they've got a corner on the truth market. Without this kind of "inner work," which consists in my simultaneously putting myself forward and relativizing myself, real community and real spiritual growth are not possible. We must both care and not care at the same moment for the moment to be free. For example, how many church communities and political action groups come to grief because of the incapacity of the participants to deal with one another in this way. Learning it is really hard work. I probably can't expect it from politicians, but I do expect it from people who know God. Its the work of detachment, self-emptying, and "fasting" — the disciplines taught by all great world religions.

OBSESSIONS

We are all trapped. We each have a false sense of what our sin is and what our virtue is. We all avoid true reality because it would destroy our illusions about ourselves. Health is actually unfamiliar and uncomfortable to all of us when we are into our compulsiveness. In that stage we "reasonably" avoid it. Health doesn't seem to "work" because we are getting all our quick but pseudo energy from unhealth!

When with the help of the Enneagram we discover our own pitfall or capital sin, we will note that it functions like a sexual obsession. Young men supposedly have sexual thoughts and feelings every ten minutes. It's just the same with Enneagram energy: it determines us at least every few minutes. Perhaps that is why it is called "passion." Every few minutes my ONE energy kicks in in some way. The ONE sticks in my limbs, in my bones, it's in my blood, it's my skin, my breath, my way of thinking, my mimicry, my gestures. For example, I can't speak without wanting to gesture sharply and clearly. That's a ONE. I can't *not* be that way. I shall always remain a ONE.

Some people want to avoid a real turnaround by saying, "I'm a little bit of a FOUR, a bit of a SIX, and a bit of a TWO." That's right, of course. We all have a little bit of everything in us. We take part in all the current social games and commit all the nine capital sins. But the crucial point is to see our one big sin. There is a key dilemma, a main root of evil, a favorite vice with each of us. It colors and flavors all areas of our life. This one pitfall is so present in our life that we ourselves do not recognize it. We were always this way. That's why we have to try to catch it "on the run," so to speak. As a rule, it's a great aha-experience. At a stroke it becomes clear why I've done everything that I've done. I see that I had the same behavior models in place even as a little boy. It's the crimson thread that runs through my life. It explains everything: why I chose certain friends, why I played a certain sport or why I didn't, and so on. To recognize and concede this is actually very humiliating. "I did all the right things for the wrong reasons!"

When we are trapped in our compulsion and our false energy, we aren't free — that's obvious. Then we let external events and other people determine our energy. They decide whether to reward or punish us for our behavior. We don't really live from within ourselves. We are not centered but live on the circumference of our own lives.

THE WAY TO SELF-WORTH

The unconditioned love of God frees us to experience ourselves as "authentically strong." I use "strength" in this connection in the intellectual-spiritual sense of the word. A biblical definition of the Holy Spirit is *dynamis*, which means "power" or "strength." We are talking about the power that gives us the certainty that God is drawing us and that we are associated with the Holy. The "devil" or evil is interested in keeping us from this experience of our power and dignity. (Perhaps we should best speak of dignity or worth, because everything connected with might, strength, and power has often been misused by the ego and hence is subject to misunderstanding.)

The Enneagram can lead us to this inner experience of dignity and power. Indeed, it unsparingly shows us our mistakes. All too often we do the right thing for false motives. But if we "eat all the way through" our compulsion and emerge again on the other side, then we stand before the depths of our self. There we find a purified passion, a chastened power, our best and true self. Tradition has called this place the "soul," the point where man and God meet, where unity is possible and where religion consists not only of words, norms, dogmas, rituals, and visits to church, but becomes a genuine experience of encounter. I am glad to pass on the Enneagram because it's one of the few tools that helps people awaken the true self so clearly. Through the Enneagram I have seen many people *really change*. For self-worth is not created; it is discovered.

WRONG WAYS AND WAYS OUT

The Enneagram defines its nine human types on the basis of nine "traps," "passions," or "capital sins." These sins can be understood as defense mechanisms that have been inculcated and built up since our early childhood as a way of coming to terms with our environment.[13] Alongside these sins, "innate" characteristics also play a role. We don't know how much is nature and how much is nurture. Neither the one nor the other is a license to hurt ourselves and others. It is amazing that with the nine sins of the Enneagrams we are dealing with the classic seven capital sins of Scholastic tradition (pride, envy, anger, sloth, avarice, gluttony, and lust), to which two further sins are added, deceit and fear, both absent from the Church's traditional teaching. I shall return later on to these "denied sins" and the implications of the denial for Western society.

One further but important warning is in order. Don't "go after" your sin directly or *you will only confirm your stance and your willfulness!* You will attack your ONE in a ONE way. You will "understand" your FIVE as another FIVE trip. You will try to "succeed" at being a redeemed THREE. The key is to recognize, name, and let go.

The oldest lists of "root sins," out of which the "actual" sins and vices spring, like branches from a tree, go back to the fifth century. John Cassian names eight root sins: incontinence, fornication, avarice, anger, sadness, bitterness, vanity, pride. Gregory the Great sees pride as the actual primal sin, radiating out into seven other sins: haughtiness, envy, anger, avarice, unchastity, incontinence, and laziness. Ultimately, however, the "sacred" number of seven became accepted.

In medieval literature and painting the seven capital sins played an important role (*Purgatorio* in Dante's *Divine Comedy*, the Parson's Tale in Chaucer's *Canterbury Tales*, Hieronymus Bosch's allegories).

The conceptual shift from "root sin" to "mortal sin" is an interesting one. The original notion of "root sins" starts off from the presupposition that the "tree of sin" has some main roots from which all other sins proceed. The Scholastic concept of the "mortal sins" deals, by contrast, more with the consequences of sin. Early on, Paul labels death the "wages of sin" (Rom. 6:23). In the Letter of James the way runs from temptation through sin to death: "Let no one say when he is tempted, 'I am tempted by God'; for God cannot be tempted with evil, and he himself tempts no one; but each person is tempted when he is lured and enticed by his own desire. Then desire when it has conceived gives birth to sin; and sin when it is full grown brings forth death" (James 1:13–15).

Finally in the First Letter of John the distinction is drawn between sins that lead to death and those that do not lead to death: "If anyone sees his brother committing what is not a mortal sin, he will ask, and God will give him life for those whose sin is not mortal..." (1 John 5:16). This distinction makes allowance for the fact that there are lesser character defects and mistakes that are tolerable, and gross forms of misconduct or misspending one's life that are highly destructive for interpersonal, communal life.

The danger of this teaching on sin is that only provable violations of moral norms are called "sin," while the depth dimension of sin remains largely ignored. That is why the Reformers renounced the distinction between "venial" and "mortal" sin. In their view the problem is not the individual sins, but the sinful person. The root sin is unbelief. The actual, concrete sins are its fruits. This justified criticism of the Roman Catholic understanding of sin had unhappy consequences in Protestant practice: Protestants understood themselves quite generally as "sinners," but this term lost all concrete content. Personal confession fell almost completely out of use. But it is not just the mere fact of our being sinners that is mortal. In our actual misdeeds death becomes concrete: they destroy our psyche, our relation to God, our interpersonal relationships, nature and the world. That sin "brings forth death," as the Letter of James says, is more than an image. Our lack of moderation kills animals and forests, our aggressiveness and fear has led to gigantic arsenals. The poor pay for the envy and greed of the industrialized nations with their death. In our laziness we allow all this to go on, as if it didn't affect us. In this book we use the old term "root sin" to stress that we need a radical renewal ("radical" comes from the Latin *radix*, root).

For many people today the concept of "sin" has become hard to understand; the very word stirs up resistance. The Church's doctrine of sin has often been used to intimidate people. Above all the Church's sexual morality was for centuries presented in a way that led to a thousand anxieties, repressions, and guilt feelings. This might suggest that we should just do without the term altogether. But that produces a vacuum that can't be filled. It strikes us as more meaningful to learn to understand the term in a new way. The German word *Sünde* contains the root *sund* (English "sunder"), which means "cleft" or "separation." The word "sin" means our separation from God, but also from our fellow human beings and from ourselves. Sins are self-chosen hardenings and fixations that prevent the energy of life, God's love, from flowing freely. This can be illustrated in particular by fear, the "root sin" of type SIX. Fear is not a moral category, but it can stand between us and God, and thus hinder love and life. In this book we understand by "sin" the self-erected blockades that cut us off from God and hence from our own positive potential. Although our sin is in part a reaction to other people's guilt, we cling stubbornly to it and in this sense are responsible for it. Along with the compilations of the capital sins, from time immemorial there have also been "catalogues of the virtues," some of which are in the Bible. The list of the seven messianic gifts of the spirit, which goes back to Isaiah 11:2 (awe or respect before God, piety, knowledge, strength, counsel, insight, wisdom),[14] and the enumeration of the nine fruits of the spirit (Gal. 5:22: love, joy, peace, patience, amiability, kindness, fidelity, gentleness, and self-control) belong to these. The best known and classic list of virtues is the combination of the four "cardinal" virtues of Aristotle (justice, prudence, temperance, and fortitude) with the three "theological" virtues from 1 Corinthians 13:13 (faith, hope, and love). These are the seven virtues that have often been represented allegorically in art (for example on the Fountain of Virtues before the church of St. Lawrence in Nuremberg). Geoffrey Chaucer (ca. 1340–1400), the greatest English poet before Shakespeare, offers an especially interesting list in the Parson's Tale from the *Canterbury Tales:* Chaucer starts from the assumption that there is at least one specific virtue as an antidote to every capital sin. Here we find ourselves closer to the Enneagram, particularly since each corresponding pair is practically identical in the Enneagram and in Chaucer.

The Parson's Tale in Chaucer's *Canterbury Tales* is a kind of guide for confession. God would like all people to be saved, but there are many ways to the heavenly city. One of these is repentance, the mourning for one's own sins and the intention of sinning no more. There are venial sins and mortal sins. Mortal sin consists in loving a creature more than God. For each of these sins there is a remedy, a healing virtue. Humility helps against pride, true love of God helps against envy, the remedy for anger is patience, laziness is overcome through fortitude, avarice through compassion, gluttony through sobriety and moderation, lechery through chastity. Confession and the reparation of guilt through alms, fasting, and bodily pain lead to eternal joys in heaven.[15] In what follows we shall speak about the "fruits of the spirit," when we describe the specific gifts or "virtues" of the nine Enneagram types. This biblical concept (Gal. 5:22), like the concept of the root sin, is connected to the image of the tree of life. Jesus says: "A good tree brings forth good fruit" (Matt. 7:17).

THE THREE CENTERS: GUT–HEART–HEAD

The nine types of the Enneagram are presented in this way for the sake of instruction:

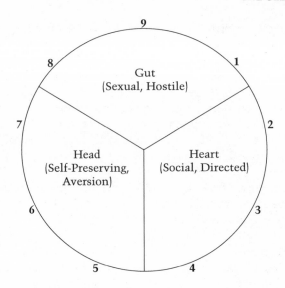

Figure 2: The Enneagram and the Three Centers

The group that embraces EIGHT, NINE, and ONE is called the group of the *gut-people*. Their center of gravity lies in the underbelly, where the "raw material" of our existence is located. It is immediate, spontaneous, felt, and intuitive. (In this sense we also speak of the "sexual types." They don't filter reality through the brain or heart first.) TWO, THREE, and FOUR are the *heart people* or the social types. Finally FIVE, SIX, and SEVEN form the group of the *head people* or the self-preserving types.

The German-American psychoanalyst Karen Horney originally started from the assumption that there were three types of people, or three "neurotic solutions," to life's conflicts: one group turns away from other people, the second group develops a hostile attitude toward other people, the third group turns toward other people.[16] Gurdjieff distinguished three areas of the body: head, heart, and gut, ascribing to them different kinds of intelligence: the mental center to the head, the emotional center to the heart, the sexual, instinctive, and motivational center to the gut.[17] In each person one of the three areas predominates.

There follows a first crude overview of the three centers. Even at this early point it becomes clear that those who belong to these different groups of people need different conversions to become whole.

Gut Center

The gut types[18] correspond to Horney's "hostile types." The bodily center that rules them par excellence is the digestive tract and the solar plexus. Gut people react instinctively. The ear and nose are their pronounced sense organs. In a new situation they first say: "Here I am, deal with me," or "How come *I'm* here?" Life is for them a sort of battle-ground. They are concerned, often unconsciously, with power and justice. They have to know who is in charge. They're mostly direct, openly or surreptitiously aggressive, and demand their own "territory." Gut people live in the present, remember the past, and hope for a lot from the future. When things go badly for them, they usually blame themselves. "I did it all wrong. I'm bad." Gut people are consciously or unconsciously ruled by aggression. On the other hand, they have little access to their anxiety and fear. They are hidden behind a façade of self-assertion. Outwardly they strike most observers as self-confident and strong, while they can be inwardly tormented by moral self-doubts.

Meditation practices in which they are entirely by themselves and in their body (e.g., Zen) are best for them. Since they follow many "instinctive" impulses, part of their task in life is to turn their generic loving into love that is specific, concrete, and entirely personal. They are always assaulted by what Annie Dillard calls "the scandal of particularity."

Heart Center

The energy of the heart people (Horney's "directed types") moves toward others. The world of subjective feelings is their domain; their theme is intersubjective relations. The heart and the circulatory system are their body center. With them touch and taste are especially pronounced. Just as gut people are concerned with power, they are concerned with being for others. They have a hard time staying by themselves. In a new situation they ask, "Will you like me?" or, "Whom am I with?" They see relationship as a task to be mastered. In this they are concerned (often unconsciously) with prestige and image. The positive side of this is that they usually have a well-defined sense of responsibility. They are ruled by what others think about them and often think they know what is good for others. While they cultivate their solicitude in an exaggerated manner, they repress their aggressions and hide behind the façade of kindness and activity. Outwardly they strike people as self-confident, gay, and harmonious, inwardly they often feel empty, incapable, sad, and ashamed.

Forms of piety that are bound up with social warmth and security (communities of prayer) have a special attraction for heart people. But they must learn above all to be alone and to pray so that they are neither noticed nor rewarded by their fellows. Jesus' saying, "When you pray, go into your room and shut the door and pray to your Father who is in secret; and your Father who sees in secret will reward you" (Matt. 6:6), holds true especially for them. Their access to God often takes place by way of a community experience. At some point, however, the walk into the wilderness and solitude must follow, so that their prayer life does not become self-deception. Dietrich Bonhoeffer says, "Whoever can't live alone should beware community."[19] Since heart people think they can do everything themselves, they have a hard time accepting redemption as a pure gift. The task of their life consists of turning the many things they hope for into real hope.

Head Center

The group comprising FIVE, SIX, and SEVEN is "top heavy." These are Horney's "aversion types." Their control tower is the brain. Their head energy, according to Horney, is an energy that draws them away from others. In every situation the members of this group first take a step backward to reflect. They're governed by their central nervous system and are in the first instance eye people. In a new situation they first want to see their way: "*Where* am I?" or "How does all this fit together?" They see life first of all as a riddle and a mystery. They have a sense for order and duty. Their attitude is as a rule unaffected and objective. They act only after thinking things over, and they go about their business methodically. In emergencies they reproach themselves for being stupid and unworthy. While their anxiety is exaggerated, they hide their feelings, especially the tender ones, often behind a facade of objectivity and uninvolvement. Outwardly they often seem clear, convinced, and clever; inwardly they often feel isolated, confused, and meaningless.[20]

Their prayer life can strike outsiders as dry, abstract, mere fulfillment of duty, but head people can actually develop warm feelings on the roundabout path of clear thoughts. Concrete forms of meditation (e.g., looking at pictures), in which they can pick something up, also appeal to these people. Head people above all have to take the step from thinking to acting, and the step from isolation to community. The second part of Bonhoeffer's saying applies to them: "Whoever is not in community, let him beware solitude."[21] Their life task consists in turning their many doubts and partial truths into faith that doesn't remain in the head, but is a confiding of the whole person.

THE NINE FACES OF THE SOUL

The main part of this book is made up of the profiles of the nine Ennea-gram types.These are rough sketches, sometimes caricatures. Exaggeration serves to make the outlines stand out boldly like woodcuts. Not all features fit all members of a specific type. This is an opportunity for readers to test themselves in the mirror of these representations. Even the insight, "I'm *not* like that" belongs to genuine self-knowledge.

The same goal is pursued with the presentation of certain symbols: To each type a series of *animals* is traditionally assigned. Real or generally recognized essential traits of these animals match the nature of each of the types. Certain *nations* also stand for individual characteristics of the types. This is not intended to stir up ethnic prejudices. Rather the purpose is a playful approximation to each form of energy, and hence this should be taken with a grain of salt. *Symbolic colors, biblical figures, saints and personalities from history, literature, and the current world scene* will likewise be mentioned, so that the picture may become more colorful and may take on flesh. These examples correspond to the authors' subjective estimate and make no claim to be authoritative. On the contrary, we would like to stimulate our readers' imagination, to make their own voyages of discovery in the polyvalent world of symbols, and to find their own illustrative material for each energy. It would be stimulating, for instance, to use the Enneagram to give names to the forces at work in fairy tales or to relate certain styles of music and dance to the nine energies.

In the following section we will begin with type ONE — we could also begin somewhere else — and go round the circle, noting how the characters and their distinguishing features change in a continuous flux. This leads us to recognize that every type also contains traits of both its neighbors, the so-called wings. We will occasionally touch on this important phenomenon; and we will address it in more detail in connection with the nine sketches.

So far there has been no proven test for tracking down one's own type. That's why it makes sense to begin by reading through all nine descriptions. To some it will immediately be clear where they are "at home." Others will need a little time. A good criterion is the following: if in reading the description of a type I get uneasy or even humiliated, it could be that I'm on home ground. The actual recognition is often bound up with a clear aha-experience, which, however, sometimes doesn't set in until after weeks and months and after conversations with others. After the recognition and humiliation of the false self, normally there will be experienced a sadness, a grief, a sometimes significant disorientation or loss of energy. This is necessary and good!

Each of the nine types embraces a broad spectrum, which we can imagine as a continuous scale that runs between the extremes of "un-redeemed" (immature, unhealthy) and "redeemed" (mature, healthy). Unredeemed persons — regardless of their type — are trapped in them-selves. Luther spoke of *homo incurvatus in se ipsum*, of "man bent in on himself. " Such people take themselves too seriously and think their perspective is the whole picture. Some have called the Enneagram "the face of God." They believe the way of redemption is to become ever more capable of leaving behind our own standpoint to look upon life from a vantage point different from our own narrow vista, once learned and now fixed. The step beyond our own point of view can easily be taken if we simply go to the "wings," or the neighboring numbers. But the further we distance ourselves from our own number, the harder it gets. The energies that have settled on the other side of the circle at first seem to us far away and alien. But how enriching it could be if we could get there internally, if we were capable of putting on all nine pairs of shoes and to look on reality from all nine sides. Then we would con-template the world, as it were, with the eyes of God. People trapped in themselves are not capable of that.

At the other end of the spectrum we find the redeemed personality. None of us has gotten there. We all find ourselves somewhere between the two poles. The older and more mature we get and the closer we come, let us hope, to God, the Center, the more we will move toward the redeemed side. To do that, by the way, we don't need to know the En-neagram. The Enneagram articulates something that spiritually mature people have always intuitively grasped and practiced.

I have already met many people who are on a believable inner path, who have done their spiritual homework. You sense it immediately when you meet such a liberated, complete person. We are all capable of, and called to, integration and holiness. One great help is some form of com-munity. Solitary fighters will rarely undergo real conversion, because they isolate themselves from those other voices and truths that challenge and complete their own perception.

Redemption is the work of God's grace, which takes place without our doing anything when we let go and expose ourselves to a greater reality, when we let ourselves fall into the Center: into God. And when we have done that, we will notice that even the letting go and opening of ourselves was not our achievement. We were "seduced" by Someone.

Unlike other authors we dispense with giving the nine types binding names as well as numbers. The classification by numbers makes it clear that we are not dealing with evaluations. All nine types are "fallen men and women" and in need of redemption to become all the more what they already are in the heart of God. No type is better or worse than the rest. All nine are in need of redemption and all nine have unique gifts that only they can bring into the community.

It has already been said that we consider the encounter with the Enneagram meaningful above all for people in the middle years of life and afterward. By this time some already have so much "inner work" behind them that many of the compulsions mentioned in the description of the types no longer fully apply to them. At around ages twenty to thirty as a rule we live according to "what works for us," which is why our behavior becomes compulsive. It is often helpful to ask yourself, "How was I when I was a young adult?"

Each of the descriptions is broken up into four sections: after a detailed *overview* of the type in question we present its specific *dilemma*. This includes its peculiar temptation, to deal with the conflicts of life in some quite definite way; the root sins, avoidances, and defense mechanisms of each type are described. The first references to the gift or fruit of the spirit, which presents itself as the opposite side of the root sin, are likewise found in this part. Finally the pitfall or fixation of each type is explained. This means its ingrained model of perception and action, the unconscious life program. In a third step there follow *symbols* (animals, countries, colors) and *examples* from literature, history, and the Bible. At the end there are references to what can contribute to each type's *conversion and redemption:* the specific calling or invitation to change, special life tasks, and suggestions for commerce with oneself. The presentation of one or another saint, that is, persons who — without denying their type — put their gifts to creative service of life, rounds out the last part. At the end of this book you will find all the terms summarized in a series of tables.

Part II

The Nine Types

TYPE ONE:
The Need to Be Perfect

Overview[1]

ONEs are idealists, driven by a deep longing for a world of truth, justice, and moral order. They are honest and fair and can spur others to work to grow beyond themselves. They are often gifted leaders, who strive to go forward, following a good model. They have a hard time accepting their own and other people's imperfections. Only when they are entirely "together" can they slowly learn to be at home in an imperfect present and to trust in the gradual growth of the good (the Reign of God).

I am a ONE myself. From early childhood we ONEs have generally tried to be model children. Even in our first years we internalized those explicit or implicit voices that demand, "Be good! Behave yourself! Try hard! Don't be childish! Do it better!" Back then we decided to earn the love of the people around us by meeting their expectations and being "good." We tried to find, develop, and stick to standards for judging what was good and bad, right and wrong. This demanding voice

35

in us never falls silent. Often one of the parents of a ONE is moral-istic, perfectionistic, or eternally dissatisfied: stingy with praise, they take above-average goodness for granted. We little ONEs produced this goodness because we didn't want to lose the love of our most important person.

Alice Miller has described the "drama of the gifted child" in her book by the same name.[2] Many parents compensate for their deficit experiences and unfulfilled dreams by trying to recoup and realize in their children what they themselves missed. So as not to lose the love of their parents, such children learn to meet the needs and expectations of father and mother. But in doing so they always lose access to their own feelings and needs and to their true selves. Many ONEs are such "gifted children."

According to Sigmund Freud, in this context a major role is played by training in cleanliness. The model child is prematurely "clean." Riso, who has attempted to harmonize the Enneagram types with Freud's categories, describes ONEs as anal retentive. This means, on the psycho-logical level, the refusal to produce a bowel movement. Such a refusal signals a blockade of the cause of dirt. Up until his "tower experience," young Luther, a classic ONE, suffered from constipation.[3]

I was mama's darling, and I didn't want to lose this preferential posi-tion. To keep my mother's attention, I met her expectations. Sometimes we ONEs make a virtue of necessity. Our self-control and our supposed moral superiority becomes a "compensatory pleasure" for giving up "lower pleasures," which we forbid ourselves to have. I can remem-ber that my mother said one day, "Wouldn't it be wonderful to have a son who was a priest?" Here I stand! Because I am a good boy, I did what mama wanted. In the days of pre–Vatican II Catholicism the best you could do to prove that you were "going the whole way," to be a truly good boy, was to become a priest.

We ONEs try to be good so that we won't be punished. We want at all costs to prevent our inner voices from condemning us. In the mean-time it was no longer my "really existing mother" who took over this role. Rather I internalized the demands of my mother: she became me and took up residence inside me. It is my own punishing voices that now accuse me when I am not sufficiently "self-sacrificing," "good," or "generous." The issue here is not necessarily objective self-sacrifice, goodness, or generosity, but what I consider to be such. The voices never fall silent and pierce me night and day with the question, "Are you good enough?" Inside us ONEs court is continually in session: we are at once prosecutor and defendant. These conflicting voices keep at us all the time, they bicker, interrupt, contradict and correct one another. Anybody who isn't a ONE can hardly imagine how exhausting it is to go through this endless inner trial.

At this point my "witness for the defense," my "objective observer," or my "lawyer" comes into play and says: "Richard, stop it. Don't drive yourself crazy with your own exaggerated standards and moral principles. And remember that these are your subjective views and not the objective truth."

ONE-children have renounced the development of their true selves to please others and earn the love of people who have sent them the signal, "You're okay only when you're perfect." ONE-children have the childhood driven out of them; too soon they have had to act like adults. Often they have had to take on responsibility, very early on, for a family in which for one reason or another one of the parents was missing; or as the oldest child they had to take over and become a role model for the younger brothers and sisters.

What's described here affects many people. There is at least a bit of this idealism, moralism, and perfectionism in almost everyone, but above all in people who have had a strongly religious education. Such an education, in its more emphatic forms, often internalizes and strengthens moralizing voices.

To take myself for an example: to this day I passionately cut coupons for special offers out of the newspaper, because my mother did that. I chase discounts, and I'd be lying if I claimed I didn't feel good doing it. Saving money is a good feeling. But what standards lie at the root of this compulsion? The whole enterprise would have a certain virtue if I gave the money I saved to the poor. But I, the Franciscan, sometimes take it to the bank — what's good about that? Still, I feel better when I can save. The imprint on my conscience from early childhood tells me that it's better, more correct, and holier to save money than to spend it.

My mother was a good German *hausfrau*. Cleanliness for her came next to godliness. This attitude is reflected in my house: at my place everything is so clean it shines, from the entrance to the back door, and even in hidden nooks and crannies. In Richard Rohr's place you can eat off the floor. I straighten up every time before I leave the city. In case I die on the way and someone enters my house, everybody should know that I was clean and orderly. Of course I could always say, "But this doesn't make any difference." Still, I feel better when everything is orderly and clean. The voices in me are convinced that cleanliness is good and dirt bad.

I like order and see immediately when something is out of place. And I feel better when everything is where it belongs. My co-workers at the Center for Contemplation and Action can tell a story or two about how I'm continually cleaning up and washing the dirty dishes. At least I can laugh about it today. I don't take it so seriously any more, and I know that it's my problem. When others don't empty out the ashtrays, I don't clean them right away, because I have since come to learn that I'm finicky in this area and have exaggerated ideals. I am still compulsive, but now at least I recognize it and don't take myself too seriously.

Dilemma

The search for perfection rules our lives and is our **temptation**. In the struggle against imperfection a ONE can turn into a Don Quixote, who tilts at windmills and dreams an "impossible dream." When we see something that approximately matches our ideal of perfection, we can get beside ourselves with joy and for a moment we're the happiest people in the world. This may be an experience of nature or art (a perfect sunset, a perfect picture, a perfect piece of music) or the meeting with a person whom — for a moment — we take to be "perfect." Something like this kindles our enthusiasm. Then as soon as we discover that this person too has weaknesses and makes mistakes, we're disappointed. ONEs are always frustrated because life and people are not what they should be. Above all, ONEs are disappointed by their own imperfection. That is why the religious way is very attractive to them: at least God is perfect.

ONEs are conscious of duty and responsibility. We are compulsively punctual. I have a clock in my head and need no alarm. When I give myself the order, "Richard, wake up at a quarter after three," then I wake up at 3:14 at the earliest and 3:16 at the latest. Most of us are pressured by time, keep an exact appointment book, and often an exact diary too. Time slips away, and after forty-six years I'm still not perfect.

We ONEs are serious people. I never tell jokes. When I try to make note of a joke, I forget the punch line. We allow ourselves relaxation and recreation only when we have thoroughly and completely finished our tasks. But that seldom happens. There's always something or other that could be improved. In the struggle for what's better there are no vacations. If we have a hobby, then it's usually a practical one that helps others or gives them joy. For example I'm fond of baking and cooking; that way I always have something in the house to offer my visitors.

ONEs are inclined to deny and punish themselves and to repress or even kill off their needs and feelings. We are by nature ascetics and Puritans, and in the final analysis we hope to redeem ourselves by at least trying to reach the ideal. "Whoever striving toils away — him we can redeem" (Goethe); this is immediately obvious to a ONE. That's why we have a terribly hard time looking away from our chores and enjoying life. We get a guilty conscience immediately. In the old days the American Puritans declared dancing and playing games to be sins. Calvin, the father of Puritanism, was a ONE. Most ONEs have a puritanical bent. That doesn't mean that I'm unhappy. I've learned over time to be glad when others are relaxed, fool around, or do nonsensical things. But I have a hard time joining in. A part of me violently resists being so unserious.

Without the help of meditation and prayer I would probably have become nothing but an obnoxious critic. I need prayer to be happy in and despite this imperfect world. ONEs must, to be sure, overcome some obstacles to find peace. When we are willing to be silent, the inner voices begin to speak all the louder. Helen Palmer quotes a type ONE woman who describes how her meditation goes:

> I am sitting in meditation, and become immediately aware of the loudness of the critic in my head. A small space of deep quiet, and I hear, "Not deep enough" or "Was better last time you sat." Then the argument starts: "Sit up straighter." "You're not trying." "Yes I am."[4]

Although it isn't simple at first, we ONEs have to learn to come to rest in order to observe the imperfection of the world (that's not hard for us) and to accept it (that's our real task in life).

On my lecture trips I have seen a lot of the world, all the pain, all the stupidity, all the deceit, all the superficiality. Does all that make me furious? Yes, but what I find in myself makes me still more aggressive. We ONEs are angry at ourselves. Anger is the **root sin** of the ONE. Had someone in my younger years asked me about my favorite sin, like all young men, I would have picked lust — and I would have been wrong. I would never have dreamed then of thinking of anger. Of all the classic capital sins anger would have been the last to occur to me.[5]

Because we ONEs are ashamed of our anger, our sin and our **avoidance** coincide. We avoid admitting the vexation that motivates and drives us, and can acknowledge neither to ourselves nor to others that we are resentful. For anger, too, as we see it, is something imperfect. Model children are not full of rage. This is our chief dilemma. Internally we are boiling with rage because the world is so damned imperfect. But we do not articulate our resentments as such. We can scarcely perceive them ourselves and certainly not stand for them. I remember arguing with people who claimed, "Admit it, you're angry." I said, "No, I'm *not!*" The very suspicion that I could be angry deeply wounded me. But others generally recognize our sin much more readily than we ourselves. That's another reason why we need binding fellowship with other people. When we are alone, we can easily surrender to the illusion of being true saints. God has given us other people so that they can keep bringing us back to the solid ground of reality. We ONEs are ashamed of our rage. We force ourselves to be "objective" and to trot out our arguments even when we're boiling inside. "I'm not annoyed at you, but actually I'd have the right, for this reason and that and the other, to be annoyed at you."

The **defense mechanism** that ONEs develop in order not to have to show their anger is reaction formation. Instead of reacting immediately and directly, within fractions of a second a process of censorship takes place within us that decides what we'll express and how.

The fact that we cannot permit our aggressions sometimes generates in us ONEs a tremendous pressure. We can be walking steam kettles. There is a repressed rancor simmering within us; it keeps thickening and attacks the voices pounding the message into our heads, "You're a good boy, a good girl. A good child isn't aggressive." The workaholism of ONEs is one of their attempts to let off steam and work off energy.

The pressure to do "good works," which ultimately drove Martin Luther the ONE to despair, is present in all ONEs. In my case it led to my becoming a notorious improver of the world. As if it weren't enough to found our own community in Cincinnati (the traditional Church wasn't good enough), we had to call it New Jerusalem, something like the perfection of perfection. Where is *the* New Jerusalem located? In Cincinnati, Ohio! Such an endeavor is the result of our ideal of perfection. Nevertheless we're never satisfied. Our inner voice continually questions our motives: "Why are you really doing this or that? You're doing it just to appear in a favorable light before yourself, others, and God." Luther is the best known example of this mechanism, which operates in a ONE. We shall come back to it again later on.

There are also very unredeemed ONEs who try to solve their dilemma differently. They can get to the point where they lead a double life. In public, where they are known and observed, they always behave correctly, morally, and blamelessly. But when they feel themselves unobserved or in a foreign environment, the repressed shadow shows itself. It can happen that they live out all the things that they otherwise deny themselves (and others). This applies to, among other things, their repressed sexual wishes. Neurotic ONEs can preach morality and live immorality, as the scandals surrounding the American televangelists have shown. Unhealthy ONEs are hypocrites. Jesus said to the Pharisees who wished to stone a woman who had been caught red-handed in adultery: "Let him who is without sin among you be the first to throw a stone at her" (John 8:7).

The special gift or **fruit of the spirit** that marks mature persons of any type is always the reverse of the root sin. The fruit of the spirit of the ONE is cheerful tranquillity. How do I get from my root sin to this gift? From my earliest years I have lived with my unacknowledged and repressed anger. When I discovered it, I became so aware of it that I learned to deal better and more constructively with my aggressiveness than most other people do! But it's still in me and always will be. I just don't take it so seriously any more. Three things have helped me personally to reach this goal: prayer, love, and nature. When I pray, I can increasingly let go of the voices of duty and responsibility and let myself drop down into God, the perfect lover. That leads me immediately to love. Love is the "bond of perfection," as Paul says (Col. 3:14). That is why I have to see to it that I fall in love with somebody or something every day, even if it's only a tree or the wonderful turquoise blue sky over New Mexico. When I don't love, the negative voices immediately get the upper hand. Finally, nature helps me: God, love, and nature are perfect. That is why almost all ONEs are nature lovers. I have seldom met a ONE who didn't like to raise flowers, work in the garden, or hike in the forest. In the ecological movement many ONEs feel at home. ONEs have a weak spot for everything that is green, grows, and blooms. Without nature, without love, and without God we ONEs can scarcely get to the space of cheerful serenity and patience, but remain aggressive idealists and ideologues who condemn others and demand that they improve themselves and be "perfect" by our lights.

Along with the serenity of the redeemed ONE, ONEs also have other gifts, once they have reached a certain degree of inner maturity. They are rational, just, and balanced. That is why they are good teachers. ONEs like to become teachers or pastors, unless they realize their love for order in professions like bookkeeping.[6] Our compulsions can give us balance. In New Jerusalem they used to tease me and say that all my sermons consisted of two columns: "on the one hand" and "on the other." We want to be fair, and so we always look at the other side. This is at once a curse and a blessing and can be explained by the fact that so many different voices are engaged in long trials in our interior courtroom. Fairly mature ONEs usually give well thought out and reasonable answers. Their opinion has already gone through the fire of their internal criticism, every if and but has already been clarified, before anything is expressed. That is why it's hard to refute ONEs.[7] They can also be very black and white. It's all clear and simple to them.

Weakly developed ONEs are often hypocritically and ostentatiously moral, continually talk with an upraised index finger and criticize everybody. They consider themselves and their ideals identical and can strike people as very arrogant and self-righteous. All ONEs live close to the edge of self-righteousness. Our friends have to remind us of this every now and then.

ONEs have a hard time making important decisions, because in the process they might make mistakes. So they're inclined to hesitate and temporize. And for that reason they often don't get ahead, because they're busy with old mistakes. They can't move on to today's business if the past hasn't been settled. In this way they become the bad conscience of a family or a people. They keep awake the memory of past guilt; they are prophets of conversion and renewal. This is one of their greatest strengths, but it can also turn them into awful pests. Riso calls type ONE "the Reformer."

The **pitfall** from which unredeemed ONEs must be liberated is their over-criticalness. They must learn to accept themselves and others without passing judgment about each and every thing. They must learn to see the beam in their own eye before they busy themselves with the mote in the eye of others, which immediately catches their attention (see Matt. 7:3–5). Immature and coercive ONEs affect other people as quietly judgmental. Others feel continually criticized by them, even when the ONE doesn't say a word. Their fellows sense this negative current of energy. People in pastoral counselling sometimes tell me, "I have difficulties opening myself before you, because I'm afraid that you're secretly condemning me." Although I don't want to, sometimes I seem to emit this energy. How can I get rid of it? In all probability I won't be able to do that completely. But I can try to build up a relationship of trust with the person in question, which will allow my capacity for criticism to serve the enlightenment, liberation, and joy of the other person, without oppressing and cutting the person down. Without such a relationship my judgments are not helpful to others and may have a destructive impact.

ONEs are inclined to understand themselves as white knights who set forth into the world to save it. ONEs know the secret pleasure of wiping out evil root and branch. St. George or the Archangel Michael, the dragon-slayers of Christian tradition, are patrons of this side of the ONE.

In relationships ONEs' energy can cause great complications. A ONE is glad to fall in love with a person who in his or her eyes is perfect. But as soon as the first weak spots show and the veneer starts peeling off, the ONE begins to carp about the other in order to change the other. ONEs can't understand why the other doesn't at least earnestly *strive* to become a "better person." Of course, if others honestly confess their mistakes, beg for forgiveness, promise improvement, and prove by deeds that they want to change, ONEs are ready to forgive generously. But the forgiveness of a ONE is seldom completely unconditional.

ONEs may carry around a list of other people's mistakes and be resentful about them. They can forgive, but they're bad at forgetting. This is connected with the fact that our anger is our source of energy and helps us to perceive ourselves. The critical potency of this anger is our contribution to each community — but it's not the whole truth. If I overidentify with my anger and sit smoldering because I consider my viewpoint the decisive contribution, at some point the others will stop taking me seriously.

Symbols and Examples

The **animal** assigned to the unredeemed ONE is the yelping, always aggressive terrier. Ants and bees symbolize the industriousness of the ONE. They are constantly busy with building up and maintaining the ideal commonwealth. Bees test all flowers and keep from all of them only the best, the honey. They remain true to their beehive and work for the growth of its community.

The symbolic **nation** of the ONE is Russia. The Russian utopians, revolutionaries, and writers like Dostoyevsky and Tolstoy embody the dream of a more perfect world and a more humane society. Mikhail Gorbachev too stands for this reformist ideal. They do not want the violent overthrow of the status quo but evolutionary change of the system. On a recent trip to Switzerland, I became convinced that it is also a ONE country: clocks, banks, and cleanliness!

The **color** of ONE is silver. Silver is a cool, sober, and clear color. It represents moonlight, which gets its brightness from the sun (the higher ideal). Like the mild silvery glow of moonlight, the redeemed ONE stands for change and growth.

Lucy van Pelt, Charlie Brown's antagonist in "Peanuts," is the caricature of the unredeemed ONE. She is continually busy changing the whole world (and particularly Charlie Brown, the eternal loser); and she refuses to accept a world that is not perfect. In one cartoon series we learn that unconditional love is the only force that can save a ONE like Lucy. Lucy is lamenting how bad the world is and how unhappy she is herself. Her brother Linus thereupon challenges her to think just once about everything she can be thankful for. That really makes her fly into a rage. There is nothing that it pays to be grateful for. Then Linus says: "At least you have a little brother who loves you." She looks at him for a moment and throws her arms around his neck, sobbing. And Linus thinks:

"Now and then I say the right thing."[8] The ONE longs for unconditional love but cannot believe it when it comes.

The monk Martin Luther (1483–1546) was at the bottom of his soul an angry young man who longed for an unconditionally loving God: "How do I get a gracious God?" was the question of his life. His anger was rightly aimed at the Catholic Church of his day, which said that this love had to be earned through indulgences, ritual performances, and good works. ONEs yearn for someone finally to come along and put an end to this tiring game. Luther had a strict father on earth and a wrathful father in heaven. And Mother Church too was strict and demanding. He was fed up with these parental voices. From a purely psychological point of view, the Reformation resulted from the entanglement of a ONE in his own compulsions. Luther longed for unconditional grace, love, and acceptance.

Erik H. Erikson got some of his most important psychoanalytical insights in his confrontation with the life story of young Luther. The ambivalent relation of the Reformer to his father is for Erikson the main cause of the compulsions and struggles that Luther was subject to in his lifetime. His father "showed the greatest temper in his attempts to drive temper out of his children."[9] The consequence was in Luther's own words, " . . . I fled him and I became sadly resentful toward him, until he gradually got me accustomed to him again." Erikson remarks, "Martin, even when mortally afraid, could not really hate his father . . . and Hans, while he could not let the boy come close, and was murderously angry at times, could not let him go for long."[10] When Luther later looked back and reported the scruples he had suffered from making his confession, he named "libido" (sexual pleasure), *ira* (anger), and *impatientia* as the sources of temptation.[11] Another psychologically revealing fact is that Luther, as already mentioned, suffered from constipation and retention of urine. There is a lot of evidence for the thesis that his "tower experience" actually took place on the toilet. Erikson remarks laconically on this: "Scholars would prefer to have it happen as they achieve their own reflected revelations — sitting at a desk" and he points to the later Luther's love of anal-vulgar language and his "capacity for dirt-slinging wrath."[12] It was as if his Reformation understanding released all the repressed anger and "filth" that had been the main cause of young Luther's pathological anxieties.

Luther, thank God, went to Paul, and found in him what he had been looking for, because Paul also was a ONE. Doesn't the apostle Paul sometimes leave the impression of being a little arrogant and dogmatic? He was a Pharisee; ONEs are born Pharisees. God transformed his root sin and made a gift of it. He used a zealous Pharisee, who managed to become a zealot for the Gospel. This is the lovable thing about Paul, the great white knight for Christ, who did everything for his Lord. But every now and then we get tired of him; we'd like to tell him, "Cool down a little, Paul. This is too much of a good thing." Especially when Paul was attacked and criticized, he could react bitterly, arrogantly, and self-righteously, and cut down his opponents with sarcasm.

In the Letter to the Galatians Paul himself reports about a significant event. He tells how he "opposed" the stormy, but fundamentally fearful prince of the Apostles, Peter (a SIX), "to his face, because he stood condemned" (Gal. 2:11). In the community of Antioch Peter had at first gone against his own grain and had eaten in public with baptized pagans — something that as an orthodox Jew he was not allowed to do. But when the "spies" of the strict Jewish-Christian "brother of the Lord," James, came from Jerusalem, he stood aloof, didn't stick to the freedom he had just demonstrated, and began to "play the hypocrite." Paul's dearest concern was to proclaim that the old frontier separating Jews and Christians had been removed by Christ. That is why he publicly called the "first man" of the Church to account. When a ONE is convinced about something, he or she doesn't waver before the thrones of princes: "Here I stand, there's nothing else I can do." Paul could have said that fifteen hundred years before Luther did. In both men we see how closely root sin and fruit of the spirit are fused together, and how God can transform our obsessions and use them for divine purposes.

Conversion and Redemption

ONEs have to learn that there isn't just one right way, but that many roads lead to Rome. That is why they have to make friends with their anger and acknowledge it, before they pass judgment on themselves and others. Unredeemed ONEs are continually looking for suitable screens onto which they can project their negative feelings and moods. As a rule this is the first person who happens to be near them. When ONEs don't acknowledge and "own" their anger they will take it out on their children, their spouse, or on an untidy house.

We ONEs are affable people, as long as we don't take ourselves too seriously. The way to do this always consists in relativizing ourselves and thus freeing ourselves from false absolutes. The greatest freedom lies in being able to laugh at ourselves, because we see that our own perception makes up only a part of the total picture.

Deep inside ONEs lives the ideal of the good, the true, and the beautiful. I would not have worked myself to death in the last few years, would not have founded a community, and would not have been there for others seven days a week if I hadn't had this ONE's energy. Nor will I apologize or cut myself down for this after the fact, because I know that God has made something good out of my ambiguous motives. I know that my love for Jesus was not the only reason why I did what I did. Part of it was Richard pure and simple, operating like everyone, from mixed motives, while thinking I am doing it for truth, justice, and the coming of the Reign of God! At this point God's humble realism appears once more. Jesus knows that the most he will get from us will be a "mustard seed" of faith, and he is satisfied. We do most things in life primarily for ourselves and struggle for self-preservation in this world. But as soon as we have the humility to concede this, the grace and love of God can fill in all the gaps. One can build only on the truth. With the Enneagram the point is to call our illusions by name and to unmask them, so that there will be room for real life instead of self-deception.

Conversion of Saul (Schnorr von Carolsfeld)
The Experience of Grace

We ONEs have to stop wanting all or nothing. I often say to myself, "this moment is as perfect as it can be." Now that I know that, I am happier and more capable of loving other people, but I am and remain a ONE. My characteristics will remain with me all my life and will get on other people's nerves. That is why I am dependent on the patience of my fellow humans and of God, and must learn to be compassionate with myself.

The **invitation** that we ONEs hear and have to make our own is hidden in the word "growth." Our love of nature is already a hint that it does us good to see things grow. What grows is not yet perfect. But it is on the way. Jesus told many parables in which sowing and harvest and the patient waiting in between point to the coming of God's Reign. They are gathered together in the Gospel of Mark, chapter 4. For example:

> The kingdom of God is as if a man should scatter seed upon the ground, and should sleep and rise night and day, and the seed should sprout and grow, he knows not how. The earth produces of itself, first the blade, then the ear, then the full grain in the ear. But when the grain is ripe he puts in the sickle, because the harvest has come. (Mark 4:26–29)

The perfect God has patience and gives us time to grow. A ONE who allows growth shares in the divine tranquillity.

In this process even the destructive anger of the ONE can be transformed into "righteous indignation." The Bible often speaks of God's anger in the face of injustice on earth. The prophets of the Hebrew Bible and Jesus are sometimes gripped by this holy wrath (the cleansing of the Temple). Paul fell into inner turmoil when he saw the many idols in Athens, and Luther broke into a rage over the trade in indulgences. Holy anger is an expression of love and may never be played off against love. It never wants to destroy, but to restore the original justice.

Ignatius Loyola (1491–1556), the founder and first general of the Jesuits, belongs to the **saints** who were ONEs. At the age of thirty the Basque knight was laid up, badly wounded after the defense of Pamplona, and in reading the legends of the saints he experienced a sweeping conversion. Finally he dedicated his arms to the Mother of God, whom he wanted to serve from then on as a spiritual knight. He cared for the sick, went on pilgrimage to Palestine, and completed a thorough course of study. To share his experiences with others he developed the Spiritual Exercises, which came under deep suspicion from the Inquisition. In 1534 he and his friends took a vow to work in Palestine for the Church or to place themselves at the pope's disposal for any other task. In 1540

the order was officially approved. Every Jesuit goes through the Spiritual
Exercises at several key moments in his life. They serve to purify the exercitant through contemplation of his own sinfulness and of the life and
suffering of Christ and the "discernment of spirits" that affect the inner
man. There is no overlooking the energy of the ONE in Ignatian spirituality: discernment of spirits, thirty days of strenuous contemplation, so
that one may become more perfect. Like all one-sided systems, this form
of piety has its particular strengths and weaknesses. Its greatest strength
is the thoroughness and conscientiousness of the self-examination, and
the readiness to submit to the tiring work on oneself and the scrutiny of
one's own motives. But this doesn't take place in a vacuum. Christ, who
gave himself up for our redemption, is the continual partner in dialogue
and the source of renewal and conversion.

Among the **lifetime tasks** of ONEs is to learn occasionally to ignore
duty, order, and the improvement of the world, and instead to play,
celebrate, and enjoy life. If ONEs dismantle their judgmentalism and
resentment and take back their projections, then compassion becomes
possible. They can learn cheerful *joie de vivre*, if they go to school with
the lighthearted SEVENs.[13]

Karl Barth, the Swiss theologian and reformer of Protestant theology
after the First World War, was a ONE. His commentary on the Letter
to the Romans was an unsparing settling of accounts with the hitherto dominant "liberal theology," which took a very optimistic view of
human possibilities. Barth protested against humankind's "pocketing"
God for its own purposes. For this reason he preached a God who is totally other and has other plans and goals than ours. Barth's multi-volume
Church Dogmatics is the most comprehensive theological *magnum opus*
of this century. This militant theologian was a positively obsessive fan
of Mozart (Mozart is a typical SEVEN). Thomas Merton describes how,
without being aware of the Enneagram, Karl Barth unconsciously drew
his creativity from the "power source" of Mozart, a type who was apparently so different from himself:

Karl Barth had a dream about Mozart.

Barth had always been piqued by the Catholicism of Mozart,
and by Mozart's rejection of Protestantism. For Mozart said that
"Protestantism was all in the head" and that "Protestants did not
know the meaning of the *Agnus Dei qui tollis peccata mundi*."

Barth, in his dream, was appointed to examine Mozart in theology. He wanted to make the examination as favorable as possible,
and in his questions he alluded pointedly to Mozart's masses.

But Mozart did not answer a word.

I was deeply moved by Barth's account of this dream and almost wanted to write him a letter about it. The dream concerns his salvation, and Barth perhaps is striving to admit that he will be saved more by the Mozart in himself than by his theology.

Each day, for years, Barth played Mozart every morning before going to work on his dogma: unconsciously seeking to awaken, perhaps, the hidden sophianic Mozart in himself, the central wisdom that comes in tune with the divine and cosmic music and is saved by love, yes, even by *eros*. While the other, theological self, seemingly more concerned with love, grasps at a more stern, more cerebral *agape:* a love that, after all, is not in our own heart but only in God and revealed only in our head.

Barth says, also significantly, that "it is a child, even a 'divine' child, who speaks in Mozart's music to us." Some, he says considered Mozart always a child in practical affairs (but Burckhardt "earnestly took exception" to this view). At the same time, Mozart the child prodigy, "was never allowed to be child in the literal meaning of that word." He gave his first concert at the age of six.

Yet he was always a child "in the higher meaning of that word."

Fear not, Karl Barth! Trust in the divine mercy. Though you have grown up to become a theologian, Christ remains a child in you. Your books (and mine) matter less than we might think! There is in us a Mozart who will be our salvation.[14]

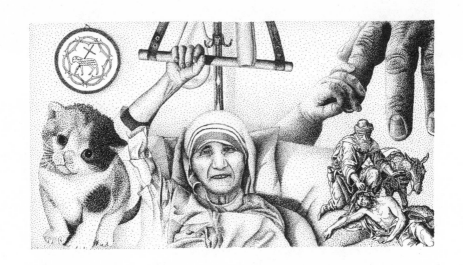

TYPE TWO
The Need to Be Needed

Overview

TWOs employ their gifts for the needs of others and care for their health, nourishment, education, and welfare. They impart a measure of acceptance and appreciation that can help others to believe in their own value. TWOs can share generously and give "their last shirt" for others. They stand by others when they have to endure suffering, pain, or conflict, and in this way they give them the feeling that someone is there for them and accepts them. The TWOs' love of neighbor and presence, however, also has dark sides that may not be recognized at first glance.

TWOs are coquettish and have an exaggerated need for validation. Some TWOs have had a childhood that seemed gray and sad to them. Real security and a feeling of having a home were sometimes lacking, or less than they needed. Other TWOs report that they have experienced only conditional love. The love of important persons in their life had to be bought by good behavior. If they met the conditions, they could, under certain circumstances, get a lot of love and security. The "beautiful"

50

childhood that these TWOs had prevents them from becoming enraged or sorrowful that they were continually being urged to exaggerated good behavior. Some TWOs also recall that early on they had the feeling of having to be a support for the emotional needs of other family members. They had the feeling that they had to make themselves useful in order to be noticed and loved. The message that they got sounds like this: "I am loved when I am tender, understanding, and ready to be helpful, and defer my own needs." With TWOs — unlike ONEs — "being good" is not a moral category. Instead, TWOs make the claim that they are "nice" and helpful; as a rule they are convinced that they are just that. This, to be sure, does not always correspond to objective reality and the perception of others. The classic picture of a TWO is the caricature of the "Jewish mother," who protects her children like a brood hen and takes care that she is used by them.[1] But woe unto them if they don't show gratitude: "How could you do that to me, after all I've done for you?" First an unredeemed TWO spoils and looks after other people, unasked and unsolicited. If this becomes burdensome or confining to others and they distance themselves instead of returning this "love," the TWO feels betrayed and exploited.

There are many jokes about priests and their housekeepers. The classic pastor's cook is a TWO. There used to be many rectories in which the housekeeper "wore the pants." I once had a secretary who was a TWO and ruled me and everyone else with her competence. She knew everything and hence was indispensable. I'm the sort of person who forgets the details; she remembered them all. When I had to go to a meeting, she informed me beforehand about the essentials. Finally the parishioners realized that if they needed information, they should go not to me but to her. She took care of me in a touching fashion, served me with body and soul. But that was also how she controlled me and kept me in line. Such is the denied and disguised manipulativeness of the TWO.

TWOs are continually holding the thermometer in the air to measure the social temperature and wind direction, because they base their identity on how others are disposed toward them and react to them. The mood gauge of TWOs rises and falls according to how much sympathy or antipathy comes their way.

At the moment I am having a visit from my little niece, who is a TWO. From morning to night she makes her entrance as if the world were a stage. She sees to it that we notice her. When she isn't being noticed or appreciated, she loses her energy. She loves and serves to get our love in return. The heart types, TWO, THREE, and FOUR are "other-directed" people, whose well-being depends in the first instance on how their environment responds to them.

In a child this is understandable and pardonable. You can spend your entire youth in this fashion. The problem begins when you keep on behaving this way as a grownup. When you are with an immature TWO for some time, you sense that they emit a needy and possessive energy. You have the feeling of being embraced by the TWO: "Notice me, stroke me." But the actual magic formula is "*Need* me."

At this point TWOs are subject to manipulation. TWOs need to be used. All you have to say to a TWO is "I need you," and all resistance fades. They fall all over you to be useful to you and to help you — even when they have neither the time nor the energy to do it. As soon as they hear the little word "need," they scrape together the last remnant of their energy to rush to help you. Later they go home and can kick themselves for letting themselves be talked into it: "Why did I let myself be exploited again? Why did I get into this stupid work group? Why did I promise to bake a cake? Besides, all that's really no fun for me anyway." But at the moment it was so beautiful to be needed that the TWOs really couldn't resist and said yes.

TWOs cry easily because they are sensitive and emotional. They are teddy bears; they like to cuddle and pet. TWOs like to talk about relationships and love. They long to be loved, to love with their whole hearts, and to be allowed to live for their beloved. Our social network would collapse without all the TWOs who sacrifice themselves for the welfare of others. They are benefactors, givers, and helpers. This is their greatest gift. But they have to resist the inclination to style themselves grandly as saints and martyrs. Some years ago, a writer who was unfamiliar with the Enneagram, Wolfgang Schmidbauer, presented this type of person in his book *The Helpless Helpers: On the Psychological Problems of the Helping Professions* and coined the term "helper syndrome."[2]

TWOs trapped inside themselves struggle with problems of identity. They change continually in order to meet the needs of whatever person may be present. This gives rise to a "multiple self " (Palmer). Hence TWOs often prefer to be together with only one other person. If several people who are close to them are present at the same time, the TWO occasionally has no idea which self to activate. Apart from such confusing situations the TWO perceives these different ego-conditions not as a problem, but as an enrichment: "Each of my friends brings out a different side in me. That is why I wouldn't want to miss any of them."

TWOs usually have a large circle of acquaintances and tend to label people as their "friends" very quickly. They guard their relationships jealously and want as far as possible to be especially important for all their friends. They are proud that so many people pour out their hearts to them; they can sense other people's needs in a positively physical sense.

Here, however, they are inclined to give good advice too quickly and to offer promising solutions. They like to flatter and affirm other people.

Dilemma

The great **temptation** of TWOs is continually to help others and in this way to evade themselves. The identity of TWOs lies, as it were, in the wishes and needs of other people, which means outside themselves. This often leads to a chaotic emotional life. Immature TWOs have a hard time finding their own center. When they are alone, the ceiling falls on their head. Meditation and prayer "in a quiet little room" for long make them anxious because nobody is there to reinforce them and be close to them, and because they are afraid to find nothing in themselves except a black hole or alarming unrest.

TWOs have a tendency to seduce other people. In thoroughly neurotic cases this can even lead to child abuse. The helplessness and neediness of children can appeal to a TWO. This need not be a question of sexual abuse. Often it's enough just to make the helpless child into a substitute object of their own needs. They direct toward this object all the love that they want for themselves but for some reason can't get. In this way basically they love only themselves. Their seeming altruism is a "legitimate" form of indulging their own egoism. TWOs have a heart for abandoned orphans. They enjoy supporting a foster child in the Third World. It's so beautiful to be needed. That is the gift and the same time the dilemma of the TWOs: they give others precisely what they want for themselves. Since there is a homeless child within them, they are especially touched by the distress of abandoned children. People who seem to be even weaker and more helpless than they give them a feeling of strength. Anyone who can help has power.

TWOs long — at least ostensibly — for fusion with others. But here too they sometimes experience this outside themselves rather than in their own lives. They continually think about who could suit whom, and they match people up. As soon as two persons in their circle of acquaintances develop romantic feelings for one another, TWOs go into action to set up or promote contacts. They can also undertake subtle attempts to prevent contacts, above all, when they fear the loss of one of the persons involved. Many TWOs like to read love novels, because life without romantic love would be only half as beautiful.

Redeemed TWOs have learned to love without conditions. The way between selfless love of neighbor and a manipulative helper complex is, to be sure, a tricky one. The demand that we deny ourselves and serve others has often been played with fast and loose, above all in the Church. Take, for example, the text given by the Bavarian pastor Wilhelm Löhe to his Lutheran deaconesses: "What do I want? I want to serve. Whom do I want to serve? The Lord in his wretched and poor. And what is my reward? I serve neither for reward nor for thanks, but out of gratitude and love. My reward is that I am allowed to. . . ."[3] Surely some of these women became real "saints," but many were twisted and exploited by the yoke of such pretensions.

In a partnership TWOs can be very possessive. Sometimes they look for partners who are weak and dependent. A classic constellation is the partnership between a TWO (usually female) and an addict. The phenomenon of co-dependence (dependence on the addiction of the partner) has been illuminated in recent years: she helps him, puts up with everything, forgives him, gives him another chance. Meanwhile she doesn't notice that this is poison for him because it lets him go on behaving as before. Unconsciously this is precisely her goal, although she would admit this neither to herself nor to others. For if he were healthy and independent, then he might not need her any more and might leave her. In many cultures, women are conditioned to be TWOs.

When immature TWOs are hurt, they can suddenly stop being sweet and pliant and show their claws. At such moments they are capable of doing frightful injury to the very person they supposedly love above all. The unredeemed TWOs' notion of love is warm, soft, and gentle. When another doesn't play along with them and torpedoes this concept, there is no escape for TWOs. Then it can happen that they suddenly turn into Furies and literally walk over corpses.

TWOs are burningly interested in the problems of others and expect people to trust them unsparingly. On the other hand, TWOs find it hard to surrender themselves. This is their pride. They may be everybody's garbage disposal, but they shy away from really depending on others. Behind this lies the shame of showing their own neediness, the fear of not being understood or being rejected, and sometimes also the feeling that "nobody likes me anyway." The threshold anxiety before a confession, a pastoral conversation, or psychotherapy is correspondingly high for them. For on the couch they would have to admit their immense need. At the same time they long for a place where they can do that without being rejected. TWOs surrender themselves only when they are very sure that the other will accept them. That is why TWOs need at least one person whom they trust enough to tell everything. In all this they want support and understanding for their conduct. Sharp or direct criticism can pull the rug out from under the feet of a TWO. To advise TWOs in a pastoral setting, you have to deal very carefully with them, and above all you must never take away the feeling that despite everything they are accepted and loved. TWOs need a great deal of acceptance and "soft" love before they are ready to let themselves be challenged by "hard love."

It's no accident that there are more women than men in group TWO. Society has encouraged and allowed women to be TWOs by, for example, idealizing female "intuition" and "devotion." Women have been told that their possibility of exercising power and influence consists in the fact that they "love." A few women have become real saints in this way. But many others become manipulative, clinging, possessive, destructive — and unhappy. The success of Robin Norwood's book *Women Who Love Too Much* seems to confirm the thesis that many women find themselves in the TWO pitfall.[4] Many women consume themselves to the point of self-abandonment for a man, consider this obsession to be love, and in the process become physically and psychologically sick (bulimia), but still can't manage to let go.

In Church circles as well TWOs can be found bustling about, and here it's particularly hard for them to break out of their role. The Gospel has often been preached as if Christianity meant everyone was supposed to become a TWO! The Sufis considered Jesus a "redeemed TWO." The Christian interpretation of the Enneagram has come to a different conclusion: Jesus Christ cannot be incorporated into the Enneagram at all, because in him we find the central features of all nine types.[5] But it's still worth noting that outsiders relate the energy of TWO to Christianity (in contrast, for example, to Islam). And despite the male hierarchy in the Church, Western Christianity is mostly a religion of women. Two thirds of the people who come to church are women. If someone by nature is a TWO and then falls into Christian circles, he or she will be continually reinforced in their compulsion. TWOs have to get permission and be encouraged to perceive their true needs, which they often don't know themselves. Otherwise TWOs will not manage to break out of their roles, which provides the rest of us with a series of pleasant advantages. We tend to maintain one another in our compulsive nature, and TWOs are classic co-dependents.

The **root sin** of TWOs is their pride. Here we see what a subtle psychology of sin is concealed in the Enneagram. It takes us behind the scene. Pride is different from conceit or narcissism. Pride is an expression of a "puffed up self," an "inflationary ego." The self-perception of unredeemed TWOs can take on downright messianic traits: "I'm more lovable than all of you; my love will save the world. I will see to it that my love saves you. I will make my love so indispensable to your life and your system that you won't be able to get along without me." Immature TWOs chum up to people with their love. The problematic side of this attitude is that they manipulate others and make them dependent precisely through their attention and considerateness.

Pride makes it hard for TWOs to find an unbarred access to themselves and to God. Real self-knowledge, awareness of their hidden self-interest, is harder for them than for others. Knowledge of sin would mean becoming aware of one's own pride, which again hinders just this awareness. Sober repentance is above all a question of "objective self-perception." TWOs have to work hard at installing an objective "inner observer," to stand up to their natural subjectivism.

TWOs also have a difficult time building up a heartfelt relationship with God. At bottom they don't need God, because they are loving and energetic themselves. Rather they're convinced that God needs them! How is God supposed to save the world without them? The pride of self-imprisoned TWOs is directed not only against their (needy) fellow men and women, but also against God. Their love will save the world!

A young theologian, who is a TWO, expressed it this way: "We TWOs are practical atheists. Only when we are sick, ruined, and lying in bed with a breakdown can we really pray from the heart, 'Lord, have mercy on *me!*' I once found myself praying, 'Lord, I have mercy on *you*'!'" TWOs expect gratitude from everybody else — including God. Because in their "love-pride" they sometimes feel like creators and conservers of life, gratitude toward life often comes hard to them. Thus they block themselves off from true joy in life.

The **avoidance strategy** of TWOs consists in suppressing their own needs and projecting them onto others. Jesus' saying, "Whatever you wish that men would do to you, do so to them" (Matt. 7:12) is — at least if it is understood at face value — poison for TWOs. In a way they do just that all the time. The pressure that they direct against themselves is transmitted to their environment and is expressed in that subtle pressure on others that is so hard to name. That is why they are ashamed. ONEs hide their anger, TWOs hide the fact that they are so needy. They are afraid of what could happen if their immense need for warmth, love, and intimacy got out of control and took off.

The needs of TWOs are as a rule sensate in nature: tenderness, sex, attachment. Other sensuous needs can easily be turned into replacements: eating, drinking, shopping till they drop. Some TWOs are chocolate addicts. After they have spent the whole day satisfying the needs of other people and repressing their own, TWOs say in the evening: "I've earned this. I have to reward myself for doing all sorts of things that I actually didn't want to do." A strikingly large number of TWOs have weight problems. Often this is a matter of compensating for unrequited love.

The **defense mechanism** of TWOs is repression. Like ONEs, TWOs repress negative impulses and feelings, especially in the realm of aggression and sexuality. To admit clearly and distinctly, "You're driving me crazy," "You turn me on," is hard for them. Both could lead to a withdrawal of love or to rejection. Nevertheless one usually senses without any trouble what's going on in a TWO. They wish neither to hide their feelings nor to show them openly. Thus they express their moods in indirect ways and see to it that they are noticed without having to take responsibility for it. An offended TWO can — without saying a single nasty word — poison the atmosphere of an entire group, and still when asked about it answer with a look of innocence, "Why would there be anything wrong with me? Nothing's wrong!"

The **pitfall** of unredeemed TWOs is obligingness or flattery. They deny themselves in order to "please" others. They are so ashamed of their own neediness, that they have to make others dependent on them in order to develop a little feeling of worth. This again leads to TWOs' developing a very independent side, which can throw the people around them into astonishment. One day they are sick and tired of being dependent on love, praise, and stroking, and they fall abruptly into the other extreme. They want to prove to all the world how independent they are; they suddenly do what they want, and fight with tooth and nail for their "freedom." This phenomenon can take on grotesque forms. But I have never yet met a TWO with whom it didn't appear at one time or other like a bolt from the blue. They will then be very stubborn.

Many problems arise for TWOs because they can't say no, and so promise more than they can keep. Afterward they get irritated at having agreed in the first place and feel guilty as well because they didn't make good on what they said they would do.

The unredeemed TWOs are under a compulsion to be used, whether by the "poor" of this world or by an important personality whom they can serve and work for. TWOs can themselves be good leadership forces if they manage to rein in their partiality and subjectivity and not surround themselves only with their favorites. TWOs are inclined to gather a circle of disciples around them, people who "understand." Critics have no great chance of penetrating this inner circle. When disciples want to break loose from the sphere of influence, this can bring about complex detachment processes. TWOs' fears of loss see to it that people who are close to them hang on by an invisible leash. In general, however, TWOs find leadership roles burdensome, because they imply so much responsibility. They are afraid of lonely, exposed positions in which they feel isolated and vulnerable to attack. A single critic who does not "play along" or "understand" is enough for a TWO to get the feeling that "everybody's against me."

The **fruit of the spirit** or gift of TWOs is humility, the reverse of pride. When TWOs reach the point where they recognize their real motives ("I give so I can get"), there comes a sobering more profound than can be imagined. When TWOs dare to endure this insight, to chew it, taste it, and digest it, then transformation and healing are possible. I recall what happened to a woman I once knew, when her mask fell and it suddenly became clear to her what kind of game she had been playing her whole life. She came three days in a row to her office hour with me, and could do nothing but cry uncontrollably. It was a real conversion. She wept over her pride and over the fact that she had always thought she was the most lovable person in the world. She promptly recognized the terrifying distance between her claims and reality. She became very humble.

The legends of the saints often talk about holy men and women weeping for their sins. In the Eastern Orthodox churches tears of real repentance are considered an infallible sign of the activity of the Holy Spirit. A cleansed person can emerge from a bath of tears. Tears shed by a TWO are normally tears of self-pity. But when a TWO can finally cry tears of self-knowledge redemption is near. At such moments TWOs recognize that they have damaged and injured other people while supposedly "wanting the best for them." This is humiliating. TWOs are redeemed from themselves the more they experience God as the real lover and realize that our love can consist only in sharing in God's love. This insight leads through a moment of deep shame to genuine humility.

False pride and false humility are twins. Genuine humility is based on a realistic self-appraisal and a healthy feeling of self-worth. False humility is actually nothing but restored and "sanctified" pride. Redeemed TWOs know their value and so don't need to be continually reinforced. Their autonomy is now no longer an act of defiance, but an expression of the fact that they have found their identity in themselves (and in God).

Symbols and Examples

The symbolic **animals** of TWO are the cat, the donkey, and the licking puppy. The cat symbolizes the ambivalence of the TWOs between distance and closeness. Cats are cuddly and get their share of petting when they feel like it. But if you want to manipulate them, they suddenly prove themselves to be free and independent. A cat can't be trained.[6] The donkey is the apparently so patient beast of burden. Jesus rode into Jerusalem not on a proud horse, but on the despised ass. At some point, however, it gets to be too much for the donkey. He can suddenly become stubborn and refractory. And when things get to be too much for him, as everyone knows, he goes on strike. The puppy symbolizes the urgent proofs of love shown by an immature TWO. After a while they seem sticky, manipulative, and repellent, because they're exaggerated.

The **country** of TWOs is Italy. The caricature of the fat Italian *mamma*, who rules the family, requires no explanation. The effort people make to *appear* warm, lovable, and charming is something one runs into in Italy at very step. If you ask someone in England for directions, the polite English will do everything to get you to your destination. If necessary, they will go along with you. In Italy they grab you by the arm (body contact is important), point with grand gestures in any direction and say "Over there!" If you follow their directions and advice, you discover that you're hopelessly lost. They present an image of attention and helpfulness. The image is more important than the facts.

The **color** of TWOs is red. It symbolizes life, power, and passion and is traditionally considered a masculine color. In Hebrew the words for blood (*dam*), earth (*adamah*), red (*adom*), and man (*adam*) derive from the same root. Red is the color of love and martyrdom. "In the pure red of the rose it is — as in the blood of Christ... — a symbol of unconditional devotion to life and the will of the Father."[7] The martyrs were often represented in red garments. As the color of fire, red represents the Holy Spirit and the Church, which was born out of the baptism of the Spirit on Pentecost. The color red also has aggressive features: it is assigned to Mars, the god of war, and to passion. Bullfighters wave a red cloth. A red flag waved in many revolutions. Red also represents the kinship of the "devoted" TWO with the aggressive EIGHT.[8]

Mary Magdalen, Martha, and John (the beloved disciple) are the symbolic figures of TWO from the **Bible.**

Mary Magdalen, the ex-prostitute, was the woman closest to Jesus. Perhaps she was the "sinful woman" who washed his feet with her tears and dried them with her hair: a woman who often loved him in life, in the hope of being loved at least once. She was the first one to meet the risen Christ. She wanted to embrace him, but he held her back: "Do not cling to me" (John 20:17). The time of physical closeness was past. Mary's love had to let go, to reach a deeper and more spiritual dimension.

Martha was one of two sisters at whose house Jesus regularly stayed. Once when Jesus was their guest, Mary sat with him, listened to him and spoke with him — something unheard of for a woman in the Orient at that time. Martha, on the other hand, fitted into the classic female role and served at table, though she had no fun doing it. She was angry that Mary gave in to her "egotistical" need, sat there, listened, and talked. Finally she snapped at her guest, Jesus: "Do you not care that my sister has left me to serve alone? Tell her then to help me." But Jesus refused to confirm her self-chosen role: "Martha, Martha, you are anxious and troubled about many things; one thing is needful. Mary has chosen the good portion, which shall not be taken away from her" (Luke 10:38–42).

"Noli me tangere" (Martin Schongauer)
Mary Magdalen and the Risen Christ

It is significant that with type TWO we think first of all of women figures. For most of the other types it is difficult to find female representatives in the Bible. The Bible reflects a patriarchal culture; its male writers often present woman in a pale, vague fashion. With type TWO it is the other way around; there are many instances of female TWOs. Still there is in the Bible one man who is a classic TWO: John.

He was Jesus' favorite disciple (whether he really was that or only would have liked to have been is not known. In any case he is called that in the Gospel of John and only there). He is the one who lay "close to the breast of Jesus" and openly showed his feelings for the Master. He is also the only man who stuck it out under the cross with the women, when all the "strong men" had fled. One of the main themes of the Johannine writings[9] is love: God is love (1 John 4:16). The last word of John before his death as a grayhaired old man is said to have been, "Little children, love one another!" His second main theme is the Incarnation, when God became flesh. John describes Jesus in his sensuousness (the washing of the feet) and is especially interested in the physical, experiential nature of salvation: "That which we have heard, which we have seen with our eyes, which we have looked upon and touched with our hands . . . we proclaim to you" (1 John 1:1–2). On the other hand, his message is in some passages highly spiritualized and mystical. For TWOs, sensuousness and spirituality are not opposites.

John, the "beloved" disciple, had a typical TWO's shadow, which is easily overlooked. But in the three synoptic Gospels it can be clearly seen. For example, he makes a bid (along with his brother James) for the best place in heaven, "at the right hand of the Master," a place he also takes at the Last Supper (the favorite position of the ambitious TWO, cf. Mark 10:37). When his love is not reciprocated, he becomes extremely aggressive: After Jesus and his disciples have been turned away from a village, he and James ask the Master: "Do you want us to bid fire come down from heaven and consume them?" (Luke 9:54).

True, John the evangelist speaks about love more than the others, but if you look carefully, you notice that this love is exclusive and applies only to the "brothers." For him "brothers" are no longer his Jewish compatriots, but only those who believe in Christ. He draws a sharp dividing line between inside and outside. The concept of "love of one's enemy" does not exist in his work. People who think differently are quickly stamped as anti-Christians. Above all he begins to damn the Jewish people, to whom he himself belongs, but who have not accepted Christ. This has to be one of the roots of Christian anti-Semitism. John has Jesus say to the Jews on one occasion, "Your father is the devil" (John 8:44) — words that Jesus surely never said. It's not far from there to those dreadful lines of Hitler: "The Jew . . . just cannot be a human being in the sense of the image and likeness of God. The Jew is the image of the devil."[10]

Conversion and Redemption

The **invitation** that redeems a TWO is the call to freedom. Real freedom, for which the TWO deeply longs, ends the game of manipulation and false love, of dependency and violent attempts at self-liberation. TWOs find their way to freedom only when they can have and accept the experience of unconditional love, the experience that in religious traditions is called "grace." A sign that this grace has arrived is gratitude. Redeemed TWOs no longer wait for God and the world to be grateful to them because they do so much for them; they can rejoice over little signs of attention. Liberated TWOs can also set other people free and be thankful for the intimacy and attention that is possible in relationships. A redeemed TWO is glad when people, about whom they were once concerned, go their own way in freedom.

One of the **lifelong tasks** of TWOs consists in achieving a certain degree of objectivity and freeing themselves from gossip, flattery, false intimacy, sentimentalism, and the continual quest for reinforcement. TWOs must take pains to practice unobtrusive service: "Can I do something for others that does not get noticed and rewarded?" When Jesus said, "When you give alms, do not let your left hand know what your right hand is doing" (Matt. 6:3) he was probably speaking to TWOs. Here is where it shows whether someone is really doing something "for God" or only to be confirmed as an altruistic and self-sacrificing person. As a rule TWOs take care that other people are informed of their good deeds. To overcome the dependency on confirmation, TWOs generally have to have — and survive — deep and painful experiences of loss. The grief work with the goal of severing symbiotic relationships can become the gateway to clearer self-perception and to freedom. Only after letting go do they notice that they can stand on their own two feet, and they're actually happy to do so.

TWOs, like all heart types, need a place of silence and objectivity, where they can be alone, where they can make friends with themselves and seriously reflect — with their heads, that is. TWOs are inclined to think with their hearts. In their aggressive phases they can, under certain circumstances, switch off their heads altogether. In such situations they don't want to hear about logic: "Stop getting on my nerves with the facts. This is how I feel now and I have a right to." A redeemed TWO can be objective and let the facts, not just the emotions, speak.

The sensitivity of TWOs to moods and feelings has a very positive re-verse side: TWOs can read from the way their partners lift their eyebrows precisely what the "weather conditions" are. That can become a burden to them, because they are immediately hurt or get anxious as soon as they sense even a hint of rejection. They have to learn to live with this emotional hypersensitivity. For this they need patience from the people around them. On the other hand, TWOs have to be continually begged: "Don't keep confusing your feelings with the objective truth."

TWOs have to look for two warning signals. When they are ashamed of their own needs, TWOs are emotionally endangered. The same is true when they begin to accuse other people or God. As soon as they have the feeling that they fall short, they need a scapegoat. It can be hell to incur the hatred of a TWO. TWOs can hate as intensely as they can love. Then they become uncommonly cruel and brutal toward themselves and others. That is the most terrible deformation of the TWOs, who are actually loving and warmhearted. TWOs must watch themselves for any movements toward shame or blame. At that point they begin to deteriorate.

TWOs have to learn to say no and to formulate their own needs clearly and distinctly. Peter Schellenbaum has investigated the mechanisms of symbiotic relationships and shown how relations can come to grief when there is no room for putting limits on them.[11] At first it feels awkward and artificial when TWOs practice saying no, marking off limits, and articulating their own needs. The first time around it's exaggerated. Just as we ONEs have to make an effort to learn to show aggression, TWOs have to train themselves to express their wishes. At first, they will overdo it, sometimes with hysteric outbursts. At this stage others have to be patient with them; after a while they'll learn a kind of homeostasis and balance.

TWOs are in the best shape when they can love and serve. In service and giving both their manipulative side and their best side appear. So it is precisely in this area that they need help and supervision, in order to develop their "fair observer," who asks, "Why are you *really* there for others?" Now and then they have to turn off the fuel supply, deny themselves to other people, and stick it out by themselves. If they practice doing good without expecting attention and rewards, they'll notice at first that this acutely impairs their motivation.

Helper syndrome, Messiah complex, martyr fantasies, relationship-addiction — all these typically TWO games sooner or later lead to the experience about which so many members of the helping professions report.

The Swedish writers Barbro Bronsberg and Nina Vestlund in their book *Burnout* shed light on the situation of professional women who break down under the demands from themselves and others. They point to widespread physical symptoms of this typical "helper's disease" and give a series of suggestions for how, for example, one can practice saying no.[12] Burnout indicates that false motives are getting their revenge. That is why TWOs have to keep on scrutinizing their motives and free themselves from their compulsions.

A redeemed TWO is very capable of love. Anyone who has the good fortune to be loved by a mature, integrated TWO has a generous servant, a wonderful lover, an enviable friend. Such people feel your pains with you and take care of you because they know the pain of relationships and loneliness. At all cost TWOs want to spare others from going through what they have gone through. This is the strength and the beauty of a redeemed TWO.

An example of a redeemed TWO, a **saint** for our times, is Mother Teresa (b. 1910). She came from an Albanian family in Skopje (today part of Yugoslavia), in which love of neighbor and helpfulness had already been writ large. At age eighteen Agnes Gonxha Bojaxhiu entered the "English Ladies," a teaching order. From the mother house in Dublin she was sent to a high school in Calcutta, where she taught geography to "higher daughters." Directly behind the school lay a completely run-down slum neighborhood. With a few of the students Mother Teresa, who in the meantime had become the director of the school and convent superior, began to go out into poor neighborhoods and take care of the sick.

She soon realized that it was not enough to help the poor and then return to the security of her own four walls. In 1946 she decided: "I have to leave the convent and help the poor by living among them."[13] Finally she got to exchange her nun's habit for the sari of the poor and was allowed to move into a hut in the slums. There she taught the alphabet to children and showed them how to wash. Former students followed her, and so the Missionaries of Charity came into existence, an order that today numbers over two thousand sisters and over three hundred brothers.

From the beginning Mother Teresa was especially infatuated with children — born and unborn. The assertion that there are too many children is, she thinks, as absurd as the claim that there are too many stars in the skies. Teresa's sisters pick up abandoned and exposed newborns and nurse them back to health. The worst thing in the world, says Mother Teresa, is feeling unwanted. That is why she insists on the right of the unborn to life and protests against abortion: "You not only kill life, but you place your ego over God. It seems to me that one can hear the cry of those children who were murdered before they came into the world."[14] Upon receiving the Nobel Prize for Peace in Oslo in 1979 she bade the invited guests heed her appeal: "For me the nations that have legalized abortion are the poorest countries. They are afraid of little ones, they fear unborn life."[15]

Early on the sisters in Calcutta began to set up hospices so that the poorest of the poor who die on the city streets could at least die with dignity: "They have lived like animals. They should at least die like human beings."[16] The sisters do not try to proselytize people by words: "The only thing that really converts is love."

In 1982 Mother Teresa criticized the West German policy toward asylum and publicly challenged the prime minister of Württemberg Lothar Spåth: "Open your doors and God will bless you." In her opinion true love must hurt and call for sacrifices. Christ meets us in the most despised individuals: "In holy communion we have Christ in the form of bread. In our work we find him in the form of flesh and blood. It is the same Christ."[17]

Today there are Brothers and Sisters of Charity all over the world. In the Ruhr district the brothers work with drug addicts; in Berlin and New York the sisters stand by AIDS victims as they die. Social structures don't interest Mother Teresa, although she understands that others could have the vocation to struggle for structural changes: "We are concerned with the individual."[18] The motto she has given her sisters is, "Do not count the cost." This the gift of redeemed TWOs: I can give something without asking whether I'll get something back.

The sisters draw their strength from silence: meditation, prayer, and celebration of the Eucharist belong to the order of the day. TWOs find action easier than contemplation. But the balance of action and contemplation redeems them from the dangerous side of their gift. In Teresa and her sisters both poles have come together.

TYPE THREE
The Need to Succeed

Overview

The special talents of THREEs often cause them to radiate an ease and assurance that inspire confidence. This allows them to spread a good atmosphere around them. They have an easy time getting jobs done efficiently and competently, aiming for and achieving personal goals, as well as inspiring and motivating other people and making it possible for them to get ahead too.

THREEs have a "sixth sense" for sizing up tasks and for the dynamic of work groups. They identify themselves with the firm (community, organization) for which they work, and have the gift of creating a good business climate and keeping the store together. They are keenly interested in connecting and "networking" the members of the group. Through their convincing charisma and the force of their arguments THREEs can gain great influence and bring the projects they believe in to success.

The THREE is the central type of the heart group (TWO, THREE, FOUR). But this does not mean that THREEs are people who manage best their emotional world. On the contrary, type THREEs have the greatest difficulties of all the Enneagram types in perceiving their own feelings. Like TWOs, THREEs are always holding an imaginary thermometer in the air to test the conditions. But unlike TWOs they don't ask, "Do you like me?" but "Am I successful? Am I getting across?" Like the former mayor of New York, Ed Koch, they forever say, "How 'm I doin'?"

As children THREEs were often loved not for their own sake but were praised and rewarded when they were successful and had special achievements to show for it. When they came home with good marks or won a football game, their mother or father said: "You're a good boy. We're proud of you." Gradually they idealized victory and success and developed the guiding motto: "I'm good when I win."

THREEs draw their life energy from their successes. THREEs are show-people, achievers, careerists, status-seekers, and handle each of their roles better than their true self, which they scarcely know. They can slip into almost any mask and act the part to perfection. The role protects and motivates them. The life of THREEs is a competitive struggle: it's a question of winning or losing. THREEs want to be winners and for that reason they often go far. A woman successful in both her career and family, who recognized herself as a THREE, describes herself as follows:

I can recall that I loved it when my father played "mental arithmetic snake" (adding and subtracting many numbers in your head one after another) with us, because most of the time I won. Not that I liked mental arithmetic; I liked to win. My sister always found this game horrible. In school I enjoyed all subjects, so long as I had good marks. The only subjects I found deathly boring were the ones like music, in which I had no prospect at all of being among the best, because we had a few superstars in the class. I thought religion teachers who gave only A's and B's were terrible, because the system of checking on performance helped me to self-determination. I never saw myself as competition for others — rather as someone who liked to get ahead on the team. Getting ahead is important. I find it hard to stand still and wait patiently for the stragglers. Often I prefer to work alone at my own tempo before I have to drag along others who can't get motivated.

THREEs can work really hard and pour all their energy into a project. They are often highly competent in their field and strike others as more competent still. People believe they have mastered their job and are convinced of their cause.

Many THREEs are also physically attractive.[1] Frequently they were handsome even as children. They were "super-kids" and heard people say again and again, "You can do it. You can make it." In many cases this became a self-fulfilling prophecy. Most THREEs seem optimistic, youthful, intelligent, dynamic, and productive.

Occupations in which THREEs go far are agents, salesmen, managers, designers, and other professions connected with the media and advertising. If they are "only" housewives and mothers, then they are super-housewives and super-mothers. In intimate relationships they tend to carry out the roles of lover or beloved skillfully: they can be romantic when romanticism is called for, sensuous when sensuality is called for. They have the tendency to become the prototype of whatever group they happen to be in and to embody the expectations and values of this group. THREE men and THREE women tend for this reason to adopt the current societal definition of "masculinity" and "femininity." For example, if the *Zeitgeist* allows the man to be domestic, soft, and tender, these features will immediately show up in the THREE man. If athletic and natural women are in demand, THREE females will soon be leading the squads of athletic and natural women.

The popular social values need not absolutely be the ones with which a THREE identifies. THREEs who join a Christian community or a radical group critical of society will not embody the values and the recognized image of society, but of their new primary relational group. Problems arise only when the THREE belongs to several groups with different lifestyles. In that case it can happen that they change their image and role with lightning speed as soon as they cross the threshold from one domain of life to another.

A good friend of mine who is a THREE has the nickname Mr. Perfect. Everything he touches seems to succeed and turns, as in the fairy tale, into gold. This friend says: "When I walk into a room where there are lots of people, I know in fractions of a second how I have to behave, how I have to appear, how I have to talk to be accepted by everybody present. Others may feel these behavior differences only as nuances; I know immediately what nuance is called for. If I leave the room and go one door down, then I can play the same game and be a completely different person."

THREEs are "cool," successful types who go through the world smiling and for whom everything they want apparently drops into their lap. In reality nothing drops into their lap. They work hard for their success. They take pains so that their plans succeed, and they commit all their energy to their efforts. But they want it to look easy and offhand and they don't let their strenuous efforts show.

THREEs are inclined to have an exaggeratedly positive perception of what they identify with. When they think that they have succeeded in something, they can send out "ad spots" for themselves in order to rake in praise, recognition, and admiration. They like to talk about their successful moments, to count up the people they were able to influence, the projects they carried through, distinctions they have won. THREEs cannot be praised enough. They suck up endorsements like a dried up sponge. Unfortunately this praise often never comes because THREEs generally strike others as so self-assured and strong that others scarcely think that these successful people are dependent on compliments. Just as TWOs do everything when they are needed, THREEs do everything for praise. Praise is the gas that makes the THREE's motor go. THREEs are even more dependent on the reactions of other people than TWOs are, though it's seldom noticed.

Dilemma

Efficiency is the THREE's greatest **temptation**. The capitalist system, which dominates the world economy, is based on the THREE dogma: "Those who exert themselves enough can work their way up." The society of the United States, the symbolic country of THREEs (see below), is an expression of this attitude. What I say about THREEs relates to all Americans, for our entire society is infected with this thinking. We admire winners and despise losers. This can be seen just by the way we deal with the army of the poor, in all their millions. Anyone who doesn't manage to make it into the mainstream of the American middle class is treated like a leper, looked upon as substandard and morally inferior. The poor do not deserve to be noticed or appreciated. In the final analysis they themselves are responsible for their failure. THREEs slip easily into "blaming the victim."

That more or less is how the credo of American society runs. The "American Gospel" of achievement, affluence, and success is so dominant and universally acknowledged that in the United States a large portion of the population of lifelong churchgoers have a value system in no way significantly different from their "unbelieving" neighbors. In fact, this attitude is carried over into the spiritual domain. Religion is increasingly becoming a kind of spiritual consumerism This is mirrored in the "spiritual" success stories of American televangelists: glowing individuals, filled with vitamins, bursting with cheerfulness and optimism and with Jesus in their hearts. Jesus is sold as a recipe for success, and the cross no longer plays any role. If the symbol of the cross is used at all, then it's "dolled up" with glow, glitter, and neon. Even Christ's death is far too quickly transformed into a story of victory. But there's no possibility of making the "word of the cross" a success story. The cross means that Christ tasted the defeat of death to the full and drank the bitter cup to the dregs. The cup does not pass Christ by. He has to taste it. A society bent on success can't follow this pattern. Middle-class culture avoids failure and defeat. We are probably the first generation in world history that has bought our way out of the experience of failure with the help of prosperity. It is a one-sided Gospel.

The **defense mechanism** of THREE is identification. THREEs protect themselves from threats by becoming fully involved in their projects, and they are reluctant to accept criticism of their group or company. In the beginning years of the New Jerusalem community I and another Franciscan who worked there with me had to present a report before a diocesan commission about what was going on in our crazy community. We were supposed to render an account to show that everything was on solid ground, that we could be trusted, and so forth. My fellow Franciscan was a THREE. He sold them New Jerusalem so beautifully it took your breath away. It sounded as if New Jerusalem were the Reign of God on earth. A very sharp-eyed priest on the commission observed: "Father, you're trying too hard. It can't be *that* good." If THREEs believe in something, then they do it without ifs, ands, or buts, and they can completely smooth out the shadow side, because "shadow" is the same as "failure."

"Failure" is the term that describes THREE's **avoidance**. There is nothing more tragic than an unsuccessful THREE, because it's traumatic for a THREE to have to deal with failing, falling short, or losing.[2] Unredeemed THREEs avoid, fear, and hate defeat like the plague. But when it does occur, they have at least three standard methods to extricate themselves. Sometimes they polish up their defeats and reinterpret them as "partial victories." Often they shift the responsibility to others. And they frequently leave the scene of the wreck as quickly as possible to plunge into a new, promising project. Unredeemed THREEs are capable of immensely overestimating themselves. They have often been so spoiled by success that in the end they themselves believe that everything they do is good and great.

The pressure to succeed that THREEs (and THREE societies) are under leads to their **root sin**, untruth or deceit. In order to win, THREEs tend to dress up the truth. The classic name for this sin is "vainglory." They create an image that looks good, can be sold, and finally will win. These are seldom boldfaced lies: rather they are the subtle nuancing, the airbrushing out of the problematic side of a project, the exaggerated stress on advantages, the creation of euphemisms (e.g., calling the MX first-strike missile "the Peacekeeper") .

Deceit or lying is lacking in the classic catalogue of the seven capital sins, as is the sin of SIX, fear. Its classification as a sin derives from the tradition of the Muslim Sufis. It is worth noting that we in the Western tradition have never unmasked and named these sins (THREE and SIX) as such. They are the deadly sins of our society, which are all the more dangerous because we don't see them. One cannot or will not recognize one's own sin.

One exception in the West is Dante, who in his *Divine Comedy* has his narrator travel through Hell, Purgatory, and Paradise. While he doesn't meet the representatives of the seven capital sins until the *Purgatorio*, he encounters the "cowards" (SIXes) at the very entrance of Hell (canto III). He places the "forgers and traitors" at the deepest point in hell (cantos XXIX to XXXIV). The latter, including Judas, who betrayed Jesus, and Brutus and Cassius, the murderers of Caesar, are frozen in the deepest circle of Hell (the ninth).[3]

Unredeemed THREEs first and foremost deceive themselves. That is why their lies are not easy to see through even for them. First, THREEs convince themselves that the lie is the truth. Then, for example, an American politician can walk up, glowing and erect, before the press microphones and explain that everything is all right — and believe it himself.

Unredeemed THREEs have no longing for depth. What's the point of depth when superficiality works and when image without content sells? THREEs thrown back on themselves are extremely pragmatic: whatever works is true. The question of objective truth doesn't even get raised. THREEs believe images to be reality itself.

In his book *The People of the Lie* M. Scott Peck has sketched out a psychology of evil from the standpoint of lying. "Evil people" or "people of the lie" are for him the ones who attack others instead of looking their own failure in the eye. Through the use of case studies from his own psychotherapeutic practice and evidence from My Lai in Vietnam (1968) he gives an impressive description of how the repression of one's own guilt and the related projection of guilt on others ends by destroying the culprits themselves. THREEs who believe their own lies belong to the most deformed personalities in existence.[4]

The bad thing is that you often blindly trust even a truly dishonest THREE. THREEs look so self-confident; they seem to know what they are doing. That's why you usually trust them. THREEs are the proverbial used car salesmen: everything is polished and shines. They speak so impressively and so quickly you can hardly follow them. Their offers often strike us as irresistible. In the end you believe that this is the best used car in the city. They can sell you everything, because they are primarily selling themselves. We like how cool and competent they are — and we buy the car because the scene is so perfectly staged and we are "cast" to be the buyer from the actor salesperson.

The **pitfall** in which the unredeemed THREE is caught is vanity. By vanity I mean that secondary, external things (packaging, clothing, outside impact) are more important than essentials (substance, person, content). Unredeemed THREEs live as if they weren't in their own body and in their own soul, but were standing alongside and watching themselves perform. THREEs are born actors. Some of them become first-class, many at least good. No wonder the actor Ronald Reagan could become president of the U.S.A. I also consider Pope John Paul II a THREE; he also was an actor as a young man. THREEs know how to use the masses. Many THREEs like to stand before crowds and audiences. Role, prestige, numbers give them a sense of success. In personal, one-on-one conversations, on the other hand, many THREEs feel rather unsure of themselves, because there people demand genuineness, vulnerability, and profundity.

The THREEs' gift or **fruit of the spirit** is the reverse of their sin: truthfulness or honesty. A redeemed THREE has found the way to truth. Such people are rare in the U.S.A., especially in the business world, where it would be to their disadvantage to change! Mr. Perfect, whom I mentioned earlier, once asked me in a personal conversation: "Richard, don't let me cheat any more. I can do such a number on myself and the world. I can put one over on anybody." He knew what he was capable of. But he had got his own number. He knew he could throw dust in people's eyes, and he was hungry for truthfulness. THREEs find the way to their gift only when they take the painful path of self-knowledge and look their life-lies, big and little, in the face and refuse to gloss over them any more. Since this is insight into one's own failure, THREEs have a very hard time with it. THREEs who have found their way to truthfulness can put their tremendous gifts to work to help other people competently and effectively and to motivate them to discover their own potential (helping them to help themselves). Redeemed THREEs manage to get groups or communities sensibly organized, get society's lies named by name, and get the truth spread "professionally and in the style of the time."

Symbols and Examples

The first symbolic **animal** of THREEs is the chameleon. THREEs are clever at adapting themselves to the expectations of their environment. This means the danger of exchanging a variety of roles and masks for their real self, to which they have no access. An unredeemed THREE whose roles and masks have been taken away can panic, can literally dissolve into nothing. A THREE woman reports that when she was in love she would spend a long time thinking what female type she should embody at her next rendezvous in order to "go over well."

A second symbol is the peacock. Some Enneagram specialists also apply the peacock to type TWO or FOUR. All heart types have something "peacock-like" about them, because with their behavior they aim at a reaction from their environment and they *present* themselves: the TWO poses as lovable and helpful, the THREE plays the role that "goes over" best, the FOUR puts in an appearance as something special. The peacock shows himself off. His vain ornaments draw attention to him. The long-term goal of counseling for heart types must be to bundle away the peacock and to dock his tail, so that it becomes clear that without his finery he is just as much a normal, ugly chicken as the rest of us.

The symbolic animal for the redeemed THREE is the eagle. The "king of the winds" is said to be the only animal that can look directly into the sun. He is a symbol for swiftness, power, endurance, and renewal: "They who wait for the Lord shall renew their strength, they shall mount up with wings like eagles. They shall run and not be weary, they shall walk and not faint" (Isa. 40:31).

The **country** of THREEs is the United States. As a citizen of this country I would like to take a somewhat more thorough look at our mentality. In the U.S. there is no motivation *not* to be a THREE. Anyone who has mastered the THREE game here will get to the top of the system. In this country THREEs become CEOs, bishops, and presidents. That is one of the reasons why we are so often disappointed by our leaders. Every now and then it dawns on us how superficially things are managed up there. All their lives these people have been so busy climbing the ladder of success that it has become the sole focus of their lives. The THREE is the prototype of the white male American — that's how young people are brought up in our country. These are the young men who become senior class president and win all the other elections. Those who don't match the THREE ideal feel inferior and insecure, as if there were something wrong with them.

We Americans have an extremely hard time seeing through the lies of our system. After the shooting down of the Iranian airbus by the U.S.S.

Vincennes, the rumor spread that Iran already had a number of mutilated corpses on hand and dumped them into the Persian Gulf to make the world believe that we had shot down a commercial airliner. Something like this could occur only to a sick THREE. America, the "kingdom of God," is exalted above any unclean motive and could never make such a mistake. This sort of deceit is part of our American system and lifestyle. It is vital for us as Americans to understand the energy of THREEs if we wish to analyze the mentality of our country. The rest of the world has an image of the "ugly American," superficial and hollow, the image of an artificial world packaged in plastic without substantial content. But we Americans cannot and will not see ourselves this way.

At this point I must say a few words in retrospect about the Reagan era. Reagan was — like many American presidents — a THREE. His election and reelection were foreseeable. If he could have run for a third term, he would have been president again. He embodied the collective essence of the United States almost perfectly. Reagan was the pragmatic, successful, attractive American without much depth. This profile matches the vanity and superficiality of the unredeemed THREE. You scratch at the veneer a little and you find — nothing. Reagan never felt or faced the pain of his own alcoholic father or his present dysfunctional family. Everything was wonderful in America!

The THREE is a type that grows out of affluence. I am sure that in Third World countries one would not meet the same percentage of THREEs as in the U.S. From their first year of life the poor have to look scarcity, failure, and defeat in the eye. They learn that you seldom get what you want, that you can't escape from pain and suffering. The United States has to go a long way to meet its false collective self, to confront it, and acknowledge its susceptibility to lies, deceit, and illusion.

The **color** of THREE is traffic-light yellow. Yellow catches the eye; it strikes us as urgent, dynamic, and eccentric. It is radiant. All this describes the redeemed THREE: "As the brightest of the colors it makes the meaning and goal of creation transparent. It makes light shine through and thereby irradiates things. Thus yellow becomes the directional element among the colors. It asks pressing questions, makes things visible, and gives answers. It guides and leads us along our way and illumines it with knowledge, meaning and insight."[5] Yellow is at the same time the most vulnerable of all colors. The slightest dirtying or cloudiness makes it appear ugly or poisonous. "As there is only one truth, there is only one yellow. Muddied truth is sick truth, is untruth. Thus the expression of muddied yellow is envy, treachery, falseness, doubt, mistrust, and insanity. In Giotto's painting *Christ Taken Prisoner* and in Holbein's *Last Supper* Judas is painted in muddied yellow."[6]

The **biblical ancestor** of all THREEs is Jacob the deceiver. Even in his mother's womb he fought with his twin brother Esau, who was the first-born. Jacob, a "civilized man," is the favorite of his mother, Rebekah, while his father, Isaac, prefers the rough hunter Esau. One evening Jacob exploits his brother's fatigue and hunger to buy his right of primogeniture, on which everything depended in the Orient at that time, for a dish of lentils. When his blind father is on his deathbed, with Rebekah's help Jacob gets his father's blessing by cheating.[7] He pretends to be Esau, and by the time his brother comes home, Isaac's blessing has already been given. Jacob has to flee from Esau's wrath to his uncle Laban in Haran. During the flight he has a dream in which he sees the heavens open and God's angels going up and down (the ladder or staircase as a symbol of ascent and descent is a message every THREE can understand.)

In Haran he falls in love with his cousin Rachel, who was "beautiful and lovely." He is supposed to serve his uncle for seven years to get her as a wife. This time he is the deceived one. On the morning after the wedding he discovers that the wrong wife has been put in his bed, namely Leah, whose "eyes were weak." But Jacob does not give up. He serves his uncle for another seven years and finally gets Rachel too.

In the meantime Laban has become a rich man through Jacob's help. But Jacob heads home. Despite all his fears he wants to go back to be reconciled with his brother. (It's a positive sign when THREEs confront their past and are ready to take the consequences of their mistakes.) As a reward for his long years of service he is allowed to take a part of the herds with him. Through a sophisticated trick he sees to it that he "has become exceedingly rich" and gets "many sheep, men and women slaves, camels and asses."

He sends messengers with lavish presents before him to assure a good reception from Esau. Jacob spends the night before the meeting alone at the river Jabbok, which his people have already forded. An unknown man comes and wrestles with him. The stranger defeats him only by an unfair blow to his hip. Even though beaten, Jacob will not admit complete defeat. When the stranger is about to leave at the break of day, he holds him tightly and says: "I will not let you, unless you bless me." The stranger gives Jacob (the deceiver) a new name: Israel (God's fighter). "For," he says, "you have striven with God and with men, and have prevailed." In the end there actually is a reconciliation between the two brothers (Gen. 25–33).[8]

Scarcely any biblical figure can be so unequivocally assigned to an Enneagram type as Jacob can. He struggles with God and with man — using every possible trick. Astonishingly God does not deny the blessing to this conflicting figure. To this day the nation of Israel has identified itself with this wrestling between humankind and God. And Israel like America is a THREE country, now incapable of seeing that they have become Goliath while Palestinian boys are the new Davids.

At first glance two other THREEs from the Bible are rather unsympathetic: Judas and Pilate. They embody the dilemma of unredeemed ambitions. According to a widespread theory, Judas betrayed Jesus to compel him to act and to force him finally to seize power as Messiah. When he realized that his calculation had gone wrong, he saw no way out except suicide. His greed for money (money as a symbol of success) fits into this picture.

The career politician Pilate was convinced of Jesus' innocence. But a just judgment might have been harmful to his professional future. In the hearing he poses the THREE's question, "What is truth?" (John 18:38) He sees right through the game, but he plays along with it, because he never makes the breakthrough from the lie to the truth that meets him in Jesus of Nazareth.

Conversion and Redemption

The **invitation** to THREEs is the call to hope. Only a hope that goes beyond ostensible successes can help a THREE acquire depth and put up with momentary failure. Paul writes: "For this slight momentary affliction is preparing for us an eternal weight of glory beyond all comparison, because we look not to the things that are seen but to the things that are unseen; for the things that are seen are transient, but the things that are unseen are eternal" (2 Cor. 4:17–18). Hope also means not basing life on one's own goals, but anchoring it in God's will and the comprehensive goals of God's Reign. Think big! Jesus says: "Seek first his kingdom and his righteousness, and all these things shall be yours as well" (Matt. 6:33).

THREEs really have to work to gain depth. They have a tendency to let their feelings atrophy. While TWOs sometimes wallow in an emotional morass, if you ask THREEs how they feel, they sometimes don't know themselves. Feelings interfere with efficiency and organization. That is why THREEs suspend their emotions while they have a task to do. But since classic THREEs are continually pursuing some project or other (sometimes three or four at the same time) the inner world too often comes to grief.

To be healed and redeemed, THREEs, like TWOs, must learn to be alone. Both need a place of silence and seclusion where there is no public feedback, no applause, and no admiration. Contemplative prayer and silent meditation are the appropriate "prescriptions." When THREEs begin to discover their inner world, in the beginning they generally make that into a project too: they want to meditate *successfully*. It takes a while before they notice that the point is to do nothing, to learn nothing, simply to exist. As soon as THREEs learn this, they will make the effort "simply to exist" and "to learn nothing" with as much success as possible. The fruitful way into the depths demands a great deal of patience from THREEs and the readiness to experience nothing in particular for quite a while.

In silence it's also important that THREEs encounter self-critically their own dishonesty and the compulsion to succeed. THREEs must above all chew and digest their shadow sides, their failure and their defeats, instead of running away from them. The confession "I've failed; I was wrong; I lied," costs THREEs an enormous effort.

It makes things still more difficult that in Western civilization THREEs are practically never challenged. Our criteria for "health" are the capacity to work, love, and enjoy. Women's magazines and the popular press in general reinforce this feeling. But THREEs imprisoned in themselves are as much in need of redemption as everyone else. It's simply harder to recognize a disease as such when everyone else calls it "health." The redemption of THREEs in our society, under certain circumstances, also means taking leave from the understanding and applause of the world around us.

Isaac B. Singer, the great Jewish-American writer and Nobel Prize winner, has sketched the fictional life-confession of a THREE in his novel *The Penitent*. The protagonist, a Jew born in Poland, has narrowly escaped the Holocaust. He emigrates to America and has a career as a businessman. He succeeds in everything, makes a lot of money, marries an attractive woman. Ultimately he takes a mistress, whom he supports, together with her daughter. When he learns that he is not her only lover, he breaks up the affair and hurries home where he catches his wife in adultery. In his disgust with life he sees only two possibilities: to commit suicide or dare to make a radical new start. He decides — despite all his religious doubts — to become an orthodox Jew and keep the commandments. His path leads him to Mea Shearim, where the strictly Orthodox Jews of Jerusalem live in accordance with the old customs. After his divorce he marries a simple Jewish girl. Through his new way of life faith slowly begins to grow in him. An unpretentious life of fidelity to the Law finally lets him find peace.

Isaac Singer says about his "penitent": "The remedies that he recommends will not be able to heal everyone's wounds, but the nature of the disease will, I hope, be recognized."[9] He attacks the superficial, successful man of the present, his "endangered family life, his greed for luxury and technical gimcrackery, his contempt for old people, his bowing and scraping before the young, his blind faith in psychiatry, his increasing tolerance of crime."[10]

Finally THREEs long, sometimes without knowing it themselves, not only for praise and recognition, but for real love. They get so much applause for their successes that in the end they think that's all they want. It takes a long time before they understand that there is more than deserved recognition: unmerited, unconditional love.

A nun friend of mine, the principal of a local high school, is a wonderful and highly competent THREE. Probably only a few people have ever seen her weak side. Several times I listened as she broke down in tears and said: "It's enough to drive you mad, Richard. Everybody elects me for all the jobs because they know I can do everything. Everybody likes me because I do everything so terrifically. I'd like just once to feel that everybody loved me for what I am. But I know that I myself contribute to making things the way they are. I seem so strong and independent and I get so much done that people always just react to what I do."

THREEs seldom cry, but now and then they can break out in very violent tears, which generally catches others completely by surprise. Their underdeveloped feeling side finally gets some air by crying. "After I cry I feel really good," says one THREE. "Before, I usually have the feeling that nobody knows me and understands me. But after crying the trouble's gone. I find that there's comfort in crying itself and that I'm comforted by God. Anyhow, nobody else can give as much comfort as an unredeemed THREE needs."

In their best moments all THREEs know that in reality they have a weakly developed sense of self-worth, that people are taking their "products." That is why to many THREEs situations like sickness and old age, where they can no longer offer anything, seem threatening. Their motto, "I produce, therefore I am," breaks down. One THREE told me: "I have a hard time coming to terms with being sick, as with really doing nothing. Even after a heart attack my father was working on his papers while he was in bed. It's crazy that even back then at fifteen I realized that this was a false compulsion. But now I react in just the same way when I'm sick." One of the **life tasks** of THREEs is to grasp sickness as a signal, a chance for transformation.

THREEs must learn to stand still now and then and stop the eternal hunt for new successes and projects. The question, "How do I actually feel?" is one that THREEs can often hardly answer. Purposeful care of the body as well as dealing with one's own dream pictures can be a bridge to the soul. Another of the life tasks of THREEs is to listen more frequently and carefully to the voice of their own feelings instead of doing what promises to get them recognition from the outside.

THREEs must above all sharpen their conscience and not allow themselves "insignificant" deviations from the truth. In the journey inward THREEs have to overcome their deep but ungrounded anxiety that behind their roles and masks there may not be any true self at all.

THREEs should also beware a hyperactive imagination that is continually busy with new projects. Instead they should undertake projects in which patient detail work is necessary and no quick results are to be expected. Like TWOs and FOURs they are in danger of immunizing themselves against criticism. Instead they should learn to search for the grain of truth in all criticism.

THREEs must confront the secret of the Cross, which is the secret of failure: out of our defeats Jesus makes *his* victories — not ours! This doesn't occur to THREEs, this doesn't work, this can't be integrated into any system of promotion. THREEs on the way to redemption free themselves from their vanity and begin to hope in God's sovereign activity, which can't be manipulated. They honestly confront their own inner emptiness and longing for love. They renounce the security won by status, money, and power. They renounce building their own reign because they hope for the coming of God's Reign.

The model of a redeemed THREE is Dorothy Day (1897–1980), the American **saint** of the twentieth century par excellence. She was born in Brooklyn, the daughter of a sports reporter, and was given a wholly non-religious education. Soon the family moved to Chicago. Dorothy's social conscience was awakened, and at age sixteen she entered the Socialist Party.

After breaking off her studies she landed as a journalist on the socialist newspaper *The Call*. She interviewed Trotsky and developed into an anarchist. Mere theories couldn't hold her interest. She had to proclaim the truth publicly (once she had recognized it), had to mobilize the masses and help them practically.

In the course of a demonstration she was arrested for the first time (all told she was imprisoned six times). Sitting in the cell awakened her interest in religion and her self-criticism. She discovered how much egotism lay behind her commitment to the oppressed. After her release she began to attend Mass regularly, while supporting herself as an artist's model and a court reporter.

Her marriage failed; then she had an affair with an atheist. Because she insisted on having their daughter, Tamara, baptized, this relationship broke up too. Her partner was "jealous of Christ."[11]

The yearning for spiritual community also led to her own baptism: "My experience as a radical and my whole political past led me... to want to join with the masses, to love and praise God."[12] But even then

Dorothy Day: Radical Christian

faith remained for her an irksome business, a loyal endurance without emotional impact.

In 1933, in the middle of the Depression, she founded *The Catholic Worker* newspaper with Peter Maurin. The paper is leftist, radical, anarchistic, pacifist, Catholic — and to this day is sold for one cent. In the very first year circulation rose to 100,000.

Along with this, Dorothy Day began to set up soup kitchens and houses for the homeless and to organize strikes. She increasingly became the conscience of the American Catholic Church and of all American Christianity. The Gospel caught fire in this woman and released an explosion of love.

Dorothy did not limit herself to giving alms, but fought — unlike Mother Teresa — for effective social changes. "This could also be read, it's true, in the papal social encyclicals, but here it was practiced, and that seemed dangerous."[13]

Even during the Second World War she remained a pacifist. After the war the archbishop of New York tried to prohibit the paper from using the adjective "Catholic." She fought back, pointing out there was a union of "Catholic war veterans." Cardinal Spellman, the enthusiastic spokesman for the Vietnam war, labeled her a communist because she supported the strike of the Church's gravediggers for higher pay.

Christian love was for Dorothy Day a matter of practice. For a long time she had difficulty with the contemplative side of faith: the struggle for the poor was for a very long time her kind of prayer. Only in nature did she — like many THREEs — find rest: nature doesn't demand and doesn't judge, it doesn't reward images.

In her last years, however, she increasingly became the silent prayer and suffered from the fact that so many socially committed young people who were part of the Catholic Worker movement were so "lacking in piety," owing to their disillusionment with the official Church. When Dorothy Day died of heart failure, masses of the poor came to her funeral and stood between the bigwigs from the Church and society — they knew that Dorothy really belonged to them. According to *Newsweek*, at her funeral there were, "no tears, only hallelujahs for her long and illuminating life."[14]

TYPE FOUR
The Need to Be Special

Overview

FOURs put their gifts to work to awaken a sense of beauty and harmony in their surroundings. They are highly sensitive and almost always artistically gifted; they can express their feelings in dance, music, painting, the theater, or literature. Everything with vital energy attracts them; they grasp the moods and feelings of other people and the atmosphere of places and events with seismographic precision.

FOURs are by nature ecumenically oriented. They reject the division of the world into "sacred" and "profane." They are more at home in the realm of the unconscious, of symbols and dreams, than in the real world. Symbols help them to be with themselves and to express themselves. They also have the gift of helping others to develop an eye for the beautiful and for the world of dreams and symbols. The ritual, well done, *is* reality for the FOUR.

FOURs too draw their vital energy from others. Their life question is: "What do you think of me? Do you notice me? Do I catch your eye?"

82

FOURs strive to be aesthetically attractive, to be exceptional, to be creative, or, in some cases, to appear esoteric, eccentric, extravagant, or exotic.

But the style and "spontaneity" of an unredeemed FOUR have something artificial about them. FOURs come out of their room and say: "I just threw a few things on in a hurry." But in fact the effects have been very carefully chosen. They deliberately put together the combination (or noncombination) of clothes and colors to stand out from the others.

The life of FOURs is primarily shaped by longing: the longing for beauty and the wish that the world and life fit together into a harmonic whole. Dostoyevsky once said: "The world will be saved by beauty." FOURs believe in this principle.

In their childhood FOURs have often had the experience of the present being unbearable and meaningless. Quite often this was connected with a very painful experience of loss. This loss can be real (death of a parent, illegitimate birth, divorce, moving and being uprooted, an undependable parent, the parents' preference for a sibling, etc.) or it can have been felt "only" emotionally. Positive role models have been missing, to some extent. Thus the child in the search for identity turns toward the inner world. Because the original source of love was missing or was too weak, new sources of love had to be created in the imagination. The longing of FOURs is directed to that lost love; it is at once a yearning to go home and to go far away. They look forward to the day when the great love will come (back), and they are convinced that this great love will redeem them.

At times the anger over a loss that has been suffered is so deep that it cannot be tolerated. Instead unredeemed FOURs direct it against themselves. They believe that for some reason they are themselves guilty for experiencing rejection and privation, and so they consider themselves "bad." Many FOURs report that they are ruled by a hidden shame. FOURs trapped in themselves will repeatedly cultivate their "badness" and thereby keep producing situations in which they are rejected or abandoned. Scandalous behavior exercises a certain charm on them; what is dark and forbidden has a peculiar power of attraction.

Most FOURs are of the opinion that society's norms don't hold for them. On the strength of their extraordinary suffering they usually feel themselves to be strangers and outsiders by nature. As such they assume the right to lay down their own norms. Many FOURs have an elitist consciousness. They try to meet special standards and feel a deficiency when that continually proves unsuccessful.

FOURs are easy to recognize. First, they have a tendency to wear odd clothes. Almost all FOURs demonstrate their melancholy side with a preference for colors such as black and violet. Some are also inclined to dress in as motley and crazy a manner as possible. Many are vegetarians, animal rights activists, feminists, and adherents to eccentric ideas about health. They often wear scarfs or berets.

Possession brings FOURs little joy. Longing is more important than having. As soon as they possess the object of their desires, they are generally disappointed. For that reason they can be very complicated love partners. A FOUR once told me her story. As a young girl she longed with every fiber of her being for her future husband. She moved heaven and earth to get him. But on the day of her wedding her romantic feelings melted into thin air. It wasn't long before she left him. At that moment she fell in love with him again. When her husband came back, the following took place: "As soon as he stood in front of the door, my love died. I reproached him for everything he had done to me. As soon as he was fed up with my wailing and turned away again to leave, my love awoke once more." To outsiders this sounds grotesque or almost funny. But it's part of the terrible dilemma in which unredeemed FOURs are caught. They can't live in the present, which is always full of ordinariness. But when their longing is realized, it is never as special as the fantasy itself was.

FOURs revere great authorities: important poets, musicians, gurus, counselors, who have something "deep" about them or are something "larger than life." Only this sort of "inner authority" counts. Formal authorities that aren't backed up by their personality make no impression on a FOUR. Their nose for the "authentic" is infallible.

All types of this group have a natural eye for beauty. That is why many of them become artists, musicians, poets, and playwrights. In the Church they are advocates and designers of creative services. They have a sense of liturgy, ritual, and shaping space. Their sensitivity to style leaves the rest of us pale with envy. Most FOURs have exquisite taste. They don't buy their paintings in Woolworth's, and they prefer to buy their clothes in a second-hand shop or a boutique rather than off the rack. They would be mortified to have to settle for cheap mass produced stuff that thousands of others wear. But like all of us, they too are inclined to exaggerate their gifts and with a certain arrogance they make other people feel their "aesthetic superiority." FOURs hate everything that is stale, old-fashioned, plain, average, styleless, and "normal."

At the same time they steal a glance of secret envy at us normal consumers who can't shine with so much class and style. FOURs have a tendency to idealize the "unwashed masses" and can write great romantic novels about the noble poor (Victor Hugo). But they do this from an ivory tower and in reality they can hardly endure living in real dirt and hard-core poverty.

The life program of FOURs could be described as an eternal quest for the Holy Grail. The Grail emerged around the end of twelfth century in Old French and Provençal literature. According to tradition it was the vessel used at the Last Supper, which Joseph of Arimathea is also supposed to have used to catch the blood of Christ.

The Grail confers heavenly and earthly happiness upon its possessor, but only the "pure" knight who is destined to do so can find it. In Wolfram von Eschenbach's *Parzifal* (ca. 1200) the Grail is a stone with marvelous powers that is guarded by angels and later preserved at the fortress of Munsalvaesche, a mixture of a Grimm brothers "table-set-yourself " and a magic holy fetish (the Grail gets its power from a host that was brought to it on Good Friday by a dove). Richard Wagner used the Parsifal legend, arbitrarily transformed in his operas *Parsifal* and *Lohengrin*.

A similar motif is the search for a specific flower, which first comes up in the *Roman de la Rose*, France's contribution to the allegory of love. The core of the poem was composed by Guillaume de Lorris (early thirteenth century). This novel in verse was probably (like Chaucer's *Canterbury Tales* and Dante's *Divine Comedy*) influenced by the Sufis; Fariddun Attar's *Birds and Flowers* and *The Conversation of the Birds* seem to have "stood at the font."[1] It describes the wanderings of the hero through an ideal landscape with a garden of love, whose walls are painted with the allegories of hatred, betrayal, greed, envy, melancholy, etc. In the garden itself the god of love dances with women named Generosity, Bravery, and Candor. Through Danger, Slander, Shame, and Fear the hand about to grasp the bud is once again held back. Even when the hero, with the help of Venus, finally gets the kiss, the opposing voices of Jealousy, Shame, Fear, and Anger resound once more. But Lady Pity and Lady Beauty come to the poet's aid.

The same motif returns in the romantic longing for the mysterious Blue Flower (Novalis), which symbolizes the striving of the human soul for fulfillment and wholeness:

> He dreamed that he was sitting on the soft turf by the margin of a fountain, whose waters flowed into the air, and seemed to vanish in it. Dark blue rocks with various colored veins rose in the distance. The daylight around him was milder and clearer than usual; the sky was of a sombre hue, filling the air with the richest perfume. But what most attracted his notice, was a tall, light-blue flower, which stood nearest the fountain, and touched it with its broad,

glossy leaves. . . . But he saw the blue flower alone, and gazed long upon it with inexpressible tenderness. . . . [2]

Dilemma

FOURs face the **temptation** to strive frantically for authenticity. Children, nature, and everything that radiates originality awakens in them the longing for the simplicity and naturalness that they lost at some point. The more unredeemed FOURs struggle to be authentic, the more they strike the people around them as mannered.

The specific **defense mechanism** of FOURs is artificial sublimation. Feelings are not expressed directly, but indirectly through symbols, rituals, and dramatic styling. This is supposed to alleviate the pain of real grief and the fear of rejection. The unredeemed FOUR is convinced that "anyone who would see me directly the way I am couldn't bear the sight."

This leads many FOURs to be more at home in their art than with other people. That is why they have to learn, really learn, the authentic capacity to love. Enthusiasm for other people can come and go. There is danger here that others will be used only as emotional releases for certain longings, memories, or dreams.

FOURs sometimes shape their lives like a *Gesamtkunstwerk*, a total work of art. Clothing, interior decoration, hobbies, circle of friends, and habits are adjusted to each other in a way that often seems accidental but in reality is carefully staged. Aesthetic points of view, which often can be appreciated only with difficulty, play the lead role here. One classic expression of the attitude is what is called "Bohemia," or an artists' milieu: melancholy music, half-wilted flowers, for example, roses or lilacs (there will be more to say about the affinity FOURs have for death and transience), incense sticks, dripping candles, the diary next to the bed. Many FOURs like to have long conversations at night over tea or red wine (since everyone else prefers white!).

The **root sin** is envy. They see immediately who has more style, more class, more taste, more talent, more unusual ideas, more genius than they do. They see who is simpler, more natural, more normal, and "healthier" than they are. There is nothing that a FOUR couldn't be envious about. Helen Palmer quotes a FOUR: "How is it that other people seem to hold hands and smile a lot? What do they have with each other that I don't have? You get on a Holy Grail search to find the something more; grasping for something that satisfied my friends, but which misses me entirely."[3]

Envy can also be expressed as jealousy, as soon as relationships come into play. FOURs often live in fear that somebody else could be more attractive, original, and interesting as a partner. This is how self-conscious FOURs sometimes appear; inside them a child is struggling with feelings of inferiority: "I don't deserve to be loved. I have to make an impression so that I'm not overlooked and abandoned again." That is why many FOURs experience the domain of close personal relations as an arena for combat and competition.

FOURs **avoid** ordinariness: everything that is current, conventional, and normal. The requirement of being like everyone else can unleash downright panic among them. That is why they refuse to change even more stubbornly than the other types. FOURs say: "But I *like* to be different. I don't want to fit in the way all the others do." FOURs have acquired their status, their circle of friends, their role, their flair, and the admiration of many people through their striking behavior. Unredeemed FOURs don't want to have anyone spoil this game for them. That is, until one day they taste its dark side. Then they notice that all this prevents them from loving. They see how eccentric they are. But it usually takes a long time before they are ready to give up their self-image. In this respect FOURs can be pig-headed. They can, of course, joke ironically or sarcastically about their moodiness and peculiarities, about their elitist affectation, and their snobishness. But the step to real self-criticism is substantially harder to take.

In the past FOURs were often thrown out of religious communities because they didn't conform. Until recently monasteries and convents used to place a high value on uniformity. Everybody wore the same brown cowl. When I gave a seminar on the Enneagram to the Franciscans in California, one person immediately struck me as a "flaming FOUR." At the end of the retreat we all met wearing our Franciscan habit, to conclude our time together with a Mass. I thought to myself at once that this man would do something conspicuous. And, sure enough, he had pinned a big red rose to his plain brown habit. FOURs have to catch your eye. It's as if they thought, "I don't know who I am if I'm like all the others. I have to stand out and in any case be different."

The **pitfall** of FOURs is their melancholy, a "sweet sadness" that lies over their whole lives like a fog. FOURs have to be depressed and suffer from time to time in order to be happy. Helen Palmer calls them the "tragic romantics." Quotations from the romantic period illustrate this: "Melancholy lays hold of you because there is no world in which you can act" (Bettina von Arnim). "Melancholy is the happiness of being sad" (Victor Hugo). The greater the pains and the depression, the more creative FOURs can become. Their pleasure in suffering has been invoked and described in countless poetic self-reflections by literary romantics from all periods and cultures:

> ...and add to this, that I taste a false sweetness in everything I suffer from. This sad state of soul is for me an abundance of pains, misery, and terror, an open path to despair.... And the crowning point of all woes is that I feed with a certain silent lustfulness on my tears and pains and only against my will do I tear myself away from them. (Petrarch, 1304–1374)

Goethe's *Sorrows of Young Werther* (1774) was the expression of his tragic-romantic *Sturm-und-Drang* period. So many young people identified with Werther that there was a wave of suicides.

FOURs often have an affinity with death, perhaps because it means the ultimate lament, the definitive longing, or also because only death can make beauty eternal. For dramaturgical reasons great love stories must almost necessarily end in death. The idea of Romeo and Juliet getting married, having children, and leading a wholly "normal" married life would be too banal; it would impair the universality and greatness of their love.

Another Franciscan whom I am friends with and who is likewise a FOUR told me the following: As a young man he used to sketch out detailed fantasies of his death. The day he died would have to be aesthetically perfect. He wanted to wait until some people whom he loved had deeply hurt him. This way he could give them the definitive punishment. It absolutely had to be springtime; then he would stand under a cherry tree in blossom and drink a poisoned cup. He would collapse, and the cherry blossoms would gently flutter down onto his body. My friend would scarcely have thought of realizing this fantasy: but such morbid reveries are not unusual among FOURs.

Romantic poems can be recognized by the way they revolve around love, beauty, and death. All other subjects are not great enough:

TRISTAN

Whoever has looked upon beauty with his eyes
Has already gone home to death,
He will be useless for service on this earth,
And yet he will tremble before death,
Whoever has looked upon beauty with his eyes.

For him the pain of love lasts forever,
For only a fool can hope on this earth

To satisfy such a drive:
Whoever has been struck by the arrow of beauty
For him the pain of love lasts forever.

Ah, he would wish to dry up like a spring,
To suck a poison from every breath of air,
And smell death in every flower:
Whoever has seen death with his eyes,
Ah, he would wish to dry up like a spring.

— August Graf von Platen, 1796–1835[4]

Since FOURs as a rule direct their aggressions against themselves, it often happens that they are disgusted by themselves and their bodies. Although they are generally very slender and attractive, they tend to find themselves too fat and too ugly. They keep trying new diet plans; the inclination to anorexia appears fairly frequently among FOUR women.

FOURs need friends and partners who will bear with them without letting themselves be drawn into the mood shifts that FOURs have. They need to experience a loyalty that stands firm. Partnership with an unredeemed FOUR is, to be sure, irritating, and requires tolerance. Since FOURs find the present — including their current partner — deficient to begin with, that partner can be exposed to a steady stream of biting criticism. Since they are on hand and easily had, those partners seem less attractive. This can even lead to FOURs' being impotent or refusing the other person sexually. Partners of an unredeemed FOUR are subjected to the hot-and-cold treatment, now seduction, now rejection. If they withdraw, they will be lured back by every means. In extreme situations this can be bound up with dramatic scenes, going as far as suicide threats. If the partner is available, then his or her faults and defects once again come into a harsh light. It's like a rehearsed dance: "If you take a step forward, I take a step back. If you take a step back, I take a step toward you."

The love affair of the Danish philosopher Søren Kierkegaard (1813–55) with Regine Olsen mirrors the tragic nature of this "disposition." Kierkegaard broke the engagement after a year, because he thought he shouldn't burden Regine with his melancholy. The conversion of this inner situation into literature led to his first aesthetic works.[5]

"Normal" quiet happiness, of the sort others — apparently — enjoy, seems to a FOUR at once attractive and repellent. For that could mean the end of the sweet wistfulness that FOURs need to feel "themselves." The inner richness of melancholy seems to be more attractive than what others carelessly call "happiness." Rainer Maria Rilke, for example, who was a FOUR, refused to begin therapy despite grave psychic disturbances. He was afraid that his true self might be destroyed by treatment and that when the devils left him, the angels might leave him too.[6]

Many FOURs vacillate between phases of exaggerated activity and others in which they are withdrawn and quasi-paralyzed. This manic-depressive structure can in some people who are highly introverted (stronger influence of the FIVE wing) turn into an altogether depressive structure. FOURs whose more success-oriented, extroverted THREE wing is dominant are by contrast often hyperactive. These two "subtypes" of FOUR do not look very similar at first glance.[7]

The depression of unredeemed FOURs is different from normal grief, which all people experience. It is bound up with the feeling of the unique-ness and vastness of their own suffering and with the unwillingness to accept help. Behind the excuse that nobody would understand them lies the refusal to mourn.[8] This is how they desperately cling to what has been lost.

Many FOURs take their feelings very seriously and are deeply of-fended when they are "hurt." Criticism of their artistic expressions can wound them in their innermost selves and drive them into retreat. On the other hand they tend to run themselves down. A painter who is a FOUR is the only one allowed to criticize his pictures.

Hollywood is an El Dorado of FOURs. Theater and film are their domain, because FOURs view their whole life as a great stage. The Oscars are shared with a handful of successful THREEs. Marilyn Monroe, Marlon Brando, and James Dean are famous FOURs among movie stars.

The biography of James Dean (1931–55), who portrayed young rebels, is almost paradigmatic. At eight years of age "Jimmy" lost his mother, who had given him dance and violin lessons. As a young man he had a precipitous theater and film career. He developed into an *enfant terrible*.

He could sit down on a chair in the middle of the street and enjoy the chorus of honking from the drivers. There are photos showing him sitting in a coffin in a funeral parlor. He always had his bongos with him; their noise drew the attention of people around him.

He used his confusion, his enigmatic nature, and his impenetrability to create his own myth: "We're fish and we drown. We stay in our world and wonder. The lucky ones are taught to ask why. Nobody knows the answer." Thoughtlessness and love of risk-taking — traits that many FOURs share — could be seen in his predilection for motorcycles and fast cars. He took part in auto races: "That's the only time I feel whole." At the age of twenty-four he died in a car crash, which he caused by

James Dean   ***Weltschmerz and Longing***   *Marilyn Monroe*

speeding. Although he made only three films, a cult sprang up after his death that persists today.[9]

Dazzling figures like James Dean invite others to project their own dreams onto them. Their lack of clarity magnetically draws other people's unsettled needs and wishes. The capacity to embody many characters and still remain nebulous makes many FOURs attractive and dangerous. If you reach out to them and try to touch them personally, you may find you are grasping the void.

Marilyn Monroe (1926–62) grew up as an orphan and was raped at the age of nine. As a sales girl, aged sixteen, she first tried to take her life. The poet-priest Ernesto Cardenal, who is likewise a FOUR and psychologically similar, writes in a moving "Prayer for Marilyn Monroe" how the girl dreamed as a child, "that she stood naked in church...before a kneeling crowd, their heads bowed down to earth, and she had to walk on tiptoe so as not to crush their heads." Cardenal prays: "Lord, in this world, contaminated with sin and radioactivity, you don't condemn a little salesgirl who dreams of being a filmstar....She hungered for love, and we offered her tranquilizers. For the sorrow of not being holy they recommended psychoanalysis.... Her love affairs were a kiss with eyes closed — and when you open your eyes, you see it was only a film kiss."[10]

The gift or **fruit of the spirit** of redeemed FOURs is harmony or
"even-souledness." At twenty-five FOURs have already lived through
all emotional spaces and experiences from agony to ecstasy. They know
all the nuances of feeling and understand the human soul better than
anyone else. If they muster the discipline to bring their emotional life
into balance, they can become impressive personalities. It's discipline
that makes the difference between a second-class "misunderstood genius" and a real artist. Great FOURs concentrate and discipline their
emotions; they can distance themselves from them and clarify them in
this way. Harmony refers to this deep, balanced, and nuanced emotional
condition. A purified FOUR can deal sensitively with real life[11] — and
not just with imaginary dramas. Such people must stop bathing in their
feelings and draining them to the dregs. They must stop playing with
their moods and foisting them on everyone else.

Healthy FOURs are capable of a depth of feeling that most of us have
no access to. If they can make this genuine emotionality fruitful, if they
can express in concentrated fashion their sense of the beautiful and the
really painful, then real works of art will be created. They no longer
serve mere self-representation, but express something universally valid.
William Shakespeare and T. S. Eliot are examples of poets in whom the
great emotions have been so purified and shaped by discipline that they
remain valid for all time. Redeemed FOURs are better than most others
at understanding and guiding people in psychic distress. They are not
intimidated by the difficult, complicated, or dark feelings of others, since
they themselves have lived through it all.

Symbols and Examples

One of FOUR's symbolic **animals** is the mourning dove, with its cooing
and complaining. If there is a style of speech by which FOURs can be
recognized, it is the longing complaint or lament. Another animal is the
basset hound, the short-legged French hunting dog with its pendant
ears and sad, bleary eyes. The eyes of most FOURs reflect an undefined
sadness, which they themselves are usually not even aware of. Even
when they smile, it's often "smiling through tears." The noble black
racing horse symbolizes the cool aesthetics of FOURs.

Redeemed FOURs are often compared with the oyster, which is an
old symbol of melancholy. Oysters transform dirt into pearls, in the same
way a purified FOUR is capable of transforming the negative and experiences of loss into something beautiful and universally valid. The writer
Robert Musil puts it this way: "Writing is like the pearl of a sickness."

FOURs are often Francophiles. France is their symbolic **country**. From time immemorial France has refused to be a country like all the others. The French are always special. The French mentality impresses non-French as refined, cultivated, and somewhat elitist. The French developed a *haute cuisine* and a *haute couture*. Everything has to be "high" and unusual. There are said to be FOURs who speak with an affected French (or sometimes a British) accent.

The **color** of FOURs is bright violet or mauve. Their shading is not precisely determined, shimmering and extraordinary, melancholic and mystical-conflicting. Violet is the liturgical color of Passiontide, the time of fasting and penance, of transformation through pain and death. In his theory of color Goethe even connected with it the terror of the end of the world: "Violet is both a symbol of the highest rapture of the soul . . . as well as of its darkest and most painful moments. . . . In its oscillations passion comes into contact with intoxication, liberation with decay, death with resurrection, pain with redemption, disease with purification, mystical vision with madness."[12] Violet is the androgynous color; it mediates between red (masculine) and blue (feminine). The redeemed FOUR embodies synthesis, mediation, and balance.

In the **Bible** we encounter the energy of FOURs in very different contexts: Shulamith, the legendary mistress of the king in the Song of Solomon, embodies the longing erotic romanticism of FOURs:

> O that you would kiss me with the kisses of your mouth!
> For your love is better than wine. . . .
> My beloved is to me a bag of myrrh
> that lies between my breasts.
> My beloved is to me a cluster of henna blossoms
> in the vineyards of En-gedi. . . .
> Behold, you are beautiful, my beloved,
> truly lovely.
> Our couch is green;
> the beams of our house are cedar,
> our rafters are pine. . . .
> Upon my bed by night
> I sought him whom my soul loves;
> I sought him, but found him not. . . .
> I adjure you, O daughters of Jerusalem,
> if you find my beloved,
> that you tell him
> I am sick with love. . . .
> My beloved is all radiant and ruddy,
> distinguished among ten thousand.

His head is the finest gold,
his locks are wavy,
black as a raven.
His eyes are like doves
beside springs of water, . . .
his lips are lilies,
distilling liquid myrrh. . . .
His body is ivory work,
encrusted with sapphires.
His legs are alabaster columns,
set upon bases of gold. . . .
His speech is most sweet,
and he is altogether desirable.
This is my beloved and this is my friend,
O daughters of Jerusalem. . . .
O that his left hand were under my head,
·and that his right hand embraced me.
Set me as a seal upon your heart,
as a seal upon your arm;
for love is strong as death,
jealousy as cruel as the grave. . . .
Many waters cannot quench love,
neither can floods drown it.

                          (from the Song of Solomon)

It is obvious that no real existing man, not even King Solomon, can match this ideal image.

Joseph is Jacob's next to last son and his favorite; for this reason his father has a many-colored cloak made for him. This is the beginning of something distinctive. His brothers envy him because of his special position. One day Joseph dreams that all his twelve brothers are out in the field binding sheaves. Only Joseph's sheaf stands up straight, while his brother's sheaves bow down before him. Another time he dreams that eleven stars, and the sun and moon, fall down before him. He tells his dream and thereby makes himself still more unpopular with his brothers. They decide to get him out of the way.

First they want to kill him, but then they sell him into slavery in Egypt. They tear up his many-colored cloak and soak the shreds in the blood of a goat, then tell their father a wild beast has torn him to pieces.

In Egypt Joseph falls into the hands of Potiphar, a high official. He avoids the amorous advances of the lady of the house; for this she has him put into prison. Even here he enjoys a special position. When two court officials who have been locked up with him have unsettling dreams, he interprets them.[13] When later Pharaoh too has dreams that none of his wise men can explain, one of his courtiers remembers Joseph. He is fetched from prison and predicts to Pharaoh seven fat and seven lean years.

Thereupon Joseph is named prime minister and is charged with storing up supplies of grain. When the lean years come, his brothers likewise appear in Egypt to buy grain. They do not recognize him. With the dramatic talents of a FOUR Joseph stages the reconciliation and the family reunion, until the story comes to the happy end described in the Bible (Gen. 36–50).

A number of the great prophets of Israel have FOUR traits as well, expressed primarily in their unusual symbolic acts. Isaiah walked naked through Jerusalem for years to point up that one day the Egyptians and Ethiopians, Israel's allies, would be dragged naked and "with bared buttocks" to Assyria. Hosea married a harlot. His marriage was a parable of the faithlessness of the people toward Yahweh in serving other gods. Jeremiah remained unmarried, at Yahweh's command, as a sign of the destruction that would befall Judah. The heart-wrenching lamentations traditionally attributed to him belong to the oldest texts of humanity in which an individual directly reflects on and formulates his psychological state.

Conversion and Redemption

The **invitation** to redemption issued to FOURs is the call to originality. FOURs find their naturalness on the way to union with God. Their striving for authenticity, their love for children and nature are early hints of this goal in life. If they can admit that they live "in God" and God "in them," their soul will come to the rest and harmony they have long yearned for.

Among the **life tasks** of FOURs is to develop a healthy realism and direct their longing toward reachable goals. FOURs have to work at seeing that their attention remains in the present and doesn't continually digress into the past or future. FOURs must find their energy without constantly slipping from one extreme into the other, without being up one minute and down the next. It must not always be euphoria or depression. Their "objective observer" has the job of asking: "Isn't a *little* joy and a *little* sadness enough — at least now and then?"

Unredeemed FOURs love ritual more than reality. They glorify their memories, which are more beautiful than the actual event was. That's why it's necessary for them to confront reality. Incarnation is called for, that is, accepting reality, even when it's ugly and dirty. There the FOURs

will truly find themselves. For this reason social commitment and working for peace and justice do FOURs good. In this they have to deal with
the dirt of the world, which cannot be aesthetically transfigured.

For redemption FOURs need to confront the real experiences of loss
in their lives, they have to admit the rage they feel against the person
in question, and they have to stop adulating him or her in the wake of
that loss. The "inability to mourn" (Alexander Mitscherlich) hampers
real liberation. Paul drives the point home to FOURs when he writes:
"Godly grief produces a repentance that leads to salvation, and brings
no regret, but worldly grief produces death" (2 Cor. 7:10).

FOURs who wish to convert can't avoid taking a critical look at their
snobbishness and their (hidden) elitist consciousness. Instead of com-
paring themselves with others, they should gratefully become aware of
their own inner treasures and share them with others. To practice doing
all this, FOURs need a network of people who won't let themselves be
manipulated by them, but remain objective and demand authentic communication. For this reason, in my experience, they are often attracted
to ONEs.

Without the FOURs the world would be deprived of the greater part
of its art and poetry. When they learn to serve others with their gifts,
they will make an important contribution toward "redeeming this world
through beauty."

Daniel Berrigan and Thomas Merton are our **saints**, the patrons of
the redeemed FOURs:

The Jesuit priest Daniel Berrigan inspired the Christian peace movement in America as no one else did. His actions were designed to get
attention. They were always symbolic, illegal, and nonviolent. During
the Vietnam War Berrigan staged the public burning of induction orders.
Another time his group penetrated the Pentagon.

Berrigan used his FOUR energy to serve humanity. Nobody else had
the idea of articulating protest in this drastic and creative way. Berrigan
put his longing and his pleasure in dramatization at the service of peace
and justice, instead of simply putting his own creative self on display.

The poet and writer Thomas Merton (1915–68), who ultimately became a Trappist monk, was born in Prades (France) into a family of artists.
At the age of six he lost his mother and began to live a restless, wandering life with his father: Bermuda, the U.S., France, England. At sixteen
he lost his father: "Thus I became a complete twentieth-century man."[14]

After finishing high school Merton began his studies in Cambridge
and soon was known for his bar-hopping, his impudent cartoons, and
his womanizing (an illegitimate child from this period later died in a
German bombing attack on London).

At the same time he was overcome by a growing disgust with himself. He went to the U.S. in 1934, moved near Harlem, joined the Communist party, and at the same time began to look into religious subjects. A Hindu fellow student recommended Augustine and Kempis to him.

In 1938 Merton was baptized a Catholic; at first his friends thought it was just another one of his crazy ideas. But he was serious about it and wanted to become a Franciscan. When he told the unvarnished truth about his life to the Franciscans, he was turned down, which deeply hurt him. But he didn't give up. He lived like a monk, gave up smoking, went on a retreat in the strictest monastery in the country, the Trappist abbey of Gethsemani, Kentucky, where along with all the other vows the strictest silence was observed.

Here he was accepted in 1941 as a postulant. Five years later his biography, *The Seven Storey Mountain*, was published, and became a sensational bestseller. It reflected the radical contempt for the world of a young (and initially very fanatical) monk and was compared with Augustine's *Confessions*. In the next thirty years some sixty more books would follow.

Monastic life became increasingly difficult for Merton. His abbot thought he was taking his subjective feelings too seriously. Finally the order even forbade him to write. Still he became a novice master. His books had drawn hundreds of young men to try out this radical life of work and prayer. They loved and revered him, although he refused to pass on blind obedience to the rule, but encouraged individual personalities with warmth and love. Ernesto Cardenal was one of his students.

Merton understood monks as people who are searching for God and want to overcome the "false self" by renouncing lies about life and artificial security. "We should let ourselves be led naked and unarmed into the center of that anxiety where we stand alone in our nothingness before God."[15]

At the same time he was becoming increasingly political he wrote essays against the Church's doctrine of the "just war" and against American militarism.

After a long struggle with the abbot he succeeded in getting permission to build himself a plain but comfortable hermitage in the woods. He began to read, to write, to receive visitors. On the occasion of a stay in the hospital he had a deeply felt love affair with a student nurse. But he was still not satisfied; he dreamed of a still more lonely hermitage in Alaska. Finally he was drawn to the Far East, since his vision of a synthesis of Christianity and Buddhism would not let go.

In 1968 he was allowed to travel to a religious conference in Bangkok;

on this journey he met Sufi mystics, Zen Buddhists, and the Dalai Lama. Both men were deeply impressed by one another. Merton died electrocuted by a defective fan in his hotel room. As the irony of fate would have it, an American military plane returned his mortal remains to the United States.

TYPE FIVE
The Need to Perceive

Overview

FIVEs, SIXs, and SEVENs are head people. They think before they act and have — or so it seems — a certain objectivity. The special talents of FIVEs consist in their being open and receptive to new facts and impressions. FIVEs are discoverers of new ideas, researchers and inventors, objective, questioning, and interested in exploring things in detail. They can be original minds, provocative, surprising, unorthodox, and profound. They are good listeners, because they pay close attention. Hence they can help others to perceive the truth more soberly and objectively. There are FIVEs who possess strong contemplative gifts. Redeemed FIVEs link their knowledge to a search for wisdom and strive for a sympathetic knowledge of the heart. They have a quiet inner power and are tender, gentle, and polite.

The primary experience of many FIVEs is a sort of emptiness. Hence they long for fulfillment. Some have had the "experience," in the womb

99

before birth, that "I am not wanted." There are FIVEs who had psychi-
cally or physically intrusive parents or who grew up in very cramped
surroundings. Their inner world was the only free space in which they
could move undisturbed. Others experienced the apparent opposite: as
children they received little tenderness and intimacy. Thus their own
capacity to show their feelings or express them physically remained underdeveloped. They sense in themselves an abyss of emptiness. A lack
of security and the feeling of homelessness and loneliness can lead to
FIVEs' creeping inside themselves like an animal that plays dead when
danger approaches.

Many FIVEs go through life and gather what they can get — in the
hope of filling up their inner vacuum. In this way FIVEs became receptive
and responsive. If TWOs are under a certain compulsion to give, FIVEs
are equally obsessed with taking.

FIVEs' passion for collecting is often directed to thoughts, ideas,
knowledge, silence, and space. There are also FIVEs whose greediness
has hardened and who can hoard the most remarkable things: books,
stamps, old newspapers, fabric remnants, toothpaste tube tops, used
milk cartons. Today they are enthusiastic about recycling.

FIVEs need a closed off and protected private sphere. They long for a
fortress in which they won't be watched and where they can think, "My
home is my castle." Most FIVEs are introverts; the exceptions prove the
rule. By nature they are monks, hermits, ascetics, bookworms, librarians,
and technical sticklers.

FIVEs often wear glasses. Their eyes already show signs of wear
before they are twenty. Their whole energy is concentrated on seeing
everything, on taking it all in. Their eyes are like vacuum cleaners. FIVEs
see everything, they hear everything — and they hold on to everything.
All activities in which one can look through lenses, such as microscopes
or telescopes, to observe, are attractive to them. Many FIVEs like to take
pictures. They like everything that allows them to play the part of observers. Many brilliant inventors, discoverers, and scientists are FIVEs.
We have to thank God that they exist. FIVEs try not to be drawn into
the whirlpool of feelings and events, but instead to develop something
like objectivity. It's important to them to maintain calm — at least externally — and to keep their emotions under control. No one is supposed
to tell by their looks that they are in a rage, have fallen in love, or are
competing with someone. All demonstrative "fuss" is odious to them.
This goes so far that they often have difficulty showing their feelings —
even when they want to. Externally this often has the effect of making
them seem snooty and cold, as if they needed nobody and felt exalted
above their fellow men and women. In reality most FIVEs have an in-

tense emotional life. But at the moment something happens it's as if their feelings are blocked and always come limping behind. At first FIVEs register it with eyes, ears, and brain; they can stand alongside the event, with seeming objectivity. As soon as they are alone, they begin to evaluate it, and once again from the head: feelings are ordered and "brought into line." That's the method by which FIVEs gradually get in touch with their emotions. Some one has said very finely that the symbolic plant of FIVEs is green lettuce, the plant that has its heart in its head.

Like FOURs, FIVEs often feel more connected to those who are absent than to those who are present. FIVEs can cherish very warm feelings for distant people. But since they seldom express these emotions in the presence of their friend or beloved, but rather announce them through little gestures, the friend or partner of a FIVE can easily get the feeling that the FIVE has no great interest in him or her. FIVEs who, as they subjectively perceive it, are already coming fully out of themselves usually strike the people around them as still relatively controlled. Friendship with a FIVE can be enriching if one doesn't expect three things: initiative-taking, continual physical nearness, or total surrender. FIVEs are afraid of giving their little finger lest people want the whole hand or even more. But anyone who is content with the little finger will find in a friend who is a FIVE a true companion, a patient, silent listener, and a fair counselor.

Many great philosophers were FIVEs: Plotinus, Thomas Aquinas, Bonaventure, Descartes, Spinoza, Feuerbach, Heidegger, Camus, Sartre. They lived for the most part in retirement and analyzed the world from the proverbial ivory tower. Concrete commitment to the specific was not their gift.

Porphyry, the disciple of the Neo-Platonic philosopher Plotinus (ca. 205–70), begins the biography of his teacher with the sentence: "Plotinus . . . resembled a man who is ashamed of being in a body."[1] Plotinus's whole philosophy is an encounter with his revulsion to the corporeal.

Thomas Aquinas (1225–1274) was called the "dumb ox" by his fellow students. He kept silent, because he didn't want to call attention to himself. It was discovered only by accident that a great philosopher lay hidden within him.[2]

An especially typical representative of the philosophizing FIVEs is René Descartes (1596–1650), the "father of modernity." As a young man he traveled a great deal and became an officer; he didn't care which cause he was fighting for. He wanted to be not an actor but a spectator. He was interested in how people killed one another and "how the weapons serving this purpose are constructed."[3] After studying the "book of the world," he withdrew into silence. He chose Holland as a

place to stay because "I could spend my whole life there without anyone's noticing me."[4] The publication of his thoughts did not interest
him. On the contrary, he wanted to remain hidden. The famous key
principles of his philosophy, "I doubt, therefore I am; I think, therefore
I am" could probably be formulated and thoroughly understood only
by a FIVE.

Ludwig Feuerbach (1804–72), the founder of modern atheism, describes his poverty-stricken student days in Erlangen as follows: "That
sort of quiet dwelling, surrounding by nature like my present one, a glass
of water in the morning, a frugal dinner at noon, in the evening a tankard
of beer and at most a radish besides: if I always had that much together,
I would never wish for more from, and on, the earth."[5]

Martin Heidegger (1889–1976) owned a hut in the Black Forest,
"sparsely furnished with wooden benches of Spartan simplicity. On the
bench in front of the hut Heidegger often sat for a long time watching the expanse of the mountains and the silent march of the clouds,
as the thoughts ripened in him." His intellectual nature was character-
ized by "heavy, deliberate thought, brooding profundity, the loneliness
surrounding him, the faint melancholy issuing from him."[6]

Along with philosophy FIVEs are by nature primarily drawn by religious mysticism. There are mystic currents in Buddhism and in the
religion of the American Indians; in Islam there is Sufism, in Judaism
Hassidism (and parts of the Kabbala), in Christianity there is the medieval mysticism of Meister Eckhart and his disciples. Mystical currents
can be found in the Orthodox churches of the East (Philokalia, the hesy-
chastic mysticism of the Mt. Athos monks), and even in Protestantism
(e.g., Gerhard Teerstegen). Mystics have been defined as the "absorp-
tion of the individual in God or the divine, or else perhaps in something
that lies behind God, a 'void' or 'non-being.' "[7] Gerhard Wehr points to
the "experience of an immediate, intuitive contact with God or with the
absolute or unconditioned."[8] Last but not least there is a strikingly large
number of women who have left an influential mark on Islamic and
Christian mysticism. It is the inner "vision," the "inner eye" to which
FIVEs find easier access than other people.

I know many religious priests who are FIVEs. Some of them are older
than I am and are still not finished with their training for any service. You
wonder: when will these people begin to do something for others and
translate their knowledge into practice? First they have to go to Chicago
and finish their degree in philosophy. Then they have to go to Rome
to write a paper on the liturgy. Next they spend a year in Jerusalem
and take up biblical and archaeological studies. They need the certainty
of really having gotten the whole picture before they feel ripe for any

undertaking. But that never happens, and so their flesh never touches the flesh of the world.

The Viennese philosopher Ludwig Wittgenstein (1889–1951), for example, first studied engineering in Berlin, after already devising, while just a boy, a new kind of sewing machine. Then he went to Manchester and devoted himself to the emerging science of aeronautics. While doing that, he noticed that he was actually interested in mathematics. So he went to Bertrand Russell in Cambridge. But he didn't stay long there either. He was drawn to a lonely farmhouse in Norway, until in 1914 he volunteered for the Austro-Hungarian army. During the war and while he was a prisoner of war in Italy he completed his *Tractatus Logico-Philosophicus*. After the war he happened upon Tolstoy and thereupon devoted himself to the Gospel and an abstemious life as a village teacher in Lower Austria. But this work didn't hold him long either. He toyed with the idea of becoming a monk and did become an assistant gardener in a monastery. Suddenly he got interested in architecture. He sketched houses, until he finally decided to get his Ph.D. after all.[9]

While FOURs tend to do everything to attract attention, FIVEs generally try to avoid anything that could draw it to them. FIVEs too can have a sort of "rehearsed" behavior. It serves the process of adaptation: "How should I behave so that as few people as possible will notice that I'm here or want something from me?" If the subject of a conversation gets too personal, FIVEs sometimes develop great skill in turning the discussion away from themselves. As soon as they have the feeling that someone wants to "sound them out," they clam up.

Many FIVEs hate words like "share" or "communicate." As soon as the demand is made in a group to exchange views spontaneously, most FIVEs let down the shades and think how they can neatly and unobtrusively pull out of the whole business. FIVEs don't want to abandon themselves and put their inmost selves on display. If they can't avoid getting involved, they generally wait before expressing themselves. Then they communicate as little as possible. But they listen well to what other people say. Nothing escapes their attention, even behind their poker face.

Many FIVEs have problems playing parental roles. The popular concept of "motherliness" wasn't invented by a FIVE. I recall a woman FIVE who came to me for counseling. She impressed me as a wonderful woman and a splendid mother. But she felt that raising children was hell. Children make permanent demands on the time, the space, and the energy of their parents while FIVEs need their private realm. That's one of the reasons why a strikingly large number of FIVEs shrink from marrying and bringing children into the world. They are afraid that these little beasts might run through the house and continually want something from them.

In monastic communities FIVEs typically want to have a little garret, ideally at the very end of the corridor. There the danger of someone's intruding into their sphere is minimal. FIVEs hate intrusiveness and intruders. If you want to find out how an otherwise so retiring FIVE can fly into a rage, you need only run through his or her room without knocking. This can really offend a FIVE. FIVEs protect their private spheres like the apple of their eye. FIVEs who live in a community must regularly retreat to be alone and refuel. Most FIVEs find too many people and too much closeness fatiguing and exhausting. They need time for themselves, to order their thoughts and feelings and to focus internally on the encounters.

Once I was in the Trappist abbey of Gethsemani in Kentucky, Thomas Merton's former monastery, where I conducted week-long exercises for the monks and introduced them to the Enneagram. After three days it was clear to me that many of these contemplative monks were FIVEs. To provoke them a bit, I said: "I always used to look up to you and admire you. I heard how you sit motionless for three hours at a time before the Blessed Sacrament. It was clear to me that you've already reached the highest stage of contemplation, because I couldn't endure sitting still for three hours and doing nothing. But now I know that most of you are nothing but FIVEs." The monks roared with laughter. They had the freedom to admit it. Many FIVEs can think of nothing more beautiful in the world than sitting there for three hours and looking at something — or nothing at all. If they sit there this way, they take their rest, nobody wants anything from them, they don't have to give anything.

What has been said might lead to the misunderstanding that all FIVEs are intellectuals, profound, wise monks or at least especially intelligent people. Unfortunately it must be added that there are perfectly stupid FIVEs too! For them too the control tower is their head, their little bit of understanding, their "logic," whatever its nature, the concept that they have of the world. What they don't understand, they don't meddle with. Unredeemed FIVEs can take on schizoid traits; they can develop forms of autism or end in nihilism — the ultimate consequence of "pure thinking" without the body, emotion, value judgments, and deeds.

The autistic person would be the full caricature of a compulsive FIVE. The film *Rain Man*, which was showered with Oscars, deals with a typical young, dynamic, upwardly mobile American THREE, who after the death of his father learns that he has an autistic older brother (Dustin Hoffman). This brother is a mathematical genius, but otherwise a prisoner of unchangeable rituals. His relationship to the outside world is mechanized.

The film shows the beginnings of a "conversion," which the extroverted THREE experiences through the encounter with his morbidly introverted brother. Conversely, the sudden devotion and challenge have a therapeutic effect on the autistic Raymond. There is an unforgettable scene where he presses his head tenderly against his brother's shoulder and so for the first time can express something like intimacy.

Dilemma

The **temptation** of FIVEs is knowledge. For FIVEs knowledge is power. Unredeemed FIVEs think they can secure their lives by being informed about everything in as much detail as possible. But the information they pick up from the outside world and store up is never sufficient. FIVEs need yet another course, another seminar, another semester, another book, another silent retreat. They are represented in disproportionate numbers at Enneagram workshops. They are fascinated by intellectual systems that explain the universe or the human soul: psychoanalytical models, theories of types, Einstein's theory of relativity, quantum leaps, the Big Bang, evolutionism, laws of heredity. That is why there are many FIVEs who are Enneagram freaks. I also know some, however, who uncompromisingly reject the Enneagram — because for them it's a spoilsport that uncovers their life program. FIVEs may have managed to shine all their lives with intellectual superiority: "I know more than other people. I understand the world better than other people. I'm above the sentimentality and emotional affectation of the others." Suddenly it turns out that they are nothing more than FIVEs and that their strength is at the same time their sin.

Part of the process of hoarding impressions and knowledge is that most FIVEs like to travel, since travel educates. They enjoy studying foreign cultures, customs, and manners, without being known or recognized. On such trips they also, on occasion, plunge into "limited adventures," because they know that such situations come without strings and can be ended at any time by departure. The actual experience takes place later when they can review their slides at home. Little souvenirs and keepsakes help them as props for memory and afterward can serve as release mechanisms for reawakening the whole event in their imagination. Some FIVEs have a collection of "totems" that cover all the important phases and events of their life.

One of the **defense mechanisms** that FIVEs like to use is withdrawal. FIVEs are afraid of nothing so much as emotional engagement. The more unredeemed they are, the more they shy away from feelings, sex, relationships that create dependency. When you touch a FIVE, he or she generally gives a start or jumps back. For this reason many FIVEs have a celibate make-up. They can choose celibacy for false motives and turn into cranky bachelors or old maids.

The great actress Greta Garbo (1905–1990) was a typical FIVE. Even in her heyday her unsociability was proverbial. In order not to attract attention she took aliases and wore disguises in public. There was no name on her door. She had body guards who had to see that nobody came too close to her. She hated to watch her own films and felt retrospective embarrassment from having exposed herself in this way. When she appeared at public receptions, she preferred speaking about abstract or political subjects, because she avoided talking about herself. She never married. Her love affairs were of short duration. In private she preferred simple clothing, almost like a nun's habit. She left some rooms of her house completely empty. From 1941 she withdrew completely from the film business in order to live like a hermit. She hid her famous face behind a hat and sunglasses.

Unredeemed FIVEs are afraid of concrete commitments. FIVEs like to stay in the abstract world of theories and ideas, but they seldom do anything to improve themselves beyond their mind. Karl Marx reproached philosophers as a group for interpreting the world instead of changing it. Abraham Maslow has pointed to the dangers of "being knowledge." By that he means an attitude that wants only to understand connections:

> Being-knowledge is without judgment, comparison, condemnation or evaluation. It is also without decision, because decision means readiness for action. . . . So long as one contemplates cancer or bacteria, full of reverence, admiration, and passive reception, enjoying rich comprehension, one is simply doing nothing. Anxiety, anger, the wish to improve the situation, to destroy or kill . . . are all cancelled. It is a not-being-in-the-world in the existentialist sense.[10]

Because of this attitude, FIVEs tend toward conservatism. The supposedly value-free research instinct has contributed to making many discoveries of brilliant FIVEs a scourge on humanity. Many scientists have refused to consider the ethical implications of their findings.

Friedrich Dürrenmatt has addressed this subject in his tragic comedy, *The Physicists*.[11] An atomic physicist named Möbius pretends to be insane because he knows that his ideas can destroy the world. In the insane asylum he meets two other physicists, a Soviet and an American, who try to abduct him. Möbius destroys his formula and convinces the other two to stay with him in the asylum — for the good of humanity. But the woman doctor in charge of the place has secretly copied the formulas and founded a company to exploit them. The shock at discovering this drives the three physicists into real madness.

When I hold retreat days with FIVEs I usually tell them: "Every time you go to confession, don't forget to say, 'I am an intellectual snob!'" At lectures and conferences FIVEs generally sit in the last row so as not to draw attention to themselves. If they were to sit in front I might suddenly direct a question to them or ask them all to stand up. Their life is like jungle warfare: they want to see but not to be seen. They are like a store detective behind a one-way mirror. He has the overview, but the shoppers don't notice that they are being observed.

Helen Palmer has dubbed the unredeemed FIVE the "unenlightened Buddha."[12] The enlightened Buddha can break free of the world and its passions, *after* he has lived and suffered through it. The unenlightened Buddha renounces his emotions because he can't and won't commit himself to them. He reaches for premature intellectual solutions and scorns the "sour grapes of the world" for false motives. For such people the practice of Zen meditation, for example, can be dangerous and can serve as immunization against the "world" and the "flesh."

The second **defense mechanism** of FIVEs is compartmentalization. Many FIVEs divide their lives into a number of segments or departments that exist in practical independence from one another. For example, they may have friends and acquaintances in every one of these areas who never learn anything about one another. So long as they limit such partial relationships to the sphere intended for them and don't try to interfere with the whole life of the FIVEs, they can be sure of getting attention and signs of devotion within the established boundaries.

"Limitation" is another key word in this context that helps us to understand the psyche of FIVEs. Because they are afraid of being co-opted and of emotional overstrain, many FIVEs feel safe only when the temporal and spatial framework of a relationship is precisely staked out. They like to know how long an appointment or meeting will last so that they can prepare themselves internally for it. They need time to get ready for exhausting encounters. They can easily feel threatened by surprise visits and unexpected assaults that personally challenge them. The sense of emotional expectation from other people strikes them as rather unpleasant. As a rule you get something from a FIVE — if you get anything at all — only when you neither expect it nor ask for it. In open conflict they have scarcely any defense mechanisms at their disposal — except for retreat and intellectual arguments.

The **root sin** of FIVEs is greed. FIVEs aren't givers. They tend to hoard both their intellectual as well as their material possessions. This is the point where they sometimes need a challenging kick in the behind: "Now it's time that you finally fork over something from your treasures."

The **pitfall** of FIVEs is avarice. They are stingy above all with themselves. They often fear that if they shared themselves, they might lose themselves. FIVEs can become misers like Ebenezer Scrooge in Dickens's *A Christmas Carol*. Avaricious FIVEs don't enjoy life, but are stingy with their possessions so that their repose and leisure will be guaranteed in the future. With some this can take on pathological features: billionaires Howard Hughes and J. Paul Getty were both famous for never allowing themselves anything despite their fabulous wealth. Most FIVEs are in fact very modest in their demands and have a natural tendency to asceticism. They always need only a bit of everything. Some even count the pieces of toilet paper in order not to waste anything. They are proud of being so modest. After all, their primary experience in life often consisted in their not getting what they actually needed. Early on they had to get used to being content with a little. From this perspective the miserliness and frugality of FIVEs are not real opposites.

The greatest gifts of FIVEs are, as always, the reverse of their obsessions: they are contemplatively gifted, they understand connections, they invent grand intellectual systems, they are good listeners, advisors, and research scholars.

FIVEs **avoid** emptiness. While outsiders often consider them mysterious and "deep," FIVEs themselves are usually afraid that they are of little value and have little real wealth in them. The fear of emptiness (*horror vacui*) is the real impetus behind much that unredeemed FIVEs do.

The gift or **fruit of the spirit** of redeemed FIVEs is objectivity. Again we see how one and the same character trait can contain a blessing and a curse. Unredeemed FIVEs *have* to distance themselves; redeemed FIVEs *can* distance themselves.

This gift of FIVEs is of great value for every community. FIVEs can be outstanding counselors. They can follow the monologues of others for hours at a time. You can talk and talk — and the FIVE seems to have an unlimited capacity to listen and absorb everything. Their ability to withdraw themselves emotionally in the process can help those seeking advice to appraise their own situation more clearly, soberly, and realistically. Because of their particular talent FIVEs can look at a very tense emotional situation objectively and say: "Now I think the issue can be viewed from this side and from that."

Detachment is at once the gift and sin of the FIVE. FIVEs are the only type with which we can use the same word to describe their greatest strength and greatest weakness.

Symbols and Examples

Symbolic **animals** of FIVEs are the owl, the fox, and the hamster.

The owl's immobile eyes are aimed forward; its hearing is very well developed. In Egypt and India the owl was a symbol of death. In Greece the owl was assigned to the goddess Athena and was considered a protector of the city of Athens ("to bring owls to Athens") and of all intellectual disciplines. Owls see everything, but they themselves are hard to locate.

As a predator the fox is a loner. It has narrow, contracting pupils. Its sense of smell and hearing is excellent. In Chinese myth the fox has a central importance. At the age of one hundred the fox became capable of changing into any form at will; at the age of one thousand its fur turned white, it had nine tails, and it was omniscient. In animal legends and poetry the fox is considered sly and crafty. In Christian symbolism it can connote deceitfulness, greed, and despair. In many fairy tales, on the other hand, it appears as a helper in time of need.

The hamster with its great cheek pouches represents the FIVE's greed and passion for collecting, the hoarding of "food" for worse times.

The symbolic **country** that we use for FIVEs is Great Britain. This is the archetype of the conservative, polite, reserved, coolly distanced English gentleman. Another side of FIVEs can be found in the form of the stingy Scot, the target of countless caricatures.

The symbolic **color** of FIVEs is blue. Blue is the color of introversion, repose, and distance, more receptive than radiant. Blue traditionally embodies the feminine. The blue background of the starry mantle worn by the Mother of God symbolizes human receptiveness to the mystery of the universe. Sky and sea, the deepest of the realms accessible to contemplation, are blue. In its dark shades it symbolizes passivity, silent contemplation, and immobility. According to Kandinsky, blue leads us away from others into our own center: "The deeper it is, the more it calls us into the infinite, awakens in us the longing for purity and finally for the supernatural."[13]

The two **biblical patrons** of FIVE are Mary, the mother of Jesus, and the apostle Thomas. Mary embodies the passivity, the receptiveness, the mystical-contemplative side of FIVEs. She is capable of receiving before she gives. At the end of the Christmas story it is reported that the shepherds told everything they had heard. "But Mary kept all these things, pondering them in her heart" (Luke 2:19). FIVEs are capable of keeping things to themselves. Secrets are safe in their hearts; they can keep silent. In the course of church history Mary was often turned into a spiritualized, untouched and untouchable virgin "without flesh and blood." Earthbound Latin American liberation theology, however, as well as other schools of thought, working from the Magnificat (Luke 1:46–55) discovers a combative Mary who is not "tame" (the text of the Magnificat was temporarily forbidden in Argentina, at least in public). In the language of the Enneagram one could say that liberation theology has discovered the EIGHT side of Mary (EIGHT — the energy of the "deed" — is the integration point of FIVE).

The apostle Thomas has entered the consciousness of Christianity above all as the post-Easter "doubter." But even before Easter he makes a brief appearance. Jesus tells his disciples that Lazarus is dead and that he wants to go to the grave. Then Thomas says to the other disciples: "Let us also go, that we may die with him" (John 11:16). Nihilistic resignation and indifference are a continual danger for FIVEs. Thomas is not with the other disciples when the risen Christ appears to them. When they tell him about it, he remains skeptical. He trusts only what he has seen with his own eyes. When Jesus again appears to the disciples, Thomas is on hand. Jesus challenges him: "Put your finger here, and see my hands; and put out your hand, and place it in my side; do not be faithless, but believing" (John 20:27). The same Jesus who had said to Mary Magdalen, the TWO, "Do not cling to me," demands that Thomas the Rationalist make body contact. While TWOs have to break away from symbiosis and develop their capacity for genuine distance, FIVEs have to go from the head to the body, from thought to the deed. According to legend Thomas later became very active. He supposedly went to India and founded the church there.

Conversion and Redemption

The **invitation** to FIVEs is wisdom. Wisdom is a deep knowledge of the connections of the world and life that must be won not only from thought but at the same time from real-life experience. Wisdom is reflected experience. FIVEs incline to "preflection": they think before they act — or instead of acting. Reflection is the subsequent intellection processing of lived life. Part of the wisdom to which FIVEs are called is also trust in God's dispensation. This means believing God capable of something greater than school wisdom ever dreamed of. It means letting mysteries remain as such instead of dissecting everything with the rational scalpel.

Among the **life tasks** of FIVEs is learning commitment and action. FIVEs have to fall in love passionately. Love is a drama for many a FIVE because in erotic attraction the longing for nearness crashes up against the at least equally strong — for them — wish for distance. It can happen that a FIVE falls head over heels in love, but during the encounter with the beloved person he or she goes numb and doesn't know how to behave. After all FIVEs often do not experience feelings until afterward. "Learning to love" is one of the great challenges of FIVEs. FIVEs who allow themselves no passion, who will not allow themselves, at this one point at least, to become "headless" are very incomplete persons.

Meditation and prayer are for FIVEs uncommonly important sources of power. FIVEs have to cultivate their inner world in order to find the courage to devote themselves to the outer world. The latter becomes possible only when the inner world is experienced as less threatening, when FIVEs have found repose and security in God and hence in themselves.

I encourage all FIVEs to meditate on the Incarnation, that is, the commitment and passion of Christ, his passion for humankind, his readiness to get his hands dirty. Christianity can't be translated into reality by sitting alone in your room with your books, which is what the unredeemed FIVE would most like to do. In Christ untouchable God has been made flesh, the God who heals human beings precisely by touching them.

A close acquaintance of mine, who is a FIVE, has discovered an ingenious way to arrive at wholeness. She became a medical masseuse because she unconsciously sensed that she had to touch the bodies of other people and be there for others. That way she freed herself from the cage of her self-involvement and isolation and opened herself to her own and others' bodies. Recently she told me: "When I do my work and deal this way with my fellow men and women, it's a part or the continuation of my prayer life." Normally FIVEs keep their energy to themselves, but this woman gives up to nine massages a day. It's a step toward her own integration.

She remains a FIVE. We all remain who we are. But on the way to healing or liberation we have to do what the Romans called *agere contra:* we have to act against the grain of our natural compulsions. This requires clear decisions. Because it does not happen by itself, it is in a way "unnatural" or "supernatural." FIVEs simply have to cut loose now and then, and in the process they make mistakes. It's no mistake to make mistakes. But FIVEs — like some other types — are afraid of that. FIVEs are afraid of doing something unreasonable. Here we see that FIVE and SIX are neighbors. Fear, the root sin of SIXes, is no stranger to FIVEs.

That's why FIVEs must dare to take the path outward. Gestalt therapy or manual labor can be helpful. Also good is every other sort of externalization of the inner world, for example, in creative artistic work (music making, painting) — even if other people are able to peek at "the soul's cards" that one holds — or in practical political and social commitment.

Although FIVEs appear self-sufficient, they need the experience of secure love in the inner world (the experience of God) and in the outer

Doubt of Thomas (Camuccini)

world (love from fellow human beings). They find psychic nurture in every encouragement that awakens inner messages, such as: "You can feel safe here. We're glad that you're here. You have a right to be here. You're welcome. You belong to us."

FIVEs have to be on their guard against arrogance and conceit, either toward others or toward God. ("If God wants something from me, God must make it clear.") They come to their most profound gift of authentic wisdom if they renounce secretiveness and artificial mystification and expose themselves to the encounter with the mystery of other people, which reveals their own mystery and sets free their own treasures. FIVEs must practice expressing emotions directly instead of storing them up for the "silent little chamber" of the soul. Temperamentally FIVEs would prefer being Buddhists rather than Christians. But precisely for them the Eastern way of world-denial and spiritualization can be a pitfall preventing them from discovering the mysteries of the Incarnation and the cross and from duplicating them in their own existence.

A representative figure for the contemplative **saints** is Hildegard of Bingen (1098–1179). Her learning was universal; she was versed in music, theology, and medicine. But she became famous because of her gift for visions. These caused her suffering, and she fell sick. Only when she wrote everything down and communicated it, did she get better. Many mystics find that only through severe struggles can they find the way to the relationship with the world that leads them out of morbid introspection into deeds. Like all FIVEs, they have to take the step from seeing to acting. But then they'll be able to become sharp-eyed spiritual and political visionaries who clearly recognize and interpret the connection between things.

Dietrich Bonhoeffer (1906–1945) took the path of the redeemed FIVE from thought to action. He was born the sixth of eight children in Breslau. His grandfather and greatgrandfather on his mother's side were famous professors of theology. His father was one of the most prominent psychiatrists of his day. "Self-control" and "objectivity" were demanded even from children in the *grand bourgeoise* Bonhoeffer family. His mother instructed the children herself, which enabled them to skip several grades.

Young Dietrich was a bookworm and an enthusiastic chess player. At age eighteen he was allowed to travel to Rome — he had already memorized the Baedeker guide to the city. Dietrich became an industrious student, signing up for lectures in many subjects. He was just nineteen when he began his famous doctoral thesis, entitled *Sanctorum communio*; in 1927 he was awarded his degree *summa cum laude*.

At twenty-two he began work as an assistant minister in Barcelona. Following that he spent a year studying in the U.S., where the encounter with racism in Harlem deeply shook him. At twenty-five he became a university lecturer. In 1933 the Nazis came to power. Right from the start Bonhoeffer clearly recognized the danger of the Führer cult (he himself always found it repugnant to have power over the souls of other people). He saw and said that the Jewish question would be the crucial issue for the Church to face in the coming years. A little later Bonhoeffer went as a chaplain to London.

When he was twenty-nine, he became the director of the illegal preachers' seminary of the "Confessing Church." In 1936 the Nazis banned him from teaching. After an extensive trip to America he caught the last ship back before the war broke out, although he already knew that the mission in Germany could cost him his head.

In 1942 he joined the circle that was planning Hitler's assassination; the intellectual had become a political conspirator. In April 1943 he was arrested. He spent two years in the Tegel prison and planned to commit suicide to avoid betraying his fellow conspirators under physical torture, of which he was enormously afraid. Shortly before the end of the war he was sent to the concentration camp at Buchenwald, where he was hanged on April 9, 1945.

TYPE SIX
The Need for Security/Certainty

Overview

People who belong to type SIX have tremendous gifts: they are cooperative, team players, reliable. In relationships one can count on their fidelity. Their friendships are marked by warm-hearted and deep feelings. They are often highly original and witty; sometimes they have a grotesque sense of humor. They do their utmost, give body and soul, for the people they love.

Redeemed SIXes know how to combine holding on to sound traditions with the readiness to take new paths. They have a sense of what is possible and what isn't. In timely fashion they discover the unsuspected weak points of a project, as they have in general a sixth sense for threatening dangers. They can be far-sighted and bold when it comes to opening up new paths and drawing new frontiers.

THREEs and SIXes have a special importance for us because their root sins were not recognized in Western Christianity as such: fear (type SIX)

115

and deceit (type THREE). So long as these two sins remain unrecognized, they are the source of great danger for our society.

Many people who have been working for a long time now with the Enneagram are convinced that in Western society the SIX is by far the most frequently encountered human type. I have had this experience and I think there are a series of reasons for it.

SIXes easily succumb to self-doubt. That makes them look ahead, fearful and mistrustful. They continually sense danger. In their psychopathic form they are victims of paranoia. If one thinks how many anxieties and dangers a little child is exposed to even before birth and then in the first weeks and months of life, we can understand that there are many people who develop the attitude that "the world is dangerous; you have to be on the lookout; I don't have enough inner authority to be up to all that, so I have to look for security somewhere outside myself."

Riso has described the torn condition of SIXes as follows:

> They are emotionally dependent on others, yet do not reveal much of themselves. They want to be close to others, yet test them first to see if they can be trusted. They worship authority, yet fear it. They are obedient, yet disobedient; fearful of aggression, yet sometimes highly aggressive themselves. They search for security, yet feel insecure. They are likable and endearing, yet can be mean and hateful. They believe in traditional values, yet may subvert those values. They want to escape punishment, yet may bring it on themselves.[1]

Some SIXes report that they could never develop primal trust because they had uncontrolled, unpredictable, violent or cold parents. Many were punished or beaten without evident reason, because the parents worked off their conflicts in this way. There were various possible consequences of this: the children either had to look for a protector whom they could trust or they had to learn to detect the slightest signs of approaching danger so they could search for cover in time, or they had to anticipate aggressively the danger that threatened.

In the first case the lack of genuine self-confidence leads to SIXes' looking around for authorities, for someone who offers security, someone who is famous or has a position of power and can tell the SIXes where the limits are. In this case SIXes need an institution (for example, the Church, the party, the state, science) or a book (e.g., the Bible, canon law, or the penal code, the Qur'an, *Mein Kampf, Das Kapital*) with infallible answers. SIXes long for certainty. They don't want to deal with impenetrable shadows and shades of gray: they want a world divided into black and white and a clearly spelled out truth they can take home with them. In the worst case the energy of SIXes produces the Nazi type, persons who want truth in totalitarian, self-righteous fashion to be the way they need it, and who are ready to carry out every order that comes "from above." At his trial in Jerusalem Adolf Eichmann said, in line with this position: "I belonged to the people who formed no judgment on their own. The words of the Führer had the power of law. I obeyed. Regardless of what would have been commanded, I would have obeyed, because an oath is an oath."

Many SIXes report breaks in their life history: they couldn't complete their studies or training. They are often overcome by a paralyzing fear of failure shortly before the examination; or they don't make progress in learning because they have to scrutinize every detail and eliminate all contradictions. They are more likely to question their own position than to defend it with certitude. The Sisyphean task of making their own opinion watertight can ultimately lead to actual failure.

Many SIXes produce situations in which they lose in the end. They are pessimists and anxious about success. If they never succeed, then the danger of envy or competition isn't so great. That is why SIXes "go around" success, pass it along to others or set themselves goals so unreachable or megalomaniacal that failure is preprogrammed. SIXes fight for their survival, but never for success, which only conceals new dangers. If they do succeed at some point, they usually forget it immediately. Every new situation is so threatening for them that the memory of earlier victories is useless.[2]

If THREEs are notorious winners, SIXes are notorious losers. This "pleasure in losing" can take on masochistic features. Woody Allen has impersonated this "loser" type in many of his films.

Most SIXes have a hard time accepting praise. They suspect there's a trick behind it, that they're being suckered. If you want to be accepted by a SIX, you should incorporate a minimum of constructive criticism in your praise: that will make it more credible.

To understand type SIX, you have to learn to distinguish between phobic and contraphobic SIXes. Both look so different that this distinction is very important.

Phobic SIXes are by nature careful, hesitant, and mistrustful. They have a hard time trusting themselves and their "instinct." As a rule they evade danger. Such people are in some ways "easy to lead" for the people around them. If they fall in with a trustworthy counselor or therapist, they're ready to be led gradually and slowly to look their anxieties straight in the eye, so that they have a good chance of becoming increasingly more relaxed, more autonomous, and more free.

Contraphobic SIXes, on the other hand, can do great damage to themselves and other people by denying and overcompensating for their
primal fear. In extreme cases they become members of, for example,
the Ku Klux Klan, far-right-wing groups, neo-Nazis, motorcycle gangs,
skinheads. Contraphobic SIXes seek out risky situations and get involved
in dangerous kinds of sports such as mountain climbing and auto racing,
because they prefer getting into "fast-forward" to continually torturing
themselves with their anxieties.[3]

They disguise the fear that is the actual driving force of their actions
and compensate for it by a put-on hardness, strength, and dare-devil behavior. Contraphobics have no access to the fear that rules them. Such
people scarcely need an occasion to fly off the handle. In extreme cases
they can scream, curse, lie, or come to blows. They can't bear much criticism or deviation from what they consider right. They doggedly defend
their interests with every means available. This can lead to completely
inappropriate modes of behavior.

Watzlawick's famous "Story with the Hammer" impressively describes the mechanism that operates with contraphobics. A man wants
to hang a picture, but doesn't have a hammer. He wants to go to his
neighbor to borrow one. Then he starts to doubt: perhaps his neighbor won't give him a hammer. Just yesterday he had given him only
a hasty greeting. "He probably has something against me. But I didn't
do anything against him, did I?" The man gradually works himself up
into a rage against his repulsive neighbor. Finally he runs over, rings the
doorbell, and shouts at the neighbor: "Keep your stupid hammer!"[4]

Dilemma

The **temptation** of SIXes is their permanent striving for security. For this
reason they love orthodox, closed systems. They have a tendency to fundamentalism, whether Islamic, Christian, scientific, green, red, or brown.
The effects of Islamic fundamentalism have stamped the Khomeini era.
Bible-wielding Christian fundamentalists fight in the United States for
God and country. For them the Bible is infallible. All fundamentalists
need an infallible source of truth. In the U.S. self-help groups of "Fundamentalists Anonymous" have lately sprung up, organized like Alco-
holics Anonymous to break loose from the intellectual imprisonment of
the fundamentalist world picture.

Two hundred years ago Enlightenment rationalistic fundamentalism began its triumphal march: science became the infallible source of
knowledge. Today we experience and suffer from the catastrophic conse-

quences of the delusion of progress. Horst-Eberhard Richter has argued that the modern myth of progress is the consequence of fear of death and the world. When faith in a loving God lost its power, there was an "abrupt shift from desperate fear to a frenzied drive for possession." Fantasies of omnipotence ("God complex") were born out of feelings of impotence. Feelings and affects were sacrificed to almighty "reason." "Instead of being the source of the deepest knowledge, they turned into an irritating factor. It became the task of the mathematical intellect to bring disturbing emotional impulses completely under control." A further consequence was that, "Instead of accepting the indispensable idea of death, our culture has invented as a replacement the phenomenon of an absolute world enemy."[5]

Thomas Meyer sees the many fundamentalisms of our time as a reaction to the "loss of consolation" owing to a skeptical, secularized modernity. People feel abandoned, because along with the liberation from religious taboos they have also lost the support the taboos once provided. Meyer calls for the removal of economic and ecological distress, so that no "green" or "neo-Nazi" fundamentalism can impose its claims of cultural hegemony.[6]

SIXes search for hierarchies, authority, and security. That's why there are more enthusiastic militarists among them than with other types. With the military there is a clearly structured hierarchical system with people who tell you what's what. You know what you must and must not do, whom you have to obey and whom to command. The pecking order is clear.

The law and everything connected with it fascinates most SIXes. Many of them seek occupations where they deal with the law — whether by protecting it or breaking it. Judges, prosecutors, defense attorneys, detectives, inspectors, police, writers of whodunits, and criminals all take part in the SIX game.

Helen Palmer calls the SIXes "devil's advocates." In canonization trials of the Roman Church the *advocatus diaboli* has to try to track down everything that speaks against the canonization. SIXes have a sixth sense for absurdities and suspicious factors.

The primary **defense mechanism** for SIXes is projection. SIXes often have a rich imagination for scenarios of apocalyptic terror and often anticipate the worst. Their mistrust leads to their tendency to project hostility, hatred, and negative thoughts onto other people, even when there is only scanty evidence for this. Thus in a partnership they can advance exaggerated notions about their partner's "unconscious motives." The mistrust that they harbor against themselves leads to imagining their own negative motives present in others as well. Such programming leads to the classic scapegoat mechanism. The hostile images of the Cold War, for example, which one hopes now belong to the past, can be understood as an expression of a global SIX syndrome.[7]

The **root sin** of SIX is fear, a sort of primal anxiety. The Bible incessantly encourages us, in the Hebrew Scriptures but above all in the message of Jesus of Nazareth, to overcome fear: "Fear not!" For have we not realized how downright demonic fear can be? Although the Bible continually summons us to decide against the voice of fear, we deny it or give it other names, such as diplomacy, prudence, or reasonableness.

Above all, individuals in positions of power who wish to control others by means of fear will always find new code names for it: "loyalty," for example, or "obedience." Many of us as children had the "virtue" of obedience pounded into our head. In reality the point was that we were supposed to knuckle under to our parents, teachers, superiors, pastors, or other people in charge. Fear was cloaked with the virtue of obedience or even with a religious vow while what took place had nothing to do with the intelligent virtue of obedience. Genuine obedience grows out of the freedom to "hear" (Latin: *ob-audire*), to make a conscientious decision and where appropriate to say no. False obedience is the rotten fruit of fear, a cover for anxiety, an avoidance of courage.

At this point I would like once more to recall the fact that we are in the domain of the head. Isn't it baffling that fear is located in the head — and not, say, in the gut or in the heart? As soon as you work with fear-obsessed persons, you notice that you're actually dealing with phantasms that persecute them. Apocalyptic scenarios are always running in their heads, visions of how everything could go wrong. Ultimately this affects the feelings and the gut; but the starting point of fear is the mind. Fear types are trapped in mind games: witness most right-wing movements with their complicated scenarios of plot and conspiracies.

The Sufis supposedly labeled the Roman Catholic Church the church for SIXes. They had the impression that the Roman system is largely based on fear, and that this has led many people to fear God, the priesthood, mortal sins, themselves, their body. The latter is palpably true if you look at the current (and still not yet overcome) Roman Catholic attitude toward sexuality. We have not been given the freedom to take risks. Mistakes were not allowed in this system. Obedience was a higher virtue than faith, hope, or even love.

The Grand Inquisitor in Fyodor Dostoyevsky's novel *The Brothers Karamazov* has Christ arrested when he returns to earth and once more heals and preaches as he did before. He reproaches his prisoner for overstraining humanity with the freedom that he saddles it with. The Church, on the other hand, has taken back this freedom out of true love of man:

"For fifteen centuries we have been wrestling with Thy freedom, but now it is ended and over for good.... [T]oday, people are more persuaded than ever that they have perfect freedom, yet they have brought their freedom to us and laid it humbly at our feet.... Thou didst reject the only way by which men might be made happy. But, fortunately, departing Thou didst hand on the work to us."[8]

In Umberto Eco's bestseller *The Name of the Rose* there is a dispute in a medieval monastery over whether Jesus ever laughed. The blind old man Jorge sacrifices the life of several monks and finally the whole monastery so that a book of Aristotle on comedy doesn't come to light. "Laughter," he says, "is weakness, corruption, the foolishness of our flesh. It is the peasant's entertainment, the drunkard's license.... Laughter frees the villein from fear of the Devil, because in the feast of fools the Devil also appears poor and foolish, and therefore controllable.... But this book could teach that freeing oneself of the fear of the Devil is wisdom."[9] Anxiety and humor, freedom and fear are incompatible. That is why theologians can't laugh at themselves or let other people laugh.

Before the Second Vatican Council the Catholic Church was very attractive to insecure people. It was a bulwark of absolute and infallible truth and security. Thank God we have *de facto* dropped that illusion. Today's Catholicism embraces the whole spectrum from Daniel Berrigan to Marcel Lefebvre. The latter, it is true, has been excommunicated. But many people long for a traditionalism, as demanded and practiced by Lefebvre.

Because there are so many people who need the illusion of security, I venture to predict that traditionalism and fundamentalism will grow. This will happen especially if we don't help people to see their "SIX pitfall" and overcome their anxiety and name it as fear instead of calling it faith or loyalty.

All this affects not only the Roman Catholic Church, but all of Western Christianity. Protestantism is a child of Catholicism and has often done the same thing to its adherents: the Church has seen to it that people are afraid of God, instead of falling in love with God. The misleading biblical concept of the fear of God has contributed its share to this disastrous development. In the classic list of the "seven gifts of the spirit," which goes back to Isaiah 11:1, there is also *timor (domini)*, fear (of the Lord). This "fear" is best translated "awe" or "reverential wonder" before the Holy Mystery. It is based on respect, not anxiety.

The possible consequences of an education that makes God simultaneously the object of love ("the good Lord") and fear are reflected in the reckoning that psychotherapist Tilman Moser has with the (Protestant) faith in God of his childhood, which he formulates in a kind of anti-prayer:

> "We should fear and love God ... " was dinned into my ears, as if the first didn't make the second almost impossible. And because your mad conditions of existence, as one whom was supposed to fear and love, engendered hatred at the same time, again had to be all the more afraid, all the more humble, all the more thankful for the reprieve, for not yet having been rejected. . . . You robbed me so thoroughly of the certainty of ever being allowed to feel right, of becoming reconciled with myself, of finding myself okay ... There was no talking in my family about psychic events, even about fears. Thus I was delivered up to your raging in me. . . . You thrive in the hollow spaces of social impotence and uncertainty. . . . For days at a time as I write the only thing that pours out of me is hatred. This morning, during a pause in writing, I suddenly gagged and puked. . . . "[10]

Unredeemed SIXes **avoid** doubt. They are fussy about upholding norms, laws, and rules and they see to it that others don't break them either.

The **pitfall** of phobic SIXes is cowardice; the pitfall of contraphobic SIXes is taking foolish risks. All SIXes at once overestimate and mistrust authorities. In their heart of hearts they feel weak and exposed. This can lead them to kowtow and submit in a sort of blind obedience. But it also leads to their joining with other underdogs to find strength in common. The strong or orthodox group helps them deny and overcome their personal insecurity. Contraphobics tend to be panicky before their fear-filled fantasies gain power over them. Then they plunge into risky undertakings or rebel with the courage of despair.

The root sin of SIXes also has a positive side: SIXes have wonderful gifts. Every community or group that has SIXes in its ranks can depend on their loyalty, self-sacrifice, and readiness to assume responsibility. SIXes, to be sure, expect from their superiors and co-workers the same loyalty and credibility for which they themselves strive. Devotion can turn to rebellion, when the admired and "infallible" leadership openly fails and their own demands are not met (e.g., Archbishop Lefebvre).[11] And then there is the fact that SIXes, because they often feel stepped on and neglected, can become passionate and courageous fighters for the cause of the oppressed (e.g., Oscar Romero of El Salvador).

The peculiar **fruit of the spirit** of SIXes is their courage. In moments of crisis SIXes can overcome their fear more easily than anyone else. SIXes have had to grapple with fear all their lives. At some point they get tired of being the eternal chicken, and they can suddenly transcend themselves in heroic fashion. One day I was standing with a group of women on the edge of the street in front of our center, where a few little children were playing. One woman was there whom most people would have called a fearful little mouse. She always seemed insecure and never took risks. That day one of the children suddenly ran out onto the street directly in front of a car that was coming quickly around the corner. Before any of us reacted, she sprang out onto the street — between the car and the child. Thank God, nobody was hurt; the car had just enough time to brake. No one would have predicted this woman to be the heroine!

A further gift of many SIXes is their well developed sense for what is "in the air." The great Enneagram specialist Helen Palmer is a SIX. She has told me that she never would have gotten her therapeutic talent and her power of empathy if she hadn't been a SIX. All her life she wondered why she constantly felt threatened and searched for explanations for her fears. "This impulse," she said, "drove me to enter into myself and explore all these energies that threaten me." Helen Palmer is one of the greatest psychics I know. She grasps the energies that issue from other people in such an immediate and uncanny way that in earlier days she would have been called clairvoyant. She simply knows what is going on in the person she's talking to. "Actually I developed this ability," she told me, "because I was afraid."

Symbols and Examples

There are very different **animals** that represent the multiple aspects of SIXes. Some like to view the phobic SIX as a hare in full flight, doubling back and forth, or as a fearful grey mouse or a shy deer. Hares are true to their post. The proverbial fear of "frightened rabbits" is actually a highly developed watchfulness that enables the animal to react immediately to every change or danger in its environment. Threatened by many natural enemies, hares have developed the protective measures important to survival: the camouflage color of their brown fur, the lightning fast back and forth flight in danger.

Symbols of the contraphobic SIX are the wolf, which needs the protection of the pack, the loyal, obedient German shepherd; the rat, which stands for the aggressive pleasure that contraphobic SIXes can develop when driven into a corner.

The **country** of SIXes is Germany. The stereotypical image of Germans corresponds to this energy. When Americans imitate Germans, they click their heels together and roar, *"Achtung!"* This grim, accurate style symbolizes the contraphobic way of reacting, the artificial self-assuredness behind which really lies uncertainty. This repression of fear has taken its revenge more than once in German history. To this day Germans have a hard time facing up to what Germans did in the name of Germany and under German orders in two World Wars because they were "just doing their duty." All this is too fear-ridden and too threatening, and so must be repressed. If the Germans don't really become aware of their history and accept it (which is what the Bible means by "conversion"), then they are condemned to repeat it. It is probably no accident that Cardinal Ratzinger, the head of the Congregation of the Faith in Rome, is a German. He sees to it that nobody deviates from the norms and rules of correct belief.

Luise Rinser, the German writer, who has been living in Italy for over thirty years, picks up Erich Fromm's distinction between "biophile" (life-loving) and "necrophile" (death-loving) people, and assigns the Italian mentality to the first, and the German mentality to the second group:

> Germany is a country of men, a country of the fathers, in which the masculine and the man have the upper hand. Germany is what may be called an animus-country, in contrast to Italy, which is an anima-country, a country of feminine qualities, the country of the madonna, the Christianized mother goddess. For me Germany is the fatherland, but Italy has become my motherland.... Things German have their greatness. Listen to Wagner's *Ring of the Nibelungs*, and you'll know what I mean.... When I... heard that Hitler was a passionate Wagnerian, I understood my intuitive rejection of him.... When Hitler ended in poison and fire, he wanted to tear all of Germany down with him into nothingness.... The fact that Hitler's necrophilia was passed on so easily to the Germans shows that it was latently present all along.[12]

The symbolic **color** of SIXes is beige brown. It doesn't strike the eye, it doesn't shine on its own, and it fits in with its environment. It's the color of the bark that protects the tree from dangers. Brown is the combination of red and green, in which dynamic red does not reveal itself. It is the color of self-denial.[13] Just like gold and silver, brown does not belong to the classic color spectrum. Still it is one of the most expressive and richly nuanced colors. It conveys closeness to the earth and security. *Humus* (earth) and *humilitas* (humility) have the same root in Latin. For this reason the medieval mendicant orders — and the Sufis before them — wore brown habits.

The **biblical representative** of phobic SIXes is Paul's disciple Timothy, the perfect follower, whom Paul must reassure. The patron of the contraphobic SIXes is the Apostle Peter.

Timothy is often mentioned in the Acts of the Apostles and the Pauline letters. As a relatively young man he was given the assignment by his mentor Paul of leading the community of Ephesus. Scholars dispute whether both New Testament letters to Timothy derive from Paul himself or were composed by invoking his name. In them, at any rate, we find the beginnings of a hierarchically structured church order. Large parts of the letters read like directives from a superior to a subordinate. While Paul's first communities were evidently much more "charismatically" and "democratically" organized, with Timothy a sort of "pastor" or functionary first makes an appearance. The name "Timothy" means "God-honoring." The direction of the community is transferred to Timothy through the laying on of hands (1 Tim.4:14). He is supposed to take care that doctrine is pure (1 Tim. 1:3–7). He is continually admonished to conduct himself in office blamelessly (1 Tim. 1:18–20). The office of bishop is mentioned here for the first time (1 Tim. 1:3–7). Theologians are justified in saying that these "pastoral letters" reflect the early Catholic Church, which was increasingly being transformed from a movement to an institution.

Peter is a contraphobic SIX. He is devoted to his master and ready to go to his death for him (Matt. 26:35). In moments of danger forward flight comes into play: when Jesus is taken prisoner, Peter cuts off the ear of a slave of the high priest (Matt. 26:51). But shortly afterward he fails pitiably by denying Jesus because of fear of mockery (Matt. 26:69–75). The confrontation between Peter and Paul described in Galatians 2:11–21 has already been mentioned in the treatment of type ONE. This is the typical collision between a reformer (ONE) and a person with an authoritarian structure (SIX) that keeps coming up in history (Luther vs. Catholicism, Gorbachev vs. hardline party dogmatists). One spiritual director told me that I probably became a priest to change and challenge the SIXes. I must admit they are the most difficult of all numbers for me to understand or tolerate — at least in their unredeemed state. It was a great achievement of the early Church that both groups showed themselves capable of compromise (see the "Apostolic Council" in Acts 15:1–35).

Peter wasn't always cowardly. There are numerous indications that in very dangerous situations he could be quite brave. When the high council orders him not to speak about Jesus any more, he says: "Whether it is right in the sight of God to listen to you rather than God, you must judge; for we cannot but speak of what we have seen and heard" (Acts 4:19–20). Later he repeats this, "We must obey God rather than men" (Acts 5:29). Ultimately Peter suffered a martyr's death for his faith.

Conversion and Redemption

There are, unfortunately, only a few SIXes who have a healthy self-confidence. The **invitation** to SIXes is faith. Faith in the biblical sense is not a set of certitudes or axioms. Ironically it is a journey into mystery — or noncertitude. It is a relationship of trust between humanity and God. God believes in us. This is the basis on which we can believe in God, without thereby losing our human dignity. God trusts us and hopes that we return the compliment. Because God has confidence in us, we can develop a healthy self-confidence.

Only a few people have gotten permission from authority figures to trust themselves. Much louder and more frequent has been the order: "Trust us! Obey us! We know what's good for you." I can still vividly recall that day when a priest for the first time allowed me to be my own authority figure and "inner authority." He begged me: "Promise me, Richard, that you'll always trust yourself." For me as a young man that was a salutary shot of genuine masculine energy. Humanly speaking, he "saved" me.

Among the **life tasks** of SIXes is learning to break free from external direction by authorities and taking over responsibility for their lives and their feelings. Above all they must dare to look their fear in the eye and call it by name. When we call the demon by name, we have power over it and can unmask it. Jesus asked the demons what their names were. As soon as the name was spoken, the spell was broken.[14] SIXes in particular have to shake off those phantasms that dominate their existence.

By nature SIXes will prefer a form of spirituality and piety that is structured, ordered, and controlled from the head: "Am I saying the right prayers? Am I saying them in the right way?" For the preconciliar Catholic Church it was always a matter of words: reading the breviary, saying the correct Latin formulas of the Mass. All this was too controlled; there was too much left brain in it.[15] Especially since women have been leaving their mark on the Church and imparting their ways of perception, forms of prayer have been developing that are more oriented toward the right half of the brain, that derive more from intuition and the body, that have more "heart." Men in Western society have hitherto felt very good with SIX energy. I am not claiming there aren't women too who are this way. But men profited from this game and laid down its rules; it is a game that to this day defines many of our institutions. That is why it will be helpful, particularly for SIX men, to emancipate themselves from hard and fast, pre-established forms of "logic" — even if at the risk of making "mistakes."

A spiritual life that helps SIXes to free themselves from their compulsions should be set up in such a way that personal trust in God and in oneself are strengthened. The point is to develop a warm, intimate relationship of the heart to the personal God, with whom one can let oneself go. To achieve this it is helpful to seek a community in which people open themselves and practice not just the abstract exchange of thoughts, but also talk about their fears and feelings.

Since the fears of SIXes are as a rule exaggerated, it makes sense for them continually to ask their friends to scrutinize these fears to see if there is anything to them. A SIX must often be reminded that many suppositions about the motives or intentions of others are projections that can be trimmed back to realistic proportions.

SIXes have to practice seriously making decisions without asking "authorities" for permission. They should also train themselves to remember their successes and to strive for more of them. Martial arts such as *tai kwan do* or judo can help in learning to react spontaneously and "from the gut," without having the time to rehearse the situation intellectually. All body movements that support a healthy self-confidence can be recommended. The important thing is that here too the SIXes find out by themselves what is best for them.

Humor and the ability to laugh at one's exaggerated fears can also contribute to driving fear away. When we laugh from the heart, fear can't remain very long. That is why dictatorships and all systems that operate on fear are afraid of nothing so much as being unmasked through laughter, mockery, and satire. Sick SIXes have no place for humor. They take themselves far too seriously.

At the Enneagram conference in Craheim one evening there was a kind of cabaret, at which the representatives of the individual types acted out themselves. The contribution made by the two SIXes demonstrates by its capacity for self-mockery how "redeemed" the individuals already are:

> Germany must stay German!
> Distrust the foreigner, distrust yourself!
> Don't say too soon what you think,
> *If* you think . . .

> First listen to what the others say . . .
> Like Timothy, ask Paul for advice,
> Stick to what the biggies teach you,
> You're not ready to stand on your own two feet.

> Be loyal!
> Loyalty and Loyola . . .
> Catholics are always welcome!

Those who swim with the current come through . . .
Those who swim with the current drown in it . . .
Those who swim with the current lose in it
What they could be
If they swam against it.

SIXes need places of security, free from fear, where they don't need
to defend themselves, where they sense they are accepted as they are.
They need a God who is not at once "dear" and "angry," who doesn't
punish them, who allows them to make mistakes and have weaknesses.
The experience of unconditional love is the one thing that in the long
run can be stronger than fear: "There is no fear in love, but perfect love
casts out fear" (1 John 4:18).

At Enneagram workshops it continually turns out that only a few
people are willing to identify themselves as SIXes, although SIX is pre-
sumably a very common type. Often people who simply cannot decide
who they are after days of reflection are either SIXes (fear of being wrong
or needing an authority to tell them) or NINEs (don't really have a focus
or don't really care). (In Craheim, for example, only two of the participants assigned themselves to SIX; by contrast fifteen said they belonged
to type FIVE.) For this reason we should stress once more: no type is "better" or "worse" than the others. Each one contains terrible and splendid
possibilities.

There is a storybook example of what can happen when SIXes find
the way to their gift:

Oscar Romero (1917–80), archbishop of San Salvador, is our **saint**
for SIXes. Romero was a classic SIX, a shy, subtle, and conservative bookworm, a waverer, a man of the system, who had followed the Catholic
party line all his life. On the day in 1977 that he was appointed primate
of El Salvador, the conservatives rejoiced, while the progressives were
frustrated and debated whether they could even celebrate the Eucharist
with this archbishop. Later Romero himself admitted that Rome had intended him to see that the progressives were "gotten rid of," since the
Vatican at the time was working toward a policy of compromise with
the Salvadoran regime.

Within three months the tables had been totally turned. The change
was sparked by the murder of a Jesuit priest, an old farmer, and an altar
boy by a sniper; and a military attack on the village of Aguilares, the
parish of the murdered priest. The soldiers desecrated their church and
refused to let Romero enter it, when he tried to save the consecrated
hosts. He later called this episode his "conversion." It became clear to
him that, "We must obey God rather than men" (Acts 5:29).

Oscar Romero: Conversion of a Conformist

This ultimate, essential loyalty henceforth got the upper hand with him over political and ecclesiastical considerations. Romero became a prophet out of obedience. At the age of sixty the best self of this man suddenly unfolded. His lifestyle changed: he began to discuss important questions with his co-workers instead of making lonely decisions. He saw the suffering of the Salvadoran people and became unusually brave. Christians, he said, had to be "bold people."

In the three years in which he was primate of El Salvador, you didn't need to go to church on Sunday: when Romero preached, every radio in the country was turned on at top volume — until the church's transmitter was blown up. Romero developed great confidence in the ability of the people to be creators of their own society and asked believers to become active themselves and "not to wait for what the bishop says on Sunday."[16] The rich oligarchy, which he constantly attacked, tried to put him down as a "psychopath." Many bishops and priests distanced themselves from him; and Pope John Paul II expressly rejected Romero's view that revolutionary violence was permitted as a last resort against long entrenched and unequivocal tyranny. Finally Romero called upon members of the army to refuse commands and to stop the repression of their own people. From then on he had to reckon with his assassination. Shortly before his death he said in an interview: "As a Christian I don't believe in death without resurrection. . . . As a shepherd I am obliged by God's mandate to give my life for those whom I love, that is, all Salvadorans, even those who are out to kill me. . . . A bishop may die, but the Church of God, which is the people, will never go under."[17]

On March 24, 1980, he was shot during his sermon. At the funeral, which eighty thousand people attended, there was a massacre by the military, to whom another thirty-nine people fell victim. To this day the official Catholic Church is split in its view of this man — but "poor people in the villages and mountains have long since declared their shepherd a saint."[18]

TYPE SEVEN
The Need to Avoid Pain

Overview

SEVENs are people who radiate joy and optimism. They are alive to the precious ingredients in every moment; they can feel childlike astonishment and experience life as a gift. In their immediacy they give the impression that there's enough of everything beautiful and good, that there's nothing superfluous. They are full of idealism and plans for the future; and they can pass on their enthusiasm to others. They help others to see and enjoy the sunny side of life. SEVENs are cheerful sorts; they have an infectious sense of humor and can laugh at themselves. When a SEVEN turns up, the children gather round. The gay SEVENs don't seem "cerebral" at first glance. Relaxed, full of good humor, imaginative, sunny, playful, with a disarming kind of charm — until one day they notice that all this also serves to protect them from attacks, anxiety, and pain.

In the course of their development many SEVENs have had traumatic experiences which they did not feel equal to. In order to avoid the rep-

131

etition of this pain in the future, they have evolved a double strategy: First they repressed or whitewashed their negative and painful experiences. Many SEVENs paint their life story in positive colors, even when the scenario was anything but beautiful: "Of course we had difficulties too, don't you? But you can't let it get you down." Secondly, they've gone into their heads and begun to plan their lives so that every day will promise as much joy and as little pain as possible. Since they are able to do a good job connecting what's pleasant with what's useful, many SEVENs achieve visible prosperity. In our society this is the most obvious way to protect themselves from pain and difficulties.

There are SEVENs with a permanent smile. Over time this can become too much for others. The SEVEN is the Pollyana type: everything's wonderful. Life is a Disneyland full of miracles and terrific surprises. SEVENs would love to live and die at Disneyland.

The SEVEN is the "eternal child." Peter Pan could be their soul image,[1] or Mercury, the messenger of the gods wearing his winged shoes, with which he disappears into a wonderful world of fantasy. We less optimistic types would like to shout to a good many SEVENs: "Get some solid ground under your feet. Not everything in life is merry, funny, and easy." Many SEVENs enjoy using phrases like: "Wonderful! The tops! Super! Classy! Neat! Can't wait for it!"

SEVENs are curious. It's as if what they already know or have is never enough. They need change, stimulation, new experiences. They always have to ferret out new possibilities of maximizing their *joie de vivre*. In their calendar there are as many beautiful and exciting dates as possible. Unpleasant tasks, on the other hand, are gladly thrust aside, put off, or ignored. If they can't be avoided, SEVENs like to cushion them with a little bit of felicity on the edge, an especially pretty music cassette for the trip to a stupid hearing, a little sidetrip to a record store as a bonbon during a boring business trip. SEVENs are "adrenaline addicts" and have champagne in their blood (Palmer). They themselves often don't notice that much of what they do is a flight from the painful abysses of their own soul.

SEVENs are not specialists, but "generalists" (Riso). They always have several irons in the fire, because they always want to leave all their options open, and unconsciously want to avoid committing themselves too deeply to a thing or a person. In depth they always see pain lurking for them. Besides, if you totally devote yourself to someone or something your own limits might become visible — and that too would be painful. Thus many SEVENs master the art of bluffing; they are all-around dilettantes and evoke the impression of being many-faceted in their gifts, of knowing all about everything. A handful of facts, cleverly combined, sometimes suffice to create a comprehensive image. Their chatter and storytelling mystifies and fascinates you.

They often have a hard time tying themselves down to one career. They don't mind carrying out several interesting jobs at the same time. They like best to be self-employed or to work in a smoothly functioning team, because they are by nature anti-authoritarian and it pains them to have their possibilities and freedoms curbed by superiors. As a rule they also don't like subordinates much either. The pressure to exercise power could lead to painful conflicts.

Dilemma

The **temptation** of SEVENs is idealism. It has several aspects. SEVENs must be sure that they are working for a good cause, one that brings joy to them and to other people. One result of this is that they deny and repress the aspects of their activity that might hurt other people. This happens especially when a collision occurs between their own need for happiness and the happiness of others. The thought, for example, that there are structural sins, which we commit as a group, because our prosperity is financed at the cost of the Third World, can stir up vehement contradiction from a SEVEN. One of their most frequent **defense mechanisms** is rationalization. A SEVEN can repress thoughts about the injustices of the world economic system, arguing that it wouldn't make the poor any happier if we gave up our money and our possibilities. The pain of a separation can be softened for a SEVEN by looking for rational reasons why a relationship failed — and quickly turning his or her attention to the positive aspects of a new situation: "Freedom's nice too!"

The death of a family member can become more bearable if you tell yourself that it was a "blessing," that the person in question had, after all, achieved many fine things in his or her life. Religious SEVENs can also find relief by thinking to themselves that this person has now been lifted up to be with God. In any case, the pain is generally not felt, but shifted. The very mechanism of rationalization shows that SEVENs are head people. This is one of the many surprising insights of the Enneagram: the happiness and joy of SEVENs are produced in the head just as the fear of SIXes is.

Under certain circumstances, SEVENs can live for years without sensing the dark side of life and the world and can label the people who place their fingers on sore points as whiners or "cultural pessimists." SEVENs usually need a very long time before they can see the shadow side of a relationship — or their own shadow side. Because they want everything to be beautiful and good, they like to fade out other aspects of reality. Like THREEs, they are in danger of ego inflation, an exaggeratedly positive view of their own person. THREEs can refuse to see failures; SEVENs can refuse to feel pain. Many SEVENs as children were literally afraid of the dark and needed a nightlamp. They don't like darkness, but primary colors and bright lights.

In retreats that I give for priests I've often had the following happen: When the week is half over and I'm beginning to bring out the bigger issues and go deep, I can predict how some of the priests of Irish descent will react. (It's mostly the Irish: Ireland is the land of the SEVENs). As soon as I talk about the need to confront their dark side and deal with their shadow, several of these men will pointedly turn away from me. Or they'll begin fooling around and telling jokes in the back rows. It's always the Irish. They surely don't want to offend me, and probably don't even notice what they're doing. They tell jokes so that they don't have to listen to unpleasantness. One of the most effective methods of avoiding pain is to laugh. "Nervous laughter," psychologists call it.

SEVENs **avoid** pain. Their method is amazingly simple: "I want to be cheerful instead of sad. I want to enjoy life." SEVENs are notorious optimists, even though they stand directly alongside the professional worriers, the SIXes. Optimism and pessimism are surprisingly not far from one another: both are intellectual mechanisms for managing the abysses and dangers of life.

SEVENs have difficulty dealing with emotional problems — their own or other peoples'. One SEVEN gave up a career in the ministry not least because he had problems with bedside counseling: "I wanted to do sick people a favor, show them new possibilities, tell them about the world outside. That's what I would have wanted from a priest. At the same time coming up against the pain and sufferings of others was terrible. I sat alongside someone who was suffering and told myself, 'I'm healthy, I'm doing all right.' I also had a bad time worrying about being rejected by the people I visited. That would have hurt *me*."

SEVENs are unhappy when others are unhappy. They need to have nice people and "good vibrations" around them. They can cheer up other people. But sometimes they also try to turn an ailing person "inside out," because they can't abide pain. When things get too "hot," too sad, or too deep, they can deftly shift the conversation off onto another track or stifle it with flourishes like, "Well, you'll be up and around in no time," or "Things aren't all that bad."

I remember a woman whose child had just entered the hospital. Her husband had lost his job that same day. As she told me all this — she *smiled*! And when the tears came, she herself realized what was happening: "Just look, Richard, I'm still smiling. I simply don't trust myself to feel the pain and I smile."

This last example shows that the cheerfulness and lightheartedness projected by SEVENs is often just put on and very deceptive. At times SEVENs themselves know that their smiles conceal a great sadness that they are afraid of. They long for someone to see through the merriment that they parade, someone to take their pain seriously. Their helpless attempts to communicate this idea to others often come to nought because they aren't taken seriously. The people around us have gotten so used to our "character" that they pin us down to quite specific ways of behaving. The closest companions of SEVENs often will simply not believe that they are screaming inside. The upshot is that the SEVENs fall back into their old game: "Just keep smiling; however things may look in there, it doesn't concern anyone" or — with self-irony — "Don't worry, be happy!" In such situations it can happen that the SEVENs relapse into the well-rehearsed clown role and suffer from the way other people amuse themselves at their cost.

But often SEVENs have already so internalized their optimism that they have problems seeing what's dark and difficult. The sin of SEVENs is intemperance or, as it used to be called, gluttony. Their motto is, "More is always better." Our society provides lots of nourishment for this slogan of an unredeemed SEVEN. The point is not simply eating and drinking. SEVENs can exaggerate everything: more eating, more drinking, more working, beginning more projects, seeking more recognition, living in more and more beautiful places, buying more, possessing more. In short, however, SEVENs have an excessive need for fun, joy, and pleasure.

When I came to Albuquerque several years ago, I initially lived with two Franciscans, both of whom were SEVENs. One evening they were visited by a Franciscan from the city, another SEVEN. There I sat, a poor serious ONE with those three wisecrackers. They began to tell all sorts of funny stories, splitting their sides with laughter. I wondered how so much grotesque and comic stuff could happen to a person in one day. One of the brothers was telling about everything he'd seen that morning in the supermarket. I said: "I was at the supermarket today too. Nothing like that ever happens to me. All you have to do is go through the store and the craziest things go on." "Well," he said, "I'm embellishing a bit." SEVENs have the gift of pumping up a comic event like a balloon. They see the comic side of a situation more quickly than others do. All that escapes me, because I'm the opposite type. I'm too serious; they're too funny. They have an uncanny flair for finding where you can have fun, where there's something to laugh about, how you can have a tremendous time.

Many SEVENs talk too much; you might call them chatterboxes. They have to work to become more "sober" and ascetic in every way. When SEVENs let someone offer them pastoral counseling, it should run like this: "If you think you have to talk this much, cut it in half. If you think you want to drink this much, half is still too much. If you think you need all these free-time activities, cross out every other one." Less is always more when unredeemed SEVENs want to be liberated from themselves.[2]

I had a SEVEN living in the house with me around the time that the film *Close Encounters of the Third Kind* was running in the movie theaters. This man had seen the film eleven times. SEVENs love science fiction, futurism, and fantasy — anything that takes them out of the present, which they always find unpleasant. That's why they have a lust to travel. They hope somewhere else there will be more happiness; the present is always disappointing.

Like TWOs, SEVENs often have to struggle with weight problems. SEVENs are often on a diet — which they hate, because it's connected with deprivation and "suffering." SEVENs love good food and often have a weakness for candy, which helps to "sweeten" life. Beyond that, TWOs, SEVENs, and NINEs are prone to addiction. SEVENs drink or take drugs to deaden the pain. The "drinker" whom Saint-Exupéry's Little Prince runs into could be a SEVEN: "Why do you drink?" asked the Little Prince. "I drink to forget." "What do you want to forget?" "That I'm ashamed." "What are you ashamed of?" "That I drink."

SEVENs are Epicureans. The enemies of the philosopher Epicurus (341–271 B.C.) said of him that he was a glutton, a sot, and a libertine (according to his philosophical colleague Epictetus). His friends, on the other hand, extolled his abstemiousness, his virtue, and his modesty. Epicurus's philosophy left room for both interpretations. For him the highest goal in life was happiness. This was made up of the absence of pain and the presence of pleasure. By "pleasure," however, he understood not so much coarse sensual enjoyment as refined, uplifting, intellectual experiences such as friendship and the exchange of ideas. It is true that he had no objection in principle to sensual pleasures, but too much of them could be counterproductive: the person who eats and drinks too much gets sick.[3]

Epicurus's ideal was the soul that is passionless and without pain. It must leave crude desires behind and press forward to the highest pleasure, namely reason. "It is not possible to live pleasurably without living rationally, beautifully, and justly, nor to live rationally, beautifully, and justly without living pleasurably."[4] Finally, there remains the problem of the fear of death. Epicurus overcomes it by declaring that death is a condition of nonsensation, nothingness — and hence not threatening. "When we are, death is not, and when death is, we are not." He is convinced that "only the knowledge that death is nothing makes transitory life delicious."[5] Epicurus's philosophy is a perfect example of how SEVENs try to eliminate fear and pain through rationality and good arguments.

Two influential present-day movements have been marked decisively by SEVEN energies: the charismatic movement within the Church and outside it large parts of what is called the New Age.

The charismatic movement is in danger of becoming a pure SEVEN movement. Charismatics often preach a theology of resurrection and glory — but they don't much want to hear about the theology of the cross; they'd prefer not looking at Jesus, the Man of Sorrows. Charismatics often seek a kind of redemption that as far as possible omits the way of the cross.

Around ten years ago I preached at a charismatic congress about the meaning of Christ's death on the cross. The faces of my audience grew increasingly long and discontented. In the end a woman came up and poured out abuse on me: "You claim to be a Franciscan? You ought to be happy and preach joy. But you talk about the cross too much. Shame on you!" Preaching on the cross, pain, suffering, and death will hardly win you bouquets among these people.

The **root sin** of SEVENs, intemperance, leaves its mark on many charismatic gatherings. If you celebrate a charismatic liturgy, you may find the community singing fourteen opening hymns and just as many at the end. There is no appreciation of restraint. And the hymn texts continually repeated at these services reflect a onesided "theology of glory." As a rule God and Christ are addressed only with titles of majesty: the Lord, the King, the Mighty One, the Risen One, the Glorious, the Most High. More is always better! Despite Jesus' admonition, "do not multiply prayers as the pagans do" (Matt. 6:7), they think that if one "Praise the Lord!" is good, then forty-five "Praise the Lords!" are better. I say all this with great respect for the gifts that have come to light in the charismatic movement. But if it doesn't discover and accept its own shadow side, then the movement will end up taking the path that unredeemed SEVENs inevitably take: to increasing superficiality.

This leads, for example, to most charismatics' avoiding social issues; this was also true, by the way, in the charismatically oriented community of Corinth, which is why Paul attacked it so sharply (1 Cor. 11:17–34). I told the charismatics ten years ago that I wouldn't appear at their congresses any more until they also dealt with themes like peace and justice. Without saying so directly, their attitude sometimes seems to be: "We don't want to grapple with these messy and pain-filled issues. We want to jump up and down, clap our hands, and sing that Jesus is Lord." My question to such groups is: "What does it *mean* that Jesus is Lord? What practical *consequences* does that have for the problems of this world?"

In the charismatic movement there is widespread use of a certain method for dealing with suffering and pain. In consists in a Christianized variety of "positive thinking":[6] believers are not supposed to mourn losses and pain, but to "thank God" even in difficult moments, even when they don't understand what God is doing. Since God has permitted this or that to happen, it must make sense; God's thoughts are higher than our thoughts. For this reason in extreme charismatic communities mourning and grief are considered expressions of unbelief and have to be repressed. The "prosperity Gospel," which has many adherents, above all in the U.S.A. and Scandinavia, sometimes goes so far as to promise Christians that as children of God they have the privilege of being rich, happy, and successful in this world. The method of continually praising the Lord leads to "successful prayer." People are encouraged to imagine ("visualize") what they want as vividly as possible and then to take hold of it "in faith." There is, of course, a great emphasis on healing in the charismatic movement — which is the taking away of pain.

It's true that in the Bible we keep meeting people who pray and who cling to God's promises ("the positive") in hard times. But that doesn't mean that suffering, pain, and temptation have been suppressed. In the Psalms human beings bring their pains and complaints before God; they struggle with God; they even dare to challenge and accuse God. In Gethsemane and on the cross Jesus struggled and suffered through the pain of death; he did not make things easier for himself with joyful praise and the help of positive thinking. He rejected the sponge with gall and vinegar, a common drug back then for dealing with pain. SEVENs should not be too quick to "visualize positively," but learn first of all to admit and express pain. The joy of the resurrection is the joy on the other side of suffering, not the joy of avoiding suffering.

The "cognitive therapy" that positive thinkers like so much pursues a similar goal. One renounces getting to the bottom of the causes of a problem (searching for it in a person's childhood, say), and instead one starts out from the assumption that "rethinking" things will make possible a new kind of conditioning. For instance, instead of constantly saying, "I'm a loser," you should build up new thinking habits by continually saying to yourself, "I am good." Helpful as this method can be as a supplementary measure, it becomes dangerous when it remains the only therapeutic approach and the past is not really gotten under control. This presents the danger of a kind of religious brainwashing that makes the person into a marionette whose strings are pulled by the "correct" truths of the Gospel. In this case the Gospel becomes an optimistic ideology that controls a person's brain while the deeper levels remain "unbaptized." For SEVENs especially this kind of counseling is downright poison. It strengthens in them a tendency that is already too dominant anyway.

Similar observations can be made in broad circles of the New Age movement. An enormous number of books and courses promise — for hard cash — harmony, enlightenment, and happiness. Many "gurus" are themselves motivated by a boundless ambition for possessions and pleasures. The more than two hundred Rolls Royces of the Baghwan are only one example of the slogan "More is better." To be sure, a seemingly joyless Christianity helped make people looking for the meaning of life susceptible to the expensive promises of harmony and happiness made by the pseudo-religious psychological market place. The "age of Aquarius," whose dawn is celebrated in New Age circles, is supposed to be marked by all-embracing goodness and harmony. Note, however, that most New Agers are "in their heads." Their approach seldom leads to a love of the poor or concern for social justice.

Helen Palmer traces the line that leads directly from the 1960s revolution of the flower children, who in the face of war and the prospect of meaningless jobs switched into a happy, delusory world of "love," to postmodern narcissism. For many "meaning-seekers" the welcome self-discovery of the individual wound up in self-involved ego trips and therapeutic navel-gazing.[7]

One symptom of this is the current orgy of "spiritual consumerism." Now that Western society has materially exploited the earth, we are currently appropriating the intellectual legacy of the East, usually without paying the price of a serious inner way. If the Enneagram is misused in this way, its primal intention is missed: to call us to take the hard, stony path of conversion. This inner way is neither cheap nor open to shortcuts.

It's not simple to criticize or challenge a SEVEN. SEVENs will patiently submit to it all with a charming smile or push it aside with a few witty remarks. In any case they don't give the impression that the criticism reaches them. SEVENs are afraid of critical thinking, because failure hurts. In this respect they resemble THREEs.

The gift or **fruit of the spirit** of SEVENs is joy. But the joy should not come at the expense of the dark side of life, and false idealism must not deny reality. Sober joy is joy in the face of and despite all the difficulties of life. It is the "nevertheless" that those who pray the Psalms hold out to God even in times of distress: "Nevertheless I am continually with thee; and thou dost hold my right hand" (Ps. 73:23). Sobriety is what makes the difference between superficial optimism and deeply grounded hope. This is the only true joy that God promises us.

Symbols and Examples

The symbolic **animals** of SEVEN are the monkey and the butterfly. As the monkey leaps from branch to branch, so SEVENs are always on the way in their search for new adventures and new pleasures. But the joy SEVENs find in practical jokes, slapstick, and nonsense also reminds us of our nearest relative in the animal world. The butterfly represents the beauty and the lightness of redeemed SEVENs. The metamorphosis of the caterpillar through the pupa to the butterfly is an old symbol in many religions for spiritual processes of transformation. Ever since the Church Fathers it has also stood for the Christian way of salvation by transformation through death to resurrection.[8]

SEVENs' **countries** are Ireland and Brazil. The Irish in particular represent this energy. Every fourth house in Ireland is a pub. The image of the Irish wake is one of singing and dancing in the face of death. When the Irish face pain they pat you on the shoulder and fill you with blarney. Ireland is the only country where you're served whiskey at nine o'clock in the morning. It's as if no effort is spared to make the day merry.

Brazil is an example of a country both enormously rich and extremely poor. Rich and poor are united in carnival, in which all trouble and care is forgotten. The cutting of the Brazilian rain forest is a good symbol of what happens when excess gets the upper hand. It raises for a short time the level of prosperity of a few people who already belong to the "haves" anyway. In the end, however, this brief "heightening of life" leads to life's no longer being possible at all.

The **color** of SEVENs is green. Green symbolizes vitality and *joie de vivre*, health and well-being. Hildegard of Bingen speaks of the "green force" or *viriditas*, from which all life springs. Green stands in colloquial language for naive and childish behavior. We call immature people "greenhorns." Unripe fruit is also green. Green reminds SEVENs that they have to work at maturing. In Christian art green is the color of Paradise and the color of the cross. In the Lady Cathedral in Zurich Marc Chagall painted a green-gold crucified Christ, surrounded by a brilliant green halo, in the middle of a green tree of life.

Wolfgang Amadeus Mozart is an **example** of a SEVEN with its radiant and not-so-radiant features. In his film *Amadeus*, Milos Forman has clearly elaborated the "monkey" side of Mozart, "God's favorite": his yen for clowning, pranks, and his erotic escapades.

Almost all his life Mozart had to struggle with extremely adverse circumstances. His extravagance led to his continually being broke. Many of his contemporaries didn't understand him. His clients made his life a hell. Nevertheless his earthy, goofy humor seldom failed him.

Mozart was, like almost all SEVENs, a glutton for appropriate work. But he could also live it up: "You know that it's carnival now . . . and I'd like very much . . . to go as harlequin. . . . Last week I gave a dance at my house. . . . We began at six in the evening and stopped at seven. What — only an hour? — No, no! Seven o'clock in the morning!"[9] Mozart sought out friends for merrymaking and scarcely entered into deeper relationships.

At the hardest times he wrote the loveliest and "lightest" music, while his more serious works were composed in periods of happiness. "In his gayest days in Vienna he . . . wrote altogether gloomy, hopeless pieces. . . . When he was having a literally filthy time, he wrote music in which one hears not the slightest echo of the great distress of those years. . . . His appetite for jokes and craziness never let up. . . ."[10] This apparent contradiction is connected with a typical SEVEN phenomenon: When the external circumstances provide enough security and acceptance, a SEVEN sometimes dares to confront the dark side of life.

The **biblical patrons** of SEVEN are King Solomon and the rich young man.

Solomon (ruled 965–20 B.C.) was the son of Bathsheba, whom his father David had brought into his harem by means of a murderous plot against her first husband, Uriah. The brilliance of Solomon's court life soon eclipsed anything the country had ever experienced. Solomon's power and splendor are proverbial: "Solomon's provision for one day was thirty cors [a cor = 6.5 bushels) of fine flour and sixty cors of meal, ten fat oxen, and twenty pasture-fed cattle, a hundred sheep, besides harts, gazelles, roebucks and fatted fowl" (1 Kings 4:22–23). Solomon is supposed to have taken in 666 hundredweights of gold per year. A gilded ivory throne adorned his palace. He had 700 wives and 300 concubines in his harem.

Solomon knew how to pacify the country, and thus to create the prerequisite for a unique intellectual, cultural, and religious flowering. By building the temple he erected a religious center for the faith of Israel. In addition he made himself a name as a poet, a talent he probably inherited from his poetic father, David.

His wisdom was as famous as his wealth. Even the Queen of Sheba (Ethiopia) came "to test him with hard questions" (1 Kings 10:1), to admire his wealth, and to increase it with guest gifts. (According to legend their relationship went beyond asking questions: the Ethiopian imperial house has traced its genealogy down to our century directly back to the encounter between these two crowned heads.)

Solomon's extravagance ultimately had fatal consequences: the women in his international harem seduced him into building temples for their gods. Finally he himself succumbed to religious syncretism: "Solomon went after Astoreth, the goddess of the Sidonians, and after Milcom, the abomination of the Ammonites" (1 Kings 11:5). After Solomon's death the kingdom of David disintegrated; it was divided into two and never recovered its old greatness and brilliance.

Several books of the Hebrew Scriptures are ascribed — no doubt wrongly — to Solomon: Proverbs, Ecclesiastes, and the Wisdom of Solomon. It is interesting that parts of Ecclesiastes reflect a kind of Epicurean worldview, which can be summarized roughly as follows: Life is ultimately meaningless; instead of lacerating ourselves with brooding, greed, or furious work, we should try to make the best of it: "Go, eat your bread with enjoyment, and drink your wine with a merry heart. . . . Let your garments be always white; let not oil be lacking on your head. Enjoy life with the wife whom you love, all the days of your vain life which he [God] has given you under the sun" (Eccles. 9:7–9).

The New Testament story of the rich young man (Mark 10:17–31; Matt. 19:16–30; Luke 18:18–30) "can positively be read as a summary of the Gospel."[11]

A man comes to Jesus, falls down before him, and asks: "Good Teacher, what must I do to inherit eternal life?" Jesus points to the ten commandments. But the man claims: "Teacher, all these I have observed from my youth; what do I still lack?" Jesus looks at him, loves him, and then says: "Go, sell what you have, and give to the poor, and you will have treasure in heaven; and come, follow me." The man's "countenance falls" at this demand and he walks sadly away, "for he had great possessions."

The rich young man can imagine what he lacks only as an addition to the material and religious wealth he already has. Jesus, on the other hand, refers him to a source of life that can be tapped only when we give up planning our own life and become poor before God. "There is no one who has left house or brothers or sisters or mother or father or children or lands, for my sake and for the gospel, who will not receive a hundredfold now in this time, houses and brothers and sisters and mothers and children and lands, with persecutions, and in the age to come eternal life" (Mark 10:29–30).

This story takes on a particular explosiveness today when a rich Western society and church stand before the injustice of the international distribution of goods like the camel confronting the eye of the needle. The Gospel "quiets the drive for material and spiritual possessions not through the promise of more possessions but through a kind of wealth that is more than a possession." It "doesn't add heavenly values to this-orldly property," but creates "a new justice in the relation of rich and poor."[12] The story of the rich young man presents a material and spiritual challenge to us all, not only to SEVENs. All hasty attempts to spiritual-ize it (and thereby blunt it) miss the point. It remains a thorn in our flesh, so long as our hearts depend on money, intellectual or material possessions, or anything else that is not God.

Conversion and Redemption

The **invitation** to SEVENs is cooperation with God. Unredeemed SEVENs think that they are the fashioners of their own happiness, and so they continually plan new ways of optimizing their lives. When they cooper-ate with God, that implies something different: they confront the reality of the world, which is always a combination of joy and pain, and they accept both sides of life. They go God's way, which leads through death to resurrection. They are capable of bringing joy and hope where grief reigns. This also implies, of course, that they actually go there and don't evade this call. It is the step from idealism to a wide-awake realism.

The gift of redeemed SEVENs is sober joy. This joy can become au-thentic and deep, if it doesn't lose itself in superficial addiction to plea-sure. Anyone who wants to put on a really beautiful celebration should hand over the responsibility for it to SEVENs. Anyone who wants to cel-ebrate a liturgy that makes people cheerful should have a SEVEN work it out.

Among the **life tasks** of SEVENs is to get wise to their overhasty ra-tionalizations. They can reach the stage where because of all the planned and organized joy they are no longer capable of rejoicing spontaneously and from the heart. Sometimes they become peculiarly frozen and tense in their efforts to avoid pain.

We should not forget that SEVENs have a SIX-wing and for this reason can be astonishingly dogmatic. These same people who were so merry a moment ago can suddenly appear narrow, absolutist, and authoritarian in their own way, above all when someone tries to spoil their mood. The merriment of unredeemed SEVENs is the result of fear and a tool of their instinct for self-preservation. Head energy always pulls back from real reality. For SEVENs it's surprising at first to notice that their energy is at bottom often a retreat from reality and not genuine commitment. They seem so committed at first glance because they constantly make a grand to-do.

It's important for SEVENs to find their way to a deep self-acceptance by discovering that they have been accepted by God and, we may hope, by a few of their fellow humans who are close to them, not only with their radiant side, but whole and entire. Then they can live realistically in the beautiful *and* painful present, instead of fleeing in daydreams to the future or the past.

Amid the hunt for possibilities SEVENs now and then feel the longing for a happiness without external props: for simply lying on the beach and enjoying the sun. They ought to try that, instead of dragging with them the usual pair of books, Walkman, notepad, and maybe even their laptop computer, in order to leave all possibilities open.

SEVENs have to learn to overcome an exaggerated fear of physical and psychological pain. Forms of meditation in which they confront their darker side can be a great help here. A time of sickness or of freely chosen limitation can become the gateway to that deep joy, for which SEVENs long. I have met several healthy SEVENs who intentionally work in hospitals or with the dying. Now their joy is in helping others avoid the pain, while still confronting it themselves.

Someone who loves SEVENs must help them to eat, chew, swallow, and digest their pain. SEVENs have to perceive their dark side, slow down their lives, stop the continual chatter, and accept the part of life that is hard and not beautiful.

William James speaks of "once-born" and "twice-born" believers: Twice-born believers go on trusting and believing, even though they have experienced pain and disappointment in their lives. Once-born believers maintain a childlike optimism, but have not lived through much pain. Perhaps the life task of a good many unredeemed SEVENs may consist in coming into the world a second time and growing up.

The **saint** of SEVENs is Francis of Assisi (1182–1226). At the beginning of his life he was the pleasure-seeking party king. But he increasingly sensed that he was in flight from himself; he withdrew more and more, and fell sick.

The meeting with the leper became the turning point in his life. In his *Testament* he tells us: "When I was full of sins, it seemed to me repulsive and bitter to see lepers." SEVENs have a natural aversion to anything that stinks, or is dirty or ugly. "But the Lord led me among them, and I dealt mercifully with them. When I went away from them, what had earlier seemed to me repulsive and bitter was transformed into sweetness for body and soul."

Here we see how Francis overcame his revulsion from his painful and dark side: He had to accept the ugly; he had to embrace pain. This is the opposite of what Francis was by nature: a rich wag, a dilettante, and a troubadour. Voluntarily he moved in the opposite direction. This led to his "extravagant" poverty. Less is more! He wanted to be the poorest, while everybody else wanted to be rich. Nevertheless he remained a merry saint and beggar. He had the same eye as ever for what was beautiful. One need only see the places in Italy where he prayed. Francis, like Mozart, needed a beautiful environment to confront his inner fears and wounds.

Many legends bear witness that the search for "perfect joy" remained the theme of his life till the end. He could rejoice in the flowers and birds, he could use a stick as a violin and dance to the imaginary melody. At the end of a life rich in privations, he could even greet death as a sister and friend. Shortly before his death he received the stigmata: the marks of the wounds of Christ appeared on his body and stamped him as a man who, along with Paul, could confess: "[We are] always carrying in the body the death of Jesus, so that the life of Jesus may also be manifested in our bodies" (2 Cor. 4:10). Francis found his authentic joy through sharing the pain of humanity, not by avoiding it.

TYPE EIGHT
The Need to Be Against

Overview

EIGHTs impress us as strong and mighty; they are capable of imparting a feeling of strength to others as well. They have a second sense for justice and truth. They instinctively know where something "stinks," whenever injustice or dishonesty is at work. EIGHTs address such situations openly and directly. They can be a rock of reliableness for others and develop a tremendous sense of responsibility and solicitude. When they commit themselves to a cause, they can bring enormous energies to bear on it. The word of an EIGHT can be trusted.

   With EIGHTs we return to the domain of the gut, which embraces EIGHTs, NINEs, and ONEs. Just as we ONEs want to be good boys and good girls, EIGHTs want to be bad boys and bad girls. Early on they got the impression that the world punishes soft tendencies, and so they put their money on hardness. As children many EIGHTs had the experience of being repressed or pushed around. They could trust no one but themselves. Children of the Holocaust and children from the slums, where you can't afford to show weakness or cry, become EIGHTs. In their cliques and gangs they have to undergo tests of courage, to prove how brave, daring, and fearless they are. Some EIGHTs also report that their parents rewarded strength: "Don't take it! Hit back! Show the other guy who's boss!" EIGHTs have developed the feeling that the strong rule the world and the weak have drawn the short straw. For this reason they have decided not to be good, not to conform, but to develop strength, to resist, to break the rules, and to order others around rather than to let themselves be ordered. Some EIGHTs have developed their attitude as a counter-reaction to parents who were too liberal and indulgent. They want to test and see just how far they have to go to get called on the carpet.

Outsiders often confuse them with ONEs because both seem to be governed by aggressions. One of the differences between the two is that EIGHTs do not apologize or take anything back. They have a hard time admitting mistakes, because that could look like weakness. ONEs pull back their punches; EIGHTs don't.

My nephew and godson is just four years old, but he can already be clearly identified as an EIGHT. My brother says: "Not once have I managed to get him to say he was sorry for anything." EIGHTs don't find it easy to ask for forgiveness: "I can punish him or even give him a spanking; it just makes him all the more hardened. Once I punished him by sending him to his room for about two hours, where he had to stay in the corner. He just stood there." Apart from my brother's dubious pedagogical methods, the example shows the inflexibility of EIGHTs: "I'll show you all. You won't get me to come down a peg." EIGHTs get energy from showing their power.

On the other hand, though the world outside may not notice, EIGHTs can deal very harshly with themselves and punish themselves severely.

EIGHTs are also frequently confused with contraphobic SIXes. Seen from the outside these types are difficult to distinguish. The aggressions of SIXes come from their head and are an expression of their anxiety and self-protectiveness. The aggression of EIGHTs comes from the gut and is directed against everything that the EIGHTs perceive as hypocrisy and injustice.

The basic experience of EIGHTs is that life is threatening or hostile, and that you simply can't trust others until there is evidence to the contrary. EIGHTs seek conflict or come right out and create it. They take the gloves off when they fight, and they're notorious fighters: if you say yes, they say no. They enjoy being against. Even if they don't always express it immediately, resistance and negation is often their first reaction to new ideas, people, and situations.

Fortunately they like to take the side of the weak. EIGHTs will not put up with false authorities and hierarchies. Their passion for justice and truth often leads them to side with the oppressed and defenseless. This is because they unconsciously know that within their own innermost self — behind a façade of hardness, invulnerability, curses, or even brutality — there is a little boy or a little girl. This inner child is the exact opposite of the strength and power they outwardly project. The feelings of tenderness and vulnerability are, to be sure, buried deep in the EIGHT. Most EIGHTs show this side to at most two or three people in their lives. With luck one of them will be their spouse, but even that isn't guaranteed. EIGHTs are insecure about this little child in themselves, but sometimes they discover that child in others and wish to protect it. This understanding is the key to understanding and disarming an EIGHT.

The self-image of EIGHTs says: "I've got power. I'm stronger than you." Male EIGHTs are often "beefy" or at least have an athletic build. Many EIGHTs are partial to expressions of strength, by which they can demonstrate power. You can find this energy in the culture of the black ghettoes in American metropolises. Even the adjective "bad" means "good" among young blacks. Similar attitudes can be observed in liberation movements and the feminist movement. People who have been pushed around and oppressed often develop EIGHT energy. Liberation theology in Latin America is largely an EIGHT theology. EIGHT energy is always taking up the cause of the little people and the poor. For the sake of justice EIGHTs are willing to fight the powers that be with every available weapon.

When EIGHTs are in power themselves, however, their subordinates often feel oppressed or pushed around, while the EIGHTs as a rule don't even notice that their behavior frightens others. They usually express their anger immediately and directly and then get on to the order of the day. The victims of their anger, by contrast, generally don't get over it quite so quickly.

EIGHTs fight as a way of making contact. We call it "confrontational intimacy." They often don't understand how this kind of contact frightens others. Because they enjoy struggles, conflict, and confrontation, they think it's the same for others. They don't notice that their blows go below the belt and are often hard to endure. Their delight in attacking, which they perceive as "playful," often strikes others as aggressive behavior, but it is actually a form of establishing contact.

When EIGHTs attack others, they often do it to shake the artificial façade of their "opposite number." They hate unclear messages and want to see what's really "there," to see where they stand. They also have to know who's a friend and who's an enemy, whom they have to fight and whom they're safe with. They have great respect for an equal enemy. Don

Camillo and Peppone, the heroes of Giovannino Guareschi's novels, are two EIGHTs. They fight for opposite value systems — both brutally and with crude means, but both with great respect for their opponent.

EIGHTs are often outstanding at playing cards and at competitive sports, because they immediately sense the weaknesses of others and take advantage of them without remorse.

Their ability instantly to unmask dishonest behavior and false strength has made some EIGHTs influential therapists and spiritual guides. They upset the false self-image of others and in this way enable what is genuine to come to light.

The notorious Russian G. I. Gurdjieff, who used parts of the Enneagram in his school, was an EIGHT. Two of his favorite methods were called "stepping on others' corns" and "offering a toast to the idiot." He zeroed in on the most sensitive points in the characters of his disciples and hacked away at them until defensive reactions appeared and gradually the disguises and masks of the "false self" could be stripped away. The word "idiot" was used in Gurdjieff's circle in the original sense and referred to a novice. At the welcoming dinner a great deal of brandy or vodka would be drunk. Alcohol had the job of breaking down the defense mechanisms more quickly. This is the sort of toast Gurdjieff used in addressing newcomers and the traits he saw in them: " 'You are a turkey cock,' he said to someone on the first evening. 'A turkey cock pretending to be a real peacock.' A few masterly movements of G's head, a guttural sound or two, and there appeared at the table an arrogant gobbler parading itself before a hen."[1]

The great Gestalt therapist Fritz Perls demanded that his clients perceive and express what was here and now, instead of escaping into the past or the future. "Here-and-Now became the smallest possible point in space and time for experiencing an inner/outer vision." This "point of intersection between past and future is the only moment in life in which I can act." Perls noted immediately when the statements of his clients didn't match their gestures or body language, and he strengthened such discrepancies to make them conscious. He called the conflicting inner voices "topdog" (the authoritarian voice) and "underdog" (the subordinate voice). As a therapist he liked to take on the role of the "opposition." He encouraged others to experience their feelings completely. With almost "mathematical precision" he succeeded in pressing forward to his patients' vital "unfinished business." In this way he led them to the bottleneck, "which had blocked the way to an essential source of life's possibilities."[2]

Chuck Dederich, likewise an EIGHT, the founder of Synanon, a group therapy for drug addicts, developed methods related to those of Gurdjieff and Perls. During the sessions at Synanon the group confronted one of the members with that person's behavior. A significant or insignificant occasion from "real life" was drawn upon. Perhaps the person in question was ten minutes late to the group session. "The one making the indictment delivers it in a scathing, righteous manner with outrageously exaggerated details. Immediately, others join in with similar incidents they have observed and everyone begins to weave a net around the indicted person to establish his thoroughly irresponsible attitudes, habits and character. Whenever he attempts to justify or defend himself, the group attacks his style of defense itself."[3] This method of dramatically playing up little incidents can be very comic; but it can also get very serious and demands a strong support group in which there is mutual trust. "In the game people work through their disagreements, express their negative feelings, carry out their quarrels and dominance struggles, let off steam and begin to explore and express new, more powerful parts of themselves."[4]

More than any other type, well-developed EIGHTs have the gift of leading other people to their real potential.

Among the EIGHTs we find great leaders and revolutionaries: Martin Luther King, Fidel Castro, Che Guevara, Jesse Jackson, and Saul Alinsky (the great American protest organizer) were and are people who charismatically inspire and motivate others to commitment. EIGHTs arouse in others the readiness to trust their leadership and to follow them everywhere. People sense in them that they will finish what they start.

While ONEs reform the system from within, EIGHTs tend to climb out of the system and throw stones at it. That too frightens people. In particular people who have a hard time admitting their own aggressiveness will be easily intimidated by an EIGHT. The aggressiveness of EIGHTs mobilizes the aggressions of the other side. For this reason it's easy to fear and hate EIGHTs.

EIGHTs sometimes seem positively to enjoy experiencing hatred and rejection. That really heats them up. They are not ashamed of playing the bull in the china shop. When I, good little boy that I am, said "shit" on my first published cassette, I immediately had guilt feelings. Good boys don't say "shit." As soon as she heard the tape, my mother phoned me to say that I shouldn't use such words. When EIGHTs say "shit," they really say it. They have fun shocking others. They enjoy making their audience twist in their seats. EIGHTs are no diplomats.

EIGHTs **avoid** helplessness, weakness, and subordination. That is why, for example, EIGHTs are inclined to view their own opinion as absolutely correct, and to be completely closed off to other arguments. They have a tendency to be overbearing and arrogant, not wanting just to stand there "weakly." They often treat their co-workers as doormats. Under certain circumstances EIGHTs go so far as to put down their opponents as vicious or retarded. Because EIGHTs know their own strengths and immediately see the weaknesses of others, they elevate themselves above other people and often construct false, unfounded hierarchies. They fit people into a friend/foe schema that seems quite inappropriate to others.

Woe betide anyone whom an EIGHT finds too self-confident. In the seminary we had a director who shot down everyone who seemed sure of himself or defended his own divergent opinion. But if you were having a really hard time, if you had failed or made a bad mistake, this same teacher was simply tremendous. That's a typical EIGHT: When you're really poor, helpless, and weak, the EIGHTs' protective instinct is aroused, and they will do anything to assist you. But as soon as you express in any way that you have power, then EIGHTs will prove that they have more power. You can never win a dispute with EIGHTs. When you bring out your big guns, they bring out still bigger ones. They can always shout louder than you.

The actual energy of EIGHTs is not anger or rage, although sometimes it can seem that way. Rather it is a passion and a total commitment to truth, life, and justice. It is a passion for the cause they believe in, or the people for whom they feel responsible.

The greatest mistake you can make with EIGHTs is to let yourself be intimidated by them and to give ground when they exert pressure in a more or less noisy fashion. Some EIGHTs begin to curse and pound on the table. You should either get fully into the fight or try to talk to the little boy or the little girl in the EIGHT. They're used to others' pulling in their horns. EIGHTs protect the weak, but they despise cowardice and softness. In such cases they can hit hard in every respect. That's their dark side. As soon as they think their interlocutors are stupid or incompetent, they finish them off, even if they are already lying on the ground. They also enjoy vulgarity and scatological humor. It's verbal power.

Many EIGHTs like hard contact sports like rugby or football. Sometimes they like to put fast cars through their paces. I heard of a football player whose kneecap was half shredded. But he kept on running and seemed almost to celebrate the pain. He could shed blood for the holy cause of football. EIGHTs can enjoy pain; they endure it better than anyone else. They stand against it heroically.

EIGHTs seldom show fear. They are generally daring and enjoy taking risks. They like to accept dangerous challenges. EIGHTs often live on the edge of catastrophe. That excites them; they're in their element.

EIGHTs are fascinating. You have to react to them, whether you want to or not. One doesn't quickly forget an encounter with an EIGHT, male or female. They are often described as "larger than life."

Dilemma

The struggle for justice is not only the strength, but also the **temptation**, of EIGHTs. This can lead to EIGHTs' appointing themselves as avengers and retaliators, because their concept of justice is "balancing out." EIGHTs start out from the assumption that the "bad" person has to be punished, even if it happens to be themselves. As soon as EIGHTs are thrown back on themselves, the danger exists that the aggressions that they otherwise turn outward will be aimed at themselves. EIGHTs always look for a guilty person to punish. Revenge and retaliation (the **pitfall** of EIGHTs) are for them ways of getting the scales of justice back in line again. Because with them it's often all or nothing, and because the world is divided into friend and foe, it can happen that EIGHTs discover their greatest enemy in themselves and can no longer trust themselves when they are confronted with their guilt. In general, however, EIGHTs feel little guilt.

The worldwide phenomenon of terrorism comes out of the energy of "retaliating justice." Self-appointed "peoples' courts" pass death sentences on representatives of "unjust regimes" or "capitalism." There is no greater torture for an EIGHT than to be isolated and thus cut off from all possibilities of external action. When put in prison, some German Red Army terrorists have taken their lives; others are prepared to do so.

The **defense mechanism** of EIGHTs is denial. Under certain circumstances EIGHTs can deny anything that doesn't fit into their concept of truth and justice. Above all they can deny and repress their own weaknesses and the limits of their power.

The **root sin** of EIGHTs is shamelessness. That is how we characterize what used to be called lust in the classic catalogue of the capital sins. EIGHTs are "red-blooded types." Once again we see what a tremendous psychology of sin the Enneagram contains. It helps us to understand better what is actually meant by lust, namely, the violation of another person for pleasure or for passion. The other is shamelessly used, taken possession of, or suppressed. Lust means that I exploit another person and do not respect his or her dignity. As Tennessee Williams once said, "All cruel people describe themselves as paragons of 'frankness.'" This sin can be manifested by EIGHTs in all areas of life. An unredeemed EIGHT has no respect for the vulnerability or dignity of another person.

Unredeemed EIGHTs can make very high moral demands on others without holding themselves to them. They sometimes swing back and forth between rigid moralism and generous *laissez-faire*. Like SEVENs they are inclined to excessive instinctual satisfaction. With EIGHTs, however, this seldom takes on particularly "cultivated" forms. EIGHTs can enjoy food, alcohol, and sex without guilt feelings; EIGHTs have guilt feelings above all when they have the impression of having been unjust and untruthful. At parties EIGHTs belong with the guests who "stick it out" and are the last to go to bed. SEVENs enjoy in order to avoid pain. EIGHTs celebrate because that is part of the well-rounded, full life. They have a positive "lust for life."

EIGHTs can enjoy power and have the need to stake their claim to it and expand it where possible. They want to be in the know, to be informed; and they get furious when they are deceived or outfoxed. If you have an EIGHT for a superior, it's better to admit a mistake at once, even if there will be a gigantic blow-out. If EIGHTs later find out that something was hidden, they can react in a way that really wounds you. Their need to check up extends to everything. They think that if you let apparently trivial items ride, that could be the first step toward everything getting out of control. For this reason EIGHTs can be fantastically fussy and insist on everything being right, down to the last detail.

EIGHTs need control over their own possessions and other people. They want to draw the lines without being dependent. This is why there are problems when they fall in love. In a partnership a minimum of adaptation is necessary: compromises must be found; personal interests have to be sacrificed. Partners who subordinate themselves to an EIGHT have found only a seeming solution; in reality they will not make the EIGHT happy. For the only people EIGHTs respect are the ones who put up resistance and stand their own ground. Besides, in a love relationship there is conflict between tender impulses and acquired hardness. Then too EIGHTs need a lot of space for themselves alone. Many EIGHTs like to hunt, fish, or mountain climb. They are the Marlboro men, who apparently need no one except themselves and nature. John Wayne is a classic EIGHT. For a love relationship this can mean, "I want to go to bed with you, but I don't want to be continually with you." That can lead to ongoing conflicts, especially when EIGHT men get together with a very attached woman.

The other side of the coin is — as always — the gift of the redeemed EIGHT: EIGHTs are passionate lovers of life. *Passio* is the Latin word that best captures the essence of EIGHT. It resonates with both the power of life and the readiness to suffer.

The **fruit of the spirit** of EIGHTs is innocence. It characterizes the little child in the EIGHT, which is unprotected and can trust. EIGHTs must learn not only to see this vulnerable and distressed child outside of themselves and to look after it there, but also to be good to the defenseless child in their own soul. This is one task for EIGHTs that is bound up with many anxieties, because it means seeing their own weakness. The prerequisite for it is sincerity. EIGHTs, who demand honesty from the people around them and who immediately unmask dishonest behavior, must learn to demand this of themselves.

For the most part EIGHTs don't like to look inside themselves to discover their tender sides. They see tenderness in others: in a little child, in an animal, in a soft, gentle girl. We can study this trait in the EIGHT caricature, the German cartoon character Obelix: "hard shell, soft core." His dog, Idefix, or a soft, tender maiden can drive the big wild man out of his head, the same man who otherwise flattens wild boars with his bare hands and slaughters whole legions of Roman soldiers.

In many of his novels Nikos Kazantzakis (1883–1957) created EIGHT types, in whom chauvinistic "manliness" is combined with *joie de vivre* and love of humanity (*The Greek Passion, Zorba the Greek*). The struggle to overcome and "spiritualize" animal passions dominates his novels *Francis of Assisi* and *The Last Temptation of Christ*.

Ernest Hemingway (1899–1961) gave the clearest literary shape to the energy of EIGHTs. His men and women are strong, self-involved, combative, adventurous, and brutal.

He himself tried all his life to present to the world an image of the "tough guy." Even as a little boy he built up a store of obscene curses that he later added to. From earliest childhood he despised tears and pain. As an ambulance driver for the Italian Red Cross in the First World War he was badly wounded: 237 pieces of shrapnel were lodged in his leg — at least according to the legend he retailed everywhere. He deadened the pain, he said, with brandy and pulled out the splinters from his flesh at night.

His enthusiasm for Spain (the land of EIGHTs) and for bull-fighting (the bull is the symbolic animal of EIGHT) never left him; Spain provides the background for many of his short stories and novels.[5] For years he wanted to be a bullfighter himself. One time he supposedly tested his courage by jumping on the back of a bull, throwing him down, and blowing cigar smoke into his eyes. Afterward, however, he was nearly gored by this bull.[6]

His passions were boxing, parties, hunting and fishing — above all catching spearfish, which can weigh upward of eight hundred pounds and are attacked by sharks; he worked up this obsession in his novel *The Old Man and the Sea*.

As captain on a yacht that he designed himself, he demanded absolute obedience from everyone who traveled with him. His outbursts of rage were feared. Above all, when his writing or his masculinity were attacked, he plotted revenge. His friend, the photographer Robert Capa, once said: "Papa [Hemingway] can be angrier than God on a bad day, when the whole human race misbehaves."[7]

On the other hand, he could be very generous when people got into trouble through no fault of their own: "To be a civilized man you need two qualities: compassion and the ability to block punches."[8]

Hemingway was married four times. He also had, according to his own account, a series of other intimate relationships with women. Toward the end of his life he fell victim to a kind of mental derangement: he was afflicted by unexplainable anxious states and could no longer write. After several failed suicide attempts, in June 1961 he succeeded in shooting himself with a hunting rifle. By this death he "snatched victory from the jaws of defeat [one more time] . . . wrote out the course of events in advance, and made the last decision his own," as Walter H. Nelson says.[9]

At any rate that's how the myth goes. In his biography, Kenneth S. Lynn attempts to disenchant the myth.[10] He proves, for example, that Hemingway himself increasingly inflated after the fact his "heroic deeds" from the First World War. Lynn describes the author as pathologically macho, a mamma's boy, who from babyhood had been so confused in his sex role that all his life he had to build up a masculine superego. As a boy he was for a long time dressed in girls' clothes, like his older sister, whom he hated all his life. His father, who was subordinate to his dominant mother, committed suicide. The biographer speculates that all his life Hemingway feared that he wasn't all man. Strong men couldn't remain alongside him. Often he challenged "rivals" to box with him, and he could hit brutally in such matches.

According to Margaret Frings Keyes, EIGHTs are ruled by inner voices that say: "Don't be you." "Don't feel what you feel."[11] If Lynn's analysis is correct, Hemingway is an example of what destructive consequences the denial of sexual identity in early childhood can have.

Symbols and Examples

The symbolic **animals** of EIGHTs are the rhinoceros, the rattlesnake, the tiger, and the bull. All these animals are aggressive and symbolize power, phallic energy, and vitality. In bullfights the Spanish *macho*, as it were, confronts his image; it is a life-and-death duel. Blood must flow; only one will survive. The image of the bullfight, which Hemingway frequently used, contains one of the great life themes of EIGHTs.

The classic **country** of EIGHT is Spain. Insight into the energy of EIGHTs helps us to understand the disastrous *machismo* of Spanish-speaking countries. True, the women of these countries know that all this is only superficial, and that behind the hard shell of their men there is a little boy. The mask of strength conceals insecurity and feelings of inferiority. But even when one sees through this mechanism, it can have extremely destructive effects: The children are afraid of the father whom they can't come close to. The wife is oppressed, degraded, beaten. The macho man has to be boss.[12]

In Spanish popular piety we find a striking bloodthirstiness, above all in representations of the crucifixion. EIGHTs want to see blood.

In societies and countries that are oppressed ("Don't be yourself") EIGHT energy can likewise become increasingly concentrated until it finally erupts in revolution.

The **colors** of EIGHT are black and white. EIGHTs want clarity. They reject intermediate tones and compromises, because they look weak. With them it's always either/or: friend or foe, good or bad, strong or weak. Black stands for absolute nothingness, for death, the end, the abyss. But it's also assigned to eros and primal chaos. White is the blinding absolute light that Moses saw in the burning bush. At the same time it symbolizes the totality of creative powers. In the Bible it is the color of innocence, of the blessed, and the angels (e.g., Matt. 17:2; 28:3). EIGHTs are people of polar oppositions: "Whoever isn't for me is against me." The number EIGHT itself consists of two poles or circles that touch at only one point. It stands traditionally for the union of opposites.

In the **Bible** EIGHTs can be found among a series of female figures in the Hebrew Scriptures, as well as among the "Judges" (Samson) and Kings (Saul and David).

The literary development of the Bible offers "rich evidence about how the historical role of women was superimposed, whitewashed, and falsified."[13] Nevertheless we do find in the Bible traces of a time in which women had the power to leave their mark on history, especially in the songs by women that are hidden in the stories of the Hebrew Bible. Thus we find traces of Miriam, a woman who had equal status as a leader with Moses and Aaron in the exodus from Egypt. After the march through the Red Sea she sings the song of liberation that is considered the oldest piece of tradition in the story of the Exodus: "Sing to the Lord, for he has triumphed gloriously; the horse and his rider he has thrown into the sea" (Exod. 15:21).

In the amphictyonic period of Israel there were charismatically gifted and divinely chosen leaders who led the troops against the enemy. Among these Judges was Deborah, about whom it is said: "The peasantry ceased in Israel, they ceased until you arose, Deborah, arose as a mother in Israel" (Judg. 5:7).

When the childless Hannah finally does bring a son, Samuel, into the world, she sings a song of liberation: "The bows of the mighty are broken, but the feeble gird on strength" (1 Sam. 2:4). We hear similar notes in Mary's Magnificat (Luke 1:46–55).

The language of biblical women becomes powerful and political when the future of their children is at stake. To protect the weak, they become combat-ready and strong.

The legendary Judge[14] Samson is presented in the Bible as a prototype of the fabulously strong hero. He doesn't fit into the scheme of pious men of God. One has to wonder about "the whirlwind of very unspiritual adventures in which Samson gets lost. In particular, Samson showed great interest in women."[15]

From his boyhood, as a sign of being consecrated to God, Samson doesn't cut his hair. As a young man he tears a lion to pieces with his bare hands. On the occasion of his marriage with a woman from the (hostile) nation of the Philistines, he kills thirty Philistines who he feels deceived him. When the Philistines bind him with bowstrings, he snaps them "as a string of tow snaps when it touches the fire." Shortly afterward he slaughters a thousand Philistines with the jawbone of an ass. When he spends the night with a harlot in the Philistine city of Gaza, the inhabitants of the city surround the house and lie in ambush for him at the city gates. But he lifts the entire city gate off its hinges and carries it up to the top of a hill.

Finally he falls in love with Delilah, who is bribed by the princes of the Philistines to ferret out the source of his strength. At first he misleads her and keeps escaping the attempts by the Philistines to checkmate him. But finally he reveals to Delilah that he will lose his power the moment that his hair is cut (this shows his little boy). As he sleeps the Philistines cut his hair off, and the "power of Yahweh" leaves him. His enemies gouge his eyes out, bind him with chains, and throw him into prison, where his hair begins to grow back. During a feast of the Philistine god Dagon they lead Samson into a great hall, where he is to appear to amuse the people. Once again he prays for divine power, clasps the supporting middle columns of the house and buries himself, together with three thousand Philistines, beneath the rubble. In this way the power struggle between Yahweh, the God of Israel, and Dagon, the god of the Philistines, is decided in favor of Yahweh (Judg. 13–16).

King Saul similarly comes to power through a divine call: Samuel the "seer" secretly anoints him as the savior of his people against the

Deborah's Song of Victory (Gustav Doré)
"The peasantry ceased in Israel until you arose, Deborah"

enemies of Israel. When the Ammonites appropriate Israelite land, the divine power latent in Saul bursts out. Saul is coming with his cattle from the fields when he hears of the inroads made by the enemy: "And the spirit of God came mightily upon Saul when he heard these words, and his anger was greatly kindled. He took a yoke of oxen, and cut them in pieces and sent them throughout all the territory of Israel by the hands of messengers, saying, 'Whoever does not come out after Saul and Samuel, so it shall be done to his oxen!'" (1 Sam. 11:6–7).

After the victory the people set up Saul as their first king. He succeeds in averting the danger from the Philistines. But he soon falls prey to melancholy, combined with fits of madness. The young shepherd boy David comes to the court to cheer the king's mood by playing his harp. David makes friends with Saul's son Jonathan and marries the king's daughter Michal. But with the instinct of the power-person Saul senses a rival in David. He tries to pin the young musician to the wall with a spear thrust. David manages to flee, gathers a group of dubious characters around him, and sets out as a guerrilla leader, serving the Philistines as a vassal. At the decisive battle on Mt. Gilboa, however, where the Philistines slay Saul and Jonathan, he is not on hand.

Now David succeeds, with Machiavellian skill and sophisticated use of political marriages, in disposing of another son of Saul's and gradually obtaining dominion over all of Israel. During his rule (1000–965 B.C.) he subjects all the neighboring peoples, including the Philistines, and makes Israel a real kingdom. He has the ark of the covenant, with the tablets of the Law, brought to Jerusalem, thereby making his capital the religious center of the kingdom. David wants to end the previous elective monarchy, in which Yahweh himself called the leaders of the people and thereby remained the "actual" king of Israel, and replace it with a dynasty.

But Amnon, his oldest son, gets caught up in an incestuous relationship with his half-sister Tamar. Absalom, the second son, has his brother murdered and enters into open revolt against his father. Absalom is captured by David's followers and killed. Finally Solomon comes to power, his son born from the questionable union of David with the beautiful Bathsheba.

The love story of David and Bathsheba sheds a peculiarly clear light on David's character. EIGHTs like David "do not necessarily allow their feelings for justice to stand in the way of their self-interest."[16] David sends Uriah, Bathsheba's husband, to the front line in battle, where he has to die. Then he takes the beautiful woman into his harem. One day the prophet Nathan comes to him and tells a story:

There were two men in a certain city, the one rich and the other poor. The rich man had very many flocks and herds, but the poor man had nothing but one little ewe lamb, which he had bought. And he brought it up, and it grew up with him and with his children; it used to eat of his morsel, and drink from his cup, and lie in his bosom, and it was like a daughter to him. Now there came a traveler to the rich man, and he was unwilling to take one of his flock or herd to prepare for the wayfarer who had come to him, but he took the poor man's lamb, and prepared it for the man who had come to him.

When David hears this story, he flies into a rage and says to Nathan: "As the Lord lives, the man who has done this deserves to die; and he shall restore the lamb fourfold." Nathan answers, "You are the man" (2 Sam. 12:1b–7a).

This is a typical EIGHT reaction. EIGHTs tend to become aggressive toward others who display a negative trait resembling the one that the EIGHT unconsciously denies. In our story the prophet Nathan represents David's true conscience and "cut[s] through these layers of deceptions and excuses in a single stroke."[17] (The story of Saul and David may be found in 1 Sam. 9–2 Sam. 24.)

Conversion and Redemption

The **invitation** to EIGHTs is mercy. Unredeemed EIGHTs are merciless toward themselves and others. Only the encounter with truth can liberate them. The truth frees them to see and accept their own weakness. From this experience they can learn to endure and accept the weakness of other people.

Because EIGHTs are afraid of their "soft core," they are seldom ready to do therapy, to work on their inner life, or to meditate regularly, in short, to set out on the "journey inward." Further difficulties arise because EIGHTs are afraid of being checked up on and manipulated by a therapist or teacher. But there are also contrary experiences. A well-known woman therapist who is an EIGHT writes: "I couldn't begin soon enough to work on myself. My EIGHT-ness saw me and struck out at me. This work on myself is uncompromising and is bearing splendid fruit. I keep getting the feedback that I am now unsparing in my unconditioned acceptance of people...."

Among the **life tasks** of EIGHTs is to confront the question of power. Power is not in itself bad: it can become a blessing or a curse. EIGHTs have to watch that they don't degrade, humiliate, or intimidate other people with their power. They have to learn to respect other standpoints, not to narcotize their feelings with alcohol and wild celebrations, to look for compromises, and to obey the same rules that they expect others to follow. Redeemed EIGHTs can protect others with their power and vitality, instead of dominating them.

Without EIGHTs this world might look still worse than it does. Thank God there are people who break through and tear down the lying façades of institutions and societies. We need them. But they have to be helped to trust their soft side. EIGHTs too have to concede when they are wrong and ask for forgiveness. Then they will notice that to do so is no weakness but real strength.

Female EIGHTs have it especially hard. Our society does "allow" men to be macho. But when a woman makes a self-confident appearance, then she's labeled a "libber" or "masculine." Women EIGHTs sometimes have problems with accepting their femaleness or anything "maternal," and with allowing themselves "soft" images (for example, the child nursing at the breast). Just as FOURs are often identified with so-called feminine energy, EIGHTs are often identified with so called masculine energy.

Male EIGHTs need access to their own female side, instead of "delegating" warmth and tenderness to women.

Martin Luther King, Jr. (1929–1968) is our **saint** and example of a redeemed EIGHT. He learned from Gandhi to trust the power of non-violence, the power of powerlessness: "Non-violence is power, but it is the right and good use of power!"[18]

In 1955–56 the Baptist minister in Montgomery, Alabama, organized a bus boycott that finally led to the lifting of segregation. After that he was arrested and convicted for actions of civil disobedience more than thirty times. After one sentencing he said: "I know that I was a convicted criminal, but I was proud of my crime. . . . My crime was trying to inspire my people with a feeling of dignity and self-respect."[19] Countless attempts on his life did not deflect him from his path. The FBI called upon him in a letter to take his own life: "You're ready, and you know it! You have a way out, and you know it!"[20]

When he became a decided opponent of the Vietnam War, many of his liberal white friends abandoned him. He was suspected as a communist — like Dorothy Day, Oscar Romero, and many other Christians who understood the Gospel as political. In 1968 King was assassinated in Memphis, Tennessee.[21]

This fearless warrior for justice had a sensitive, soft side and was plagued all his life by self-doubts. As a young man he had twice tried to commit suicide. He could not handle his sexuality; "other women" weighed down on his marriage. It is comforting to know that "saints" and biblical figures too had a shadow side that they couldn't cope with and — like all of us — are imperfect, but "on the way."

TYPE NINE:
The Need to Avoid

Overview

NINEs are peacemakers. Their gift of accepting others without prejudice makes people feel understood and accepted. NINEs can be unbiased arbitrators, because they can see and appreciate the positive aspects of both sides. Their sense of fairness may make them committed fighters for peace and justice. They express harsh truths calmly and so matter-of-factly that it's easy for others to "swallow" these truths. In the presence of a NINE many people find it easy to come to rest themselves.

It's no accident that the NINEs are situated at the vertex of the Enneagram, because in a certain way NINE describes the original and unspoiled human essence. We would probably all be NINEs, if we hadn't grown up in a technologically "civilized" world. I reached this conclusion when I was in Africa, the Philippines, and other parts of the Third World. When you get to the villages there and meet the so-called natives, the original human race as it has populated our planet since the beginning of time, anyone who knows the Enneagram is immediately struck by the thought that most of these people are NINEs.

One can review what happened with the Africans who by nature were NINEs and then were dragged as slaves to America's THREE society. I can readily understand why in our Western performance-oriented society they stand as "failures." Our game is not their game. Our rushed existence, our rat race, and our careerism don't correspond to what they understand by life.

The fictional speeches by the South Sea chieftain Tuiavii from Tiavea, which were published in the popular little book *The Papalagi* (1920), describe Western industrial society from the standpoint of a South Sea Islander. The "papalagi" is the white man whose life and activity the "primitive" doesn't understand. Thus the way Western people deal with time is extremely strange to him: "Assume the white man . . . would like to go out into the sun or travel in a canoe on the river or love his girl, he mostly spoils his pleasure by fastening onto the thought: There is no time for me to be merry. . . . He names a thousand things that take his time, he squats grumbling and complaining about a job . . . that he has no joy in. . . . But then if he suddenly sees that he does have time, that it's there after all, or give him another time, again he gets no pleasure from it, he's tired from work without joy. . . . There are papalagi who claim they have never had time. . . . That's why most of them run through life like a thrown stone. . . . "[1]

The so-called civilized nations have declared this original attitude toward life a sin, which they call laziness or indolence. But in the case of this lack of drive we are dealing rather with a kind of internal vagueness. NINEs have a hard time understanding their own nature. First they have to find out what they actually want and become conscious of who they are. The consequence is that they are, so to speak, "everywhere and nowhere." They are generalists, can do a little bit of everything, but are never masters. They master something of everything, but nothing totally. They lack focus and determination. A young German theologian, who is a NINE, reports:

> I am an all-arounder. I can ski a little, surf a bit, motorcycle somewhat, play a few guitar chords, sing tolerably, dance quite well, preach to some extent, listen very well, handle children a little, understand English to a degree, my French will do, even a few phrases in Italian from vacation; swimming's good enough for a backyard pool, diving, mountain hiking, imitating dialects, performing skits (if I force myself); I'm also good in theology, but I got "only" a B on the exam. In grammar school I once had a re-

port card in which there were "only" B's — that may have looked peculiar. Somewhat handy, know a bit about computers, motors, wood-working — all for domestic consumption. Oh, yes, I forgot fishing and water sports.

Sometimes NINEs simply lack courage, or they don't consider themselves important enough to display their talents in front of other people. So they can fade themselves in and out of everything without being much noticed. If somebody else broaches a subject, they take it up, though not necessarily with great passion. If their partner changes the subject, they address that. NINEs like to swim with the current.

Many NINEs report that in their childhood they were overlooked or "swamped." They were ignored or rejected if they expressed their own opinion. The interests of their parents or their siblings seemed to take precedence over theirs. They learned that not even their outbursts of rage were registered. For this reason they decided to keep their anger to themselves. Other NINEs found themselves as children in such a difficult and apparently insoluble situation that they had to try to maneuver between the fronts and to "understand" both sides, in order not to be caught between two grindstones. In this way they developed a fine flair for the needs and interests of everyone else and could sense these better than their own needs. On this point NINEs resemble TWOs. Other NINEs have experienced a dull harmony without great highs, lows, and challenges; or were so spoiled that early on they became very comfortable. In school they seldom developed great energies. The young theologian just quoted tells us:

In the first class we had contests in mental arithmetic. The first one to get the solution was allowed to call out the answer. I was slower; I remained in the bottom third. For this reason I considered myself a bad arithmetician, and my career in math was over. I remember horrible math classes in high school. I just barely got by. I refused to strain myself. Instead I used my energy so I wouldn't have to learn anything and I could pay just enough attention. It was like that in other subjects too. From the outside it looked as if I had slept through school time, but today it seems to me that it must have taken enormous amounts of energy to avoid real work.

NINEs are lovable; one simply has to like them. Sometimes, however, they seem so charming and elastically soft that they are scarcely graspable as persons. Most of them will not change the world, because they prefer the path of least resistance and are afraid of decisions that might pin them down. They like to put off important responsibilities and avoid everything that is too hard and takes too much energy. They often consider themselves simple and uncomplicated and present themselves accordingly. This makes dealing with NINEs easy. NINEs are honest; they have no hidden motives. They say what they feel, even if they have to sweat before discovering it in themselves. But then what they say is really what they mean. Some NINEs report that they sometimes actually feel an inner compulsion to answer questions honestly. Afterward they may get angry for having given themselves away to someone who actually wasn't worthy of their trust.

Dilemma

The **temptation** of NINEs consists in belittling themselves — especially in their own eyes. At first glance NINEs seem humble. In reality this often conceals false modesty and fear of revealing themselves. Because they are often not very convinced about themselves, they like to stay in the background and cultivate the self-image of not being anything special. They can enter a room and then leave it without anyone taking notice of them. They don't draw the attention of others to them, and do nothing to make themselves conspicuous. NINEs are dependent on others' noticing them and coming up to them. When this happens, they are surprised ("Oh, you noticed me!") and can come out of their inner hiding place.

For this reason there aren't many prominent NINEs. Because NINEs don't take themselves so seriously, they are often overlooked by others. Ex-president Gerald Ford is a NINE. One immediately asks: Gerald Ford? Who was that? Somehow one doesn't remember him.

The **defense mechanism** of NINEs is narcosis. Because they often don't feel adequate to the many strains and challenges of life, they take refuge more than other types do in some sort of addiction. They have a hard time getting going and so are easily tempted to think: "Maybe it'll help me if I drink a little glass or smoke a little joint." NINEs seek stimulants and strong sensations from outside, because they find it difficult stimulating themselves.

NINEs sometimes give the impression of being absent-minded or slightly befuddled. If nothing is happening around them, they can even suddenly fall asleep in broad daylight. Sleep can be the ideal place to retreat to when life gets too trying. On the other hand they often struggle with insomnia at night.[2]

In distressing situations NINEs often withdraw. They don't want to burden other people, and they don't take into account that someone may understand them and may be able to help them — or that anyone at all might be interested in their problems. But when they get to the point of deadlock, at which they can no longer move at all, they absolutely need outside help. Love and attention are true wonder drugs in getting worn-out NINEs back on their feet again. This love, however, can only be a start. The life task of NINEs consists in discovering and developing their feelings of self-worth and their own inner drive, in order to become independent of continual outside impulses.

The **root sin** of NINEs is laziness. The monks of earlier times spoke of *acedia*:

> The demon of acedia, also called the noonday devil, is the most troublesome of all. He attacks the monks at the fourth hour and besieges the soul until the eighth hour. At first he causes the sun to move slowly or not at all so that the day seems to have fifty hours. Then he drives one to look out the window continually and to spring forth from his cell to look at the sun, to see whether it is still far from the ninth hour, to see whether a brother might not be coming. He further infects one with aversion to the place where one lives and to the way of life itself, to manual labor, with the idea that love has disappeared among the brothers, and that there is no one to console one ... [The demon] paints a picture of how long life lasts, and shows him [the monk] the hardships of asceticism. ... [3]

NINEs are by nature easy-going, with weak instinctual drives. This can make others see red. They have problems with taking the initiative, developing projects and perspectives, tackling jobs and carrying them through. They do everything in order not to tie themselves down and not to be tied down by others. For this reason you have to work out clear "contracts" with them: "By April the 19th, twelve noon, this and that have to be taken care of." Then they'll take care of the job — though not a day sooner. As soon as they're left a lot of free space for self-determination, usually nothing will move ahead.

The **pitfall** of NINEs is laziness and comfort. The attitude of many NINEs is: "The thing isn't worth the effort. Why should I stand when I can sit? And why should I sit when I can lie down?" And somehow they are right. I know NINEs who have told me: "You're working yourself to death, Richard, and I'm not — and in the end it all boils down to the same thing for both of us. Why do all you people make yourselves so crazy?" It's hard to avoid the logic of this. The motto of NINEs is, "Take it easy. Cool down. Relax. In the end it makes no difference whether you wear yourself out or not — and it's better not to wear yourself out." This is the laziness of NINEs.

You can be friends with a NINE and for six months there will be no sign of life. Then if you write or call the person, the NINE is pleased as punch that you've thought of him or her and want to talk. Unredeemed NINEs, at least, seldom think of taking the first step themselves and establishing contact. That can lead you to think that they don't like you. But as soon as you take the initiative toward a NINE, you notice that the NINE rejoices and reacts — though not necessarily right away. (If the reaction is connected with an obligation, like writing a letter, for example, that can be neglected for a while longer.) It seldom occurs to NINEs to take the first step.

Parents who are NINEs sometimes have problems actively attending to their children. This can easily give children the wholly false impression that their parents don't care about them. But as soon as the children take the initiative, their NINE parents react and then can be very loving and tender.

NINEs keep getting taken in by themselves. A young woman reports the following episode. She was in a bookstore and came upon a book with the significant title *Hesitation*. She debated back and forth whether to buy it. When she finally left the store with the book in her pocket, she knew that she would never read it. That's a NINE.

For years I had a spiritual director who was a NINE. He maintained that "we NINEs are at bottom great cynics about ourselves and about human nature. We believe that we're worth nothing, and that ultimately nothing is worth anything. We tend toward resignation. Anyone who wants to help a NINE has to look to do something about this deep-seated cynicism." The personality structure of NINEs is also called passive-aggressive. The attitude, "We don't commit ourselves," actually conceals a negative message. At bottom it contains an arrogant view of oneself and the whole world: "You're not worth my driving myself crazy." We should not forget that NINEs, like other gut persons, belong to Karen Horney's "hostile types" and bear within themselves a deep distrust of life. With them, however, it is really well hidden. NINEs express passive aggressiveness above all in a certain stubbornness. When NINEs don't want to do something, they don't want to do it. Wild horses can't get them to do something that's too complicated or strenuous.

NINEs **avoid** conflicts. Aside from stubbornness and sleep they have at least two other possibilities of indirectly communicating their displeasure, without exposing themselves to violent emotions: sitting it out or retreating. NINEs can persistently refuse to contribute anything toward changing a situation. NINEs won't move from the spot and hope that the problem will somehow solve itself. Or they withdraw and in this way document their annoyance. Since NINEs sense quite precisely what others expect of them, their anger can also be expressed by acting as if they noticed nothing. They simply don't comply with unspoken expectations. That is the only form of "dissimulation" to be expected from a NINE. Nonviolent resistance comes naturally to a NINE.

It will take a long time before NINEs directly express their rage. Either they provoke the other person by their passivity for so long that the other explodes and thus opens up the possibility for a confrontation, or the explosion of the NINE is "prepared for" by a long process. At first the position of the other person strikes NINEs as plausible and acceptable. Only in a longish testing phase do they realize that they just don't agree. Next the NINEs have to ascertain internally that the outburst of anger is justified. Then — and only then — can there be a volcanic explosion of wrath that generally throws the people around the NINE into astonishment and terror, because they have gotten used to thinking that the NINE is so easy to handle.[4]

NINEs do not load their heads down with unnecessary ballast. They long to cast off unnecessary burdens and to find something clear and simple. NINEs like a book or lecture if it's lucid and concrete. Everything that's complex and too abstract they find boring. They seek simplicity because they are looking for their own simple center and are afraid there might be nothing there.

Unredeemed NINEs can avoid everything: life, the world, evil and good, even themselves. NINEs have none of the defense mechanisms at their disposal that the other eight types use to try to protect their inner self from the assaults of the world outside. As "children of paradise," they live in a world whose dangers and allurements they don't feel up to. This defenselessness means that almost everything that approaches NINEs from the outside world is exhausting and draining. They spend their energy avoiding or deadening inner and outer conflicts and suppressing strong feelings. While they are outwardly composed and have a calming effect on others, it can sometimes happen that they are seething and boiling inside. NINEs can also experience inner repose. These are the most beautiful moments of their lives.

In partnerships NINEs often find that they are torn back and forth between strong wishes for fusion (symbiosis) and a deep-seated wish for autonomy. The upshot is that the step to final commitment in a relationship is difficult for them and it can take years before all reservations have been dropped. It's likewise difficult to give up and let go of an existing relationship: "If I can't live in this person and through this person — how am I to live at all?" NINEs find their way to real love when they have found their way to their own center, out of which they can meet a partner without fusing with him or her.

Unredeemed NINEs are especially anxious in the face of uncontrollable energies like sex and aggression. Because both are bound up with conflicts, NINEs tend to keep them under control so that they largely drop away as motive forces. The result is an all-encompassing laziness. Many NINEs are highly gifted, but their gifts often aren't actualized because they neglect to bring them forward.

In Jesus' famous parable of the Pounds, we were completely unable to see the third servant, a NINE, as the hero of the story. With our capitalist and success bias, we idealized the capital of the oppressor king. (Jesus is talking about Archelaus, who enlisted others in his exploitation of the poor. See Luke 19:11–27.) Actually the third servant, whom Western Christianity always considered the "nonachiever," is a classic presentation of a nonviolent resister who refuses to play the game and suffers the consequences. This is exactly what Jesus is teaching the disciples. He makes a NINE the hero, to communicate the price that must be paid for the coming of the Reign of God. The world will reward cooperation and it will punish noncooperation. Get ready for persecution, Jesus is telling his disciples, "who imagined that the Reign of God was going to show itself then and there" (Luke 19:11). THREE cultures are almost incapable of understanding or appreciating NINES. That is probably why nonviolent resistance had to be retaught to the Christian West through Gandhi, an Indian (whom I suspect was also a NINE — with two intense wings!).

In NINEs there are two possibilities placed close together: to lead a beautiful, interesting life, full of feeling, a fulfilled, lovable, truly human and "holy" life — or not even to begin living and so to remain with nothing to show for their lives. Jesus depicts the second possibility with terrible dramatic force. The two German proverbs sometimes quoted in this context, "If you do nothing, you do nothing wrong," and "You don't sin when you're asleep," are unfortunately not true. More than other types, NINEs are inclined to commit sins of omission. Even laziness can be fatal.

If the Roman Catholic Church is a SIX system, liberal Protestantism in particular displays many features of NINE. It avoids clear dogmatic statements, tries to please everybody, to be open to everyone and everything. The lack of a clear profile that one frequently encounters in Protestant piety is one of the reasons why many people are turning their back on this form of Christianity, which strikes them as a "supermarket of possibilities," and sometimes makes pluralism an end in itself. It is, however, also true that many people find this openness agreeable, and see the Protestant Church as free space in which they are simply allowed to be themselves. If it is not to become irrelevant, Protestantism must continually reflect on its Reformation roots (ONE) and, alongside a shapeless openness that welcomes and embraces everyone and everything, must keep alive the question of truth and justice (EIGHT). These are the necessary wings of the NINE.

The gift or **fruit of the spirit** of NINE is, surprisingly, the deed, a form of decisive action. At first NINEs waver and hesitate, putting off everything. But if they reach a decision, then it happens in a moment of absolute clarity. Without further considerations, without revision or the least doubt, they know in a flash what's involved, they will do it, and no one will be able to stop them.

My example here is a young man I once lived with. As pastor in the community I was also an active matchmaker — that's my TWO-wing. I knew that this lad, with whom I lived in the same house, had his eye on a certain girl. I kept approaching him and asking, "Have you spoken with her yet?" But he kept dodging: "No, no, not yet, everything in its time." This went on for at least a year — and the fellow was twenty-seven. One evening, he came up to me and said: "Richard, I talked to her. We're going to go out!" After the first date I encouraged him to take her out again. So they met again and again, and that too lasted a few years. I kept digging my hooks in: "Are you going to pop the question tonight?" Answer: "No, no, not yet, don't pressure me, Richard!" And again he came up quite unexpectedly one evening and said: "Now I've asked her. We're getting married!" He knows what he wants with simple clarity. The matter is decided once and for all and becomes a deed.

The positive side of their striving for harmony is that NINEs are excellent mediators and peacemakers. They want a world in which people can live with very little conflict and in peace with one another. What they are looking for themselves they also wish for everyone else. They don't believe that there are unbridgeable oppositions.

Precisely because NINEs themselves often have no clear standpoint, they are capable of shifting themselves to, and accepting, any standpoint whatsoever. Through their whole style they convey the impression, "I can understand both sides and bring them under one umbrella; then after all you'll have to do that too." Many people report that in the presence of a NINE they come to rest in some inexplicable manner and can relax. It really is hard to be truly aggressive when a NINE is there. NINEs often don't understand this themselves, because they can feel inwardly torn and unsettled and don't believe that they of all people are radiating peace.

NINEs are a great enrichment for the peace movement and for groups fighting for justice. One must not forget that NINEs have two energy-laden high-tension wings, EIGHT and ONE, that bristle with passion and commitment to justice and a better world. NINEs are gentle prophets. Their peaceful radiance is disarming. They can work very effectively precisely because they are indirect. ONEs and, above all, EIGHTs frighten others away; people feel threatened by them. NINEs, by contrast, awaken trust. People are much more willing to let them "get away with things."

Among the classic figures in world literature is the prototype of a NINE, Ivan A. Goncharov's *Oblomov*. The novel was published in 1859.[5] Oblomov, a landowner, who lives in Petersburg far from his estate of Oblomovka, vegetates away, passive, idle, and irresolute. His bed and an oriental dressing gown are his world. More than two hundred pages go by before the "hero" finally leaves his bed.

Seven persons appear in the course of the morning and try to get him up. "In an analogy to the seven deadly sins they all embody worldly temptations and weaknesses."[6] But all their alluring offers can't really motivate Oblomov. He sinks into a dream of lost paradise and the intact world of the Oblomovka he knew in his childhood.

Finally Oblomov's German friend, Stolz (pride) appears, and gets him to plunge into social life. But Oblomov misses there the "center around which everything turns"; he notices the emptiness, boredom, and meaninglessness of the active life.

Only his love for Olga wakens Oblomov, turning him into a "madman, possessed by passion." Olga knows what she wants. Oblomov falls hook, line, and sinker for her mind and will. But he doesn't stay the course. In the long run this woman is too exhausting for him. She will marry him only if he promises to "stay the course." By contrast, he calls upon her to, "Take me as I am, love the good in me!" Olga can't do that.

With his motherly landlady Agafya ("the good") the idyll of his childhood finally awakens, as it were, to new life. "As it once did in Oblomovka the life of Oblomov flows gently on in the cycle of religious and secular feast days and ends one day silently, without pain and without fuss."[7]

The Russian orthodox emigrée Tatiana Goricheva stresses that Oblomov has a "hidden and paradisiacal soul," and wants "to live from the inside out," but of course does not take this step.[8] Nevertheless his dream of paradise, his "utopia" is important. Oblomov's ideal is for Goricheva (a Christian) "realer than all the maxims of everyday life."[9]

The Munich dramatist Franz Xaver Kroetz, who has been involved with Goncharov's protagonist for decades, leaves the question open in his play *Oblomov* whether the "vice" of "Oblomovism" might not be a virtue. Obviously he inclines to this view, because he shapes the role

of Oblomov — in contrast to his antagonists Stolz and Olga — with a
great deal of sympathy.[10]

Symbols and Examples

NINE **animals** include the elephant, who stands around in the zoo not
doing much, who doesn't seem especially aggressive; it is known for
having a very gentle disposition but can be very resentful. Also included
are, of course, the sloth, all whales, and above all the dolphin. Whales
and dolphins are the animal patrons of the redeemed NINE.

A great deal has been written about whales and dolphins in recent
years. The fascinating world of these animals deserves a detailed presentation. The splendidly illustrated book *Continent of the Whales* by
Heathcote Williams is a hymn to this species, which the author calls
"extraterrestrials who have already landed on our planet."[11]

Whales spend three times as much time playing as they do searching for food. They are musical and have a highly complicated system
of understanding that is evidently continually evolving. Their ears are
twenty times more sensitive than the human ear. The brain is often at
least comparable in size and complexity to the human brain; the brain
of the finback whale is six times larger than the human brain.

Whales maintain the ecology of plankton. Without whales plankton
would proliferate wildly and deprive the ocean of oxygen. Whales repro-
duce only to the extent that nourishment is available for their offspring.
The males woo their loves with songs and daredevil stunts. If a whale
calf dies prematurely, the mother carries it on her back until the dead
body falls apart.

Whales and dolphins have saved people's lives. As far as we know, no
whale has ever attacked a human. Humans, by contrast, have launched
a "holocaust of the seas" against the whales, to butcher their precious
bodies. "Because the whale has no enemies in the sea, a whale refuses to believe in an attack, like the Indians once and the Australian
aborigines."[12] The Eskimos say, "It does humans good to think about
the whale."[13]

We humans can learn from the whales that intelligent creatures can
survive without extirpating one another and without destroying the environment for their own purposes. This nonaggressiveness is seldom
found among humans; redeemed NINEs embody it more than all others.

The **country** of NINEs is any country at all before it was ravaged by
civilization. An often used ethnic image is Mexico, more particularly the
Mexican wearing a sombrero, taking a siesta in the afternoon. This image

too is meant only as an illustration and is not intended to stir up popular prejudices. Actually Mexicans are caught in the tension between EIGHT and NINE, according to their own assessment.

The **color** of NINEs is gold, the color of gods, kings, and saints. Buddhist monks wear saffron-colored robes as a symbol of enlightenment. Just as gold has to be sought in the depths of the earth, NINEs have to seek for their gifts and bring them to light. The golden age and the golden city are archetypal images for peace, happiness, harmony, and fulfillment.

The **biblical patron** of NINEs is the "unwilling prophet," Jonah.[14] He receives the command from God to go to the Assyrian city of Nineveh, the quintessence of godlessness, and to proclaim God's coming chastisement. Jonah wants to escape this unpleasant assignment and boards a ship headed in the opposite direction, to Tarshish. God makes a storm come up. Shipwreck seems inevitable; all the sailors plead to their gods to be rescued. Only Jonah is asleep in the hold: the captain has to go wake him up. The sailors cast lots to find which one of the passengers is responsible for the disaster, and the lot falls on Jonah. He himself proposes that they pitch him into the sea, which they at first refuse to do, but finally agree to.

The storm immediately stops. A great fish swallows the prophet. He survives in the belly of the beast and three days later is spit up on the shore. Now he carries out his charge and preaches that the city will be destroyed in forty days. Surprisingly the people listen to him. The king, the whole people, and even the animals begin to fast and put on penitential garments.

God regrets the decision to destroy the city and decides to spare it. This displeases Jonah. Again he wants to die. He leaves the city and sits under a canopy of leaves he has rigged up, to see whether the destruction will come after all. God makes a castor oil plant grow, which provides shade for Jonah and under which he can take a siesta. This special attention delights the prophet. But on the next morning a worm gnaws on the root of the shrub so that it wilts. The hot east wind plagues Jonah; once more he wishes to die. But God gives him a lesson in unconditional love: "You pity the plant, for which you did not labor, nor did you make it grow, which came into being in a night, and perished in a night. And should I not pity Nineveh, that great city, in which there are more than a hundred and twenty thousand persons who do not know their right hand from their left, and also much cattle?" (Jonah 4:10–11).

Jonah's laziness is really resignation and infatuation with death. Neither his own life nor the life of the city of Nineveh mean anything to him. Sleep and death seem to end all of life's conflicts. God challenges Jonah to deeds of love that can redeem both the prophet and the city.

Jonah and the Whale (woodcut, c. 1470)
The Unwilling Prophet

Conversion and Redemption

The **invitation** to NINEs is (unconditional) love. NINEs need the experience of being wanted, of being important, of having something to give. They have to learn that others — God and their fellow men and women — believe in them, so that they can believe in themselves. Redeemed FIVEs can love unconditionally like no other type (e.g., Etty Hillesum). The behavior of unredeemed NINEs often resembles this total love: Because condemning others or disputing with them means stress and conflicts, the acceptance of other people is sometimes the path of least resistance. Again we see how ambivalent every gift is: in this case there is a danger that NINEs will accept even completely unacceptable conduct by other people in order to spare themselves the bother of a confrontation.

NINEs know better what they don't want than what they do want. For this reason they can best decide, when they have different options, by testing and eliminating everything that runs up against inner resistance from them. The possibility that survives this process of selection should then be tried out.

Among the **life tasks** of NINEs is overcoming their secret cynicism. NINEs have to learn to believe that there is a golden kernel in them and that they have an energy source that makes them capable of acting purposefully and decisively. NINEs are gut types. They have to act boldly, enjoying the risk, in order to experience themselves. As long as they sit around and ponder, they will become ever more deeply resigned and finally get bogged down. Their energy needs a point of orientation. They need something on which to focus all their power. NINEs report that it makes them happy when they finally manage to distinguish essentials from nonessentials, to set clear priorities and to act consistently.

The positive side of the double-edged longing NINEs feel for harmony and rest is the wish to bring together everything that is resistant, complex, and unresolved, to unite and integrate the opposites. NINEs seek wholeness. The psychoanalyst Carl Gustav Jung was a NINE. He thought that one of his most important responsibilities was to make a contribution to the integration of the human soul: good and evil, masculine and feminine; he tried to unite everything. He also discovered the "collective unconscious," that deepest ground of the soul in which opposites are cancelled out, because there all persons are equal and "one." NINEs feel deeply connected with the primal Ground of Being. They can help others to find their way back to this Ground.

It helps NINEs when they consciously struggle to find their own standpoint instead of orienting themselves toward others. Ordered structures and an invariable daily routine prevent all one's energy from being used up in planning; they stop continual new distractions from delaying the "main thing." NINEs should not abandon themselves to passive fatalism, should not let themselves go, roll into a defensive ball, or even give themselves up. It is a difficult but rewarding task for NINEs to be consistent in guiding to completion projects they have begun. Instead of wishing and planning for many things, they should try to take the closest, most obvious job in hand, and make the first step.

Helen Palmer also recommends that NINEs feel and express rage and aggressions in their imagination until they have loosed the blockages.[15]

Redeemed NINEs may be the only ones to whom we could entrust the world with a good conscience, without having to fear that they would enrich themselves, exploit others, or seek their own advantage. They are the last ones who would rouse themselves or develop the necessary ambition to climb to influential positions.

An ideal example of a redeemed NINE, a twentieth-century **saint**, is Pope John XXIII (1881–1963), the "pope nobody would have thought capable of anything."[16] Angelo Roncalli came from a large, poor peasant family and all his life kept the frugality of the peasant's son. He was passionately attached to the cause of the poor. In his first position as secretary to the bishop in Bergamo he supported striking metallurgical workers. He was completely lacking in ecclesiastical ambition; he would have most liked to become a country pastor.

But things turned out otherwise. In 1925 he was sent as the Vatican's ambassador to Bulgaria and shortly after that to Istanbul. In these years he had to mediate continually between the interests of the Roman Catholic Church and an environment made up of people of different faiths (Orthodox and Islamic). He was called the "Monsignore with the motto, 'Let us have understanding for each other.' " During World War II he contributed to the rescue of two hundred thousand Jews from the Nazis by the fabrication of false baptismal certificates.

In Rome meanwhile he had apparently been forgotten. So everyone — and most of all Roncalli himself — was surprised when he was sent as nuncio to Paris in 1944. Again there were difficult tasks of mediation. The Catholic Church had become too tied up with the German occupation force and had to be "de-Nazified" to recover its credibility. He mastered this responsibility with a great deal of skill and irresistible charm.

At the age of seventy-two Roncalli became patriarch of Venice. Finally he could once again be near people. His episcopal palace always had its doors open. The cardinal traveled about using public transportation and sought out contact with ordinary men and women. In 1958 after a long, tough struggle at the conclave he was elected a "transitional pope" — obviously as a compromise candidate and because of his advanced age of seventy-seven. And he did become a transitional pope, but in an altogether different sense from what people had in mind. He saw to it that the Church underwent a radical reform and completed the transition into the twentieth century.

John XXIII knew what he wanted: an opening of the Church to the world, simplification and humanization of ecclesiastical manners, cooperation: "Simplify what is complicated, and don't complicate what's simple" was a motto for him — and for every NINE. He one day surprised his cardinals with the idea of holding a council. From then on he stubbornly and unwaveringly pursued this inspiration (decisive action!).

His goal was to bring "fresh air" into the Church. Through the Council the Church received fresh impulses, dialogue with the world religions and with atheists began, the bishops got more say, and the position of the laity in the Catholic Church changed fundamentally.

The "good pope," as everyone had come to call him, was above all occupied by world peace. During the Cuban missile crisis he secretly mediated between Khrushchev and Kennedy. His peace encyclopedia, *Pacem in terris*, contained sentences like this: "Hence justice, sound reason, and a sense of human dignity demand that the worldwide arms race cease; that furthermore the weapons that already stand available in various states be simultaneously reduced on both sides; that nuclear weapons be forbidden and finally that an effective, reciprocal supervision of disarmament be agreed upon."[17]

Statements like the following read like the profession of faith of a redeemed NINE: "Patience and rest, these are two beautiful qualities. To be always busy and not to suffer from haste, this is a piece of heaven on earth. Apart from the will of God there is nothing interesting to me." And, "Angelo, don't take yourself so seriously!"[18]

Part III

Inner Dimensions

REPENTANCE AND REORIENTATION

The Enneagram distinguishes between gut, heart, and head types (sexual, social, self-preserving), depending on which life center the person is primarily defined by. At the same time each individual is a microcosm in which all three centers are found and at times "function" in a specific way: All nine types think, feel, and act, have a sex drive, a desire for self-preservation, and social impulses. All nine types commit errors of the mind and errors of the heart. In the section that follows we will turn to each of the centers and show which specific mistaken attitudes and developmental possibilities are found in each type. In this way much of what has just been discussed in the description of the types will be systematized once again.

Pitfalls and Invitations

When Jesus called people to repent, he did so with the words:"The kingdom of God is at hand! Repent and believe in the Gospel!" (Mark 1: 15). The Greek word *metanoiete*, which is found at this point in the original text of the New Testament, means literally "Change your mind, think differently!" Or as I like to put it, "Unlearn!"

Jesus invites people to see the world and God in a completely new and different way. He calls them to break out of their customary ways of thinking and to dare "new thinking," which takes into account the Good News that the reign of divine love is near.

The Enneagram spells out the **pitfalls** or deadends in our thinking. At the same time it gives each type a specific invitation or call to conversion. In Enneagram literature these invitations are called "holy ideas" or "ideas of the higher spiritual center." The term "invitation," which we have chosen, emphasizes on the other hand that we understand the call to freedom primarily as a message from God and not our own doing. Instructions and explanations for each pitfall and invitation are contained in the descriptions.

We should note that the triangle that connects the central types of gut, heart, and head centers with one another is formed by the three "theological" virtues that Paul mentions in 1 Corinthians 13:13: "So faith, hope, and love abide, these three; but the greatest of these is love." With

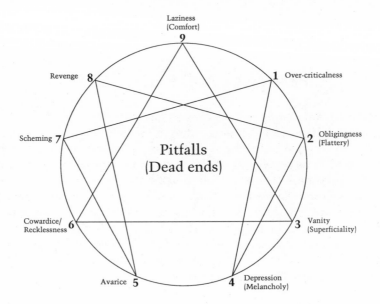

Figure 3: The Pitfalls

Figure 4: Invitation (Calling)

the Enneagram too love is "the greatest." It stands at the top, marking the beginning and the end of the circle.

Root Sins and Fruits of the Spirit

Root sins are emotional compulsions or mistaken attitudes. "Sin" means a separation or failure to reach a goal. The nine sins promise advancement in life, but in reality they produce just what they are trying to prevent: loneliness, absurdity, emptiness. They separate us from God, from our fellow humans, from the creation, most of all from ourselves. They prevent us from reaching the goal of our lives: reconciliation with ourselves, with our neighbors, and with God.

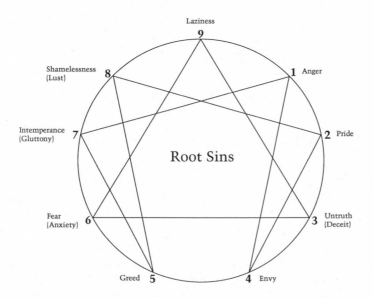

Figure 5: Root Sins

The nine fruits of the spirit are images of redeemed passion or sin. They can't be produced; rather they can only be allowed to grow. They are gifts of divine grace. This does not condemn us to passivity. Paul challenges the Corinthians to "strive for the higher gifts of grace!" (1 Cor. 12:31). Such striving can take various forms: we can ask God for gifts; we can also begin to live "as though" we already had those gifts. These fruits are an expression of our being unmarred by the power of sin.

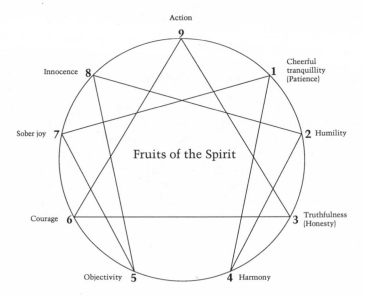

Figure 6: Fruits of the Spirit

Subtypes: Sexual–Social–Self-preserving

The three natural impulses are associated with the passions: the sex drive, the social impulse, and the drive for self-preservation. These passions are the raw material of our being; they are therefore unconvertible. Attempts to kill off these impulses, as ascetics in every era have tried, lead to the truncation of the whole person. Our position is that one must learn to control the passions so they don't destroy our lives but serve them. Our impulses sometimes seem like evil monsters, lurking uncontrollably in the lower regions of our souls. The symbol of the dragon is used over and over again to describe the nature of the desires. One can attempt to slay the dragons — as St. George and the Archangel Michael did. But there is also another possibility: in the legend of Martha it is reported that the saint tamed a dragon, so that he followed her willingly. The story is told of Francis of Assisi that he made friends with the wolf of Gubbio, whom all the world feared. It is in this sense that we suggest taming the dragon and embracing the wolf.

The Enneagram presupposes that every person is dominated by one of three natural impulses. Thus for each of the nine types there are three subtypes. The particular life situation has a very strong influence in determining which subtype a person belongs to at any moment. It is to be assumed that in their professional life people will mainly live out their social subtype, in partnership their sexual subtype, and in the moments of solitude and withdrawal their self-preserving subtype.

Sexual Subtypes

ONE: *Jealousy*. Sexual ONEs try to control their partners. They watch every step their partner takes and fear that others might be more attractive to their partner. Inside they boil with jealousy and fear of loss, but are unable to admit and express this "imperfect" feeling. The jealousy comes from the fear that another could be more perfect and therefore more attractive. Sexual ONEs can extend this zeal to their "cause" too and be very hot-headed, as Paul was, before his conversion, "breathing threats and murder against the disciples of the Lord" (Acts 9:1).

TWO: *Seduction/Assault*. Sexual TWOs constantly try to produce signs of affection and closeness and, for example, do everything to create an attractive environment for a rendezvous. With all their might they try to ignore and overcome objective obstacles that make a relationship impossible. So no rational arguments do any good ("Love conquers all!"). The love of the sexual TWO consists mainly in overcoming obstacles. As helpers they are dominant, take others by the hand, and know what is best for their clients.

THREE: *Masculinity/Femininity*. Sexual THREEs try to represent the ideal sexual image of their time and group. They play the male or female role perfectly, as required in their neighborhood or society. Sexual conquests are important for their self-esteem as symbols of success.

FOUR: *Competition*. Sexual FOURs establish their self-esteem through comparison with others. They are therefore tempted to beat on their own turf those whose favor they want to win, in order to impress them. The other side often considers this hostile competition. The destructive side of unredeemed sexual FOURs becomes apparent when they seduce others only to drop them later. The successful seduction serves as proof that they are equal or superior to the desired person.

FIVE: *Confidence*. FIVEs trust only a few other people. They share their secrets only in very important relationships. They invite only one person whom they really trust into their "fortress." For them, sexuality is a nonverbal form of communication that relieves them of the difficult task of putting their feelings into words. Sexually oriented FIVEs give the impression to the people around them of being "cool" and self-assured. Such FIVEs can seem very convincing to others and thereby gain influence with them.

SIX: *Strength/Beauty*. The vulnerability of an intense relationship mobilizes the mistrust of the SIX. As a rule the sexual SIX man is somewhat contraphobic. Through a certain coldness, hardness, and put-on strength, he can prove that he is in control. The sexual SIX woman can play out her power through the art of seduction. She enjoys playing the role of the soft, shy doe that seems unapproachable. In this way she can at the same time attract and repel her "other."

SEVEN: *Susceptibility*. The sexual SEVEN enhances the actual experience of the relationship through distinct fantasies, which are more important than facts. Sexual SEVENs are fetishists: a "turn-on" can be more interesting than an experienced, lived relationship. In sexual relationships they are open to their partner's impulses, as long as they do not involve pain, too much profundity, or strenuous demands.

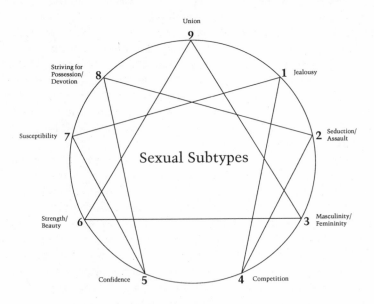

Figure 7: Sexual Subtypes

EIGHT: *Striving for Possession/Devotion*. Sexual EIGHTs want to control and possess everything, including their partners. They expect them to devote body, soul, and spirit to them. They are prepared to return the same devotion when they have the feeling that their partner is equal to them and will not exploit this "position of power." There are EIGHT men (not just in the comics, like Hägar and Helga) who are strong in the outside world, but subjugated to their wives at home. Sexual EIGHTs believe in fast cars, an endless supply of liquor, beautiful women and men. They are proud of their toughness and are the most rebellious of all types.[1]

NINE: *Union*. The sexual type NINE would like most of all to live in and through another, be it a person or God. They perceive the feelings of others more clearly than their own, and physically sense exactly what the loved one is going through. Sexual NINEs make their partner happy and become happy themselves through the reflection of this happiness. Of course their partners shouldn't overstrain them: the relationship shouldn't demand too great an effort on the part of the NINE.

Social Subtypes

ONE: *Nonadaptability*. ONEs are not prepared to identify themselves unconditionally with a social system that's defective. If they did, they would feel as if they were covering up those defects. Rather they see their task as the constant reform of the system, and they have a tendency to moralize. At the same time, they are afraid that the people in charge might have something to reproach them with. This is the position of critical solidarity and of "yes, but...."

TWO: *Ambition*. Social TWOs strive for social influence. Like John the disciple they want to be near the master and to participate in his power. They themselves do not need to be successful, but they want to play an important role in the lives of significant people. Social TWOs have an infallible instinct for who the "important people" are, and they seek to be close to them.

THREE: *Prestige*. Social THREEs want to succeed and have social prestige. They are trendsetters and opinion-makers and have a nose for "what's in the air." Social THREEs can formulate group consensus before the problem has even been discussed. Their roles and ways of behaving can change on short notice like a chameleon, and in this way they can maintain a good public image. Their behavior is determined by the possible reactions of others, whose approval is of vital importance to them.

FOUR: *Shame*. Social FOURs are ashamed without quite knowing the reason why. Unredeemed social FOURs feel misunderstood. They believe that they are despised by others and fear that other men might be able to read their thoughts and feelings and condemn them because of this. They are also afraid that their outward appearance might be rejected. That they can't live up to their own high standards also makes them ashamed. Social FOURs turn on their often irresistible charm in order to relieve the social pressure that burdens them.

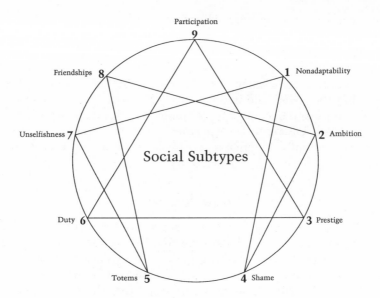

Figure 8: Social Subtypes

FIVE: *Totems*. For social FIVEs, it is important to belong to some kind of "in-group" that is interconnected through esoteric knowledge of the same (abstruse) interest and is closely tied in with a "guru." They seek the nearness of other people in the know and of the group. They are hoping for recognition from the true masters of their guild. Social FIVEs enjoy participating in a code language known only to insiders. This subtype strives for titles, degrees, and other symbols of spiritual power.

SIX: *Duty*. Social SIXs do their duty and obey the laws of a group in order to win its approval. They are also very sensitive about minor rule violations, which in their opinion weaken the system. Uniforms (civilian ones too) and correct behavior help to keep the group together. In two-person relationships SIXes also try to abide by the rules that in their opinion reflect the value system of the other. Social SIXes are conservative and can react very anxiously when innovations are to be introduced.

SEVEN: *Unselfishness*. Social SEVENs can, in time of need, roll up their sleeves and make great sacrifices for their family, group, company, or their nation. Their optimism tells them that all restrictions are only temporary steps designed so that everyone will soon be happy again and many new opportunities will be waiting on the doorstep. For a "good cause" and the well-being of humanity, SEVENs will even give their life.

At the same time SEVENs are aware that every sacrifice limits their own possibilities.

EIGHT: *Friendships*. Social EIGHTs value harmonious relationships. They want everyone to be "happy" and to have no cause for doing injustice to one another. They cultivate friendships and are always ready to give their friends the shirt off their back. Social EIGHTs can be outstanding leaders who hold the community together and let the weaker members rely on them for support.

NINE: *Participation*. Social NINEs want to be there and to belong. When they pull themselves together to join a community, they enjoy the fact that they can continually profit from the life-energy of others and that they themselves don't have to think about how they are going to kill the time. They are apt to give only a part of themselves to group activities and have to learn how to participate more actively and completely.

Self-preserving Subtypes

ONE: *Anxiety*. Self-preserving ONEs are anxious about succeeding. A single error could ruin everything. They feel that because of their imperfection they have earned their failure, for imperfection is evil. ONEs live in perpetual fear that they could make a mistake that would be ruinous. Because of this, when they speak they tend to interrupt and correct themselves constantly.

TWO: *Privilege*. Self-preserving TWOs assume that they have earned special privileges on account of their kindness, holiness, and friendliness ("I have the right to . . . "). They assume that others have to reward their attention and devotion. Self-preserving TWOs are afraid of getting the worst of it if they themselves do not make sure that they're in front. Behind the selfless façade of the TWO stands a person who hates to give up anything.

THREE: *Security*. Self-preserving THREEs try to secure their status, their success, and their reputation. Money and possessions guarantee the future. THREEs are ready to make great sacrifices for this security. They work hard to maintain or improve their social status. Social decline and professional or financial failure conjure up anxious visions that must be kept away by any means.

FOUR: *Resistance*. Self-preserving FOURs stubbornly refuse to give up their self-image of being something special. Anyone who gets in their way and tries to change them has to plan on meeting resistance. Self-preserving FOURs feel misunderstood; they withdraw and suffer in silence. Their imagination is ruled by lamenting the tragedy of their existence.

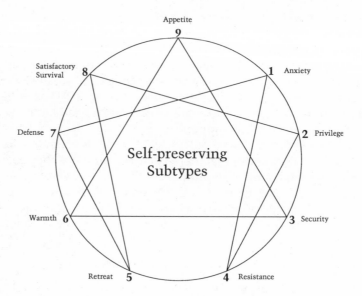

Figure 9: Self-preserving subtypes

FIVE: *Retreat.* "My home is my castle": for their self-preservation self-preserving FIVEs need a private sphere to which they can with-draw undisturbed and undistracted by the expectations or the presence of others. In the hours of retreat they recharge their batteries so that they can better deal with the stress of meeting others. In this restricted area they can hide themselves and attend to their often quite unusual thoughts.

SIX: *Warmth.* Self-preserving SIXes radiate warmth and friendliness in order to disarm potential assailants. The behavior of self-preserving SIXes is connected with their deep mistrust and resembles that of TWOs: "If others like me, then they won't attack me." Occasionally they use a grotesque sense of humor in order to win the affection of others.

SEVEN: *Defense.* In order to minimize the threat of potential enemies and those who would disturb their own intact world, self-preserving SEVENs like to surround themselves with like-minded people who de-fend the same interests and are enthusiastic about the same goals. The family is especially important for this subtype. These SEVENs are group fanatics; their group could be an entertainment committee or a bowling club, a choir or a charismatic prayer group — where people have fun together: "Together we're unbeatable."

EIGHT: *Satisfactory survival.* Self-preserving EIGHTs find it unjust when they don't get what they "deserve." Through control of their environment EIGHTs try to stand up to the threats on their "property rights." They can't bear it when details aren't "just so." Today somebody forgets to buy toothpaste, tomorrow the whole system may collapse.

NINE: *Appetite.* Self-preserving NINEs mitigate the menaces of life through narcotics, whether food, drink, or television. If they are, for example, busy finishing an interesting novel, they can forget the world around them and neglect their own tasks and responsibilities. These NINEs are the "neglected children" who are afraid to come off badly. They store up a supply (of food, drink, books), which calms them. They collect things they never use, but are there in case they're needed. Self-preserving NINEs can be totally exhausted after short spurts of activity or after completing minor jobs.

IDEALIZED SELF-IMAGE AND GUILT FEELINGS

The presupposition of the Enneagram that there are nine basic types of people opens the way for a host of questions: How is it that in each of these nine groups there could still be such different people? Are there mixed types? Doesn't each person have traits of all nine Enneagram numbers? How can I tell to which group I belong? What must I do to overcome my compulsions?

We have already wrestled with some of these questions. In this, the third part of the book, we want to try systematically to delve deeper. Beyond this, we will also add a few aspects that were omitted from the description of the types for the sake of clarity.

Based on our predispositions, parental and environmental influences, as well as societal factors, all of us create in the course of our development certain ideals, whose realization we pursue. Our self-image is determined largely by these ideals, which we also use to measure other people.

Feelings of guilt arise when we do not live up to these ideals.

Likewise we reproach others if they disregard our ideals. Unfortunately these internalized accepted ideals are often false or at least exaggerated. It is in just this attempt to realize our ideals that we are in danger of running right into the dead-end of our pitfall and sins. For the most part we develop guilt feelings only when we don't achieve our ideals, not when we "fall into the trap."

TWOs, for example, develop guilt feelings when they have the sense that they are not doing enough for others. Their identification with the

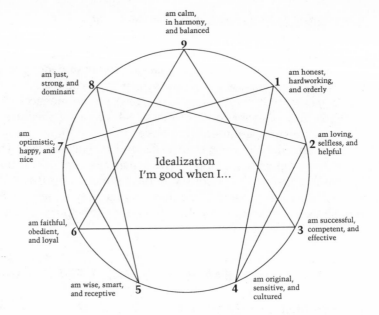

Figure 10: Idealization

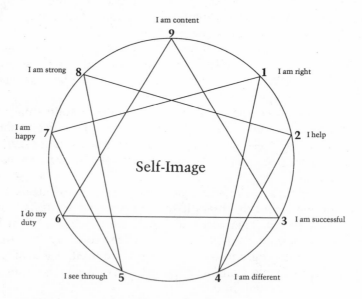

Figure 11: Self-Image

role of helper, however, is exactly the point where they fall prey to their pride.

The principles of idealization can be formulated like this: "I'm good when I...." The two following diagrams contain the nine idealization statements and the nine self-images. These "self-definitions," by the way, can be very helpful for many people in determining their own Enneagram type.

TEMPTATION — AVOIDANCE — RESISTANCE

For the sake of clarity, here again are the specific temptation, avoidance, and resistance mechanisms of the nine types in diagram form:

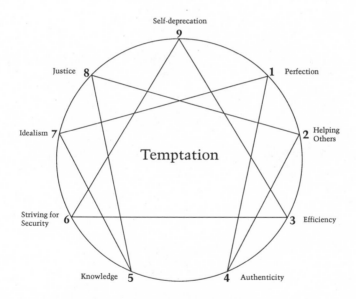

Figure 12: Temptation

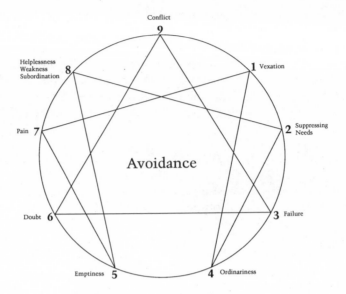

Figure 13: Avoidance

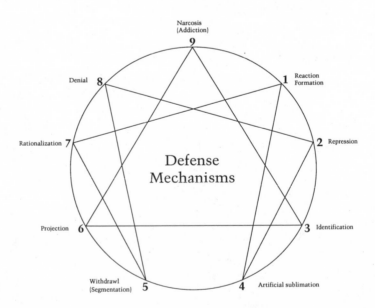

Figure 14: Defense Mechanisms

THE TRIPLE CONTINUUM

Unredeemed — "Normal" — Redeemed

It has already been mentioned that each of the nine types represents a continuum, that is, within each type there are various gradations. They run between two poles: on the one side is the immature, unredeemed, or sick personality, on the other side the mature, redeemed, or healthy personality. Between the two poles lies the path of maturity and redemption. The "normal" or average representatives of a type are located between the two extremes. We deliberately use psychological terminology (maturity) *and* religious language (redemption) to describe the same process, because with an authentic inner path, psychological and spiritual development are not divorced, but rather support and presuppose one other.

We all — ideally — go through a process of integration. But there are also phases in life of stagnation or relapse into an immature stage (regression, disintegration). Redeemed and unredeemed aspects of our personalities, moreover, are mixed within each of us.

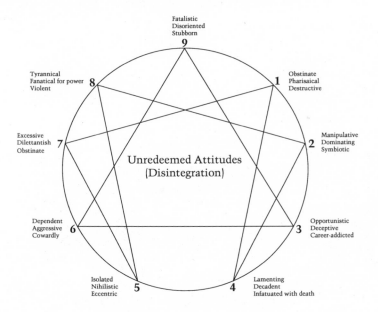

Figure 15: Unredeemed Attitudes

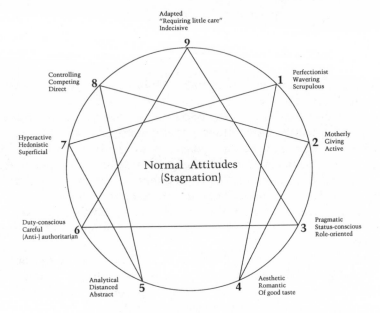

Figure 16: Normal Attitudes

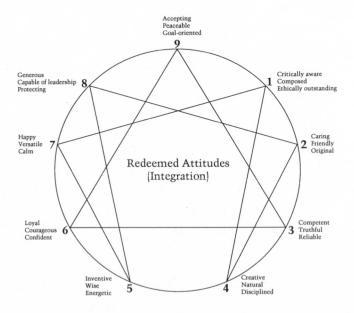

Figure 17: Redeemed Attitudes

The Wings

In the following two sections, we touch on that part of the Enneagram that cannot be rationally substantiated. The truth of the following claims can only be determined through experience: It has been shown that people who work on themselves with the help of the Enneagram's theories change themselves for the better. Therefore there is a lot of support for the claim that no one created or invented the Enneagram, but rather that we have here an intuitive discovery of regular spiritual and psychological patterns.

The entire circle that the Enneagram describes is a kind of gradual overlapping; each energy melds into the next. The Enneagram does not make jumps between the individual types. As a consequence, each number contains something of each of its neighboring numbers, which help to determine it and balance it out. The two types directly neighboring me are my "wings." FIVE, for example, contains parts of its FOUR and SIX wings. While FIVEs are primarily determined by their own energies, blockages, and gifts, there are still two neighboring "theaters of war." The energies in the wings balance out the primary energy. There are, however, those who even say that the primary energy is formed by the tension from the wings! I have found this to be very true in several cases.

The work with the wings is an important first step in the integration of the whole personality. ONEs, for example, who are nothing but ONEs will easily become arrogant, self-righteous, and hypocritical. They will want to make clear to the world what is right and what is wrong. The TWO wing evens that out. It makes sure that the ONEs not only keep to their moral ideals, but also seek the love and affection of other people and try to serve them. The NINE wing on the other side evens out the workaholism of the ONE. The workaholic has a lazy wing that — when it comes into its own — assures the necessary recovery.

In the first half of life, usually one of the wings is developed. One of the tasks for the second half of life is to turn to the as yet underdeveloped second wing. Even people who know nothing of the Enneagram will do this unconsciously.

The fact that each type has two wings is helpful in determining the actual Enneagram number. Many "novices" waver among two or three numbers that are next to one another. If it's only two numbers, then what they have is probably the actual type and one of the wings. If it's three numbers, then often the middle one is the actual type. Those who vacillate between two numbers that are separated by a third, for example between NINE and TWO, should look to the middle number (in this case,

With wing NINE	ONE	With wing TWO
Intolerant	Unredeemed	Hypocritical
Impersonal	Normal	Controlling
Just	Redeemed	Compassionate

With wing ONE	TWO	With wing THREE
Judgmental	Unredeemed	Calculating
Ambitious	Normal	Adapted
Encouraging	Redeemed	Friendly

With wing TWO	THREE	With wing FOUR
Malicious	Unredeemed	Arrogant
Attractive	Normal	Pretentious
Sensitive	Redeemed	Intuitive

With wing THREE	FOUR	With wing FIVE
Manic	Unredeemed	• • • • • • •
Addicted to success	Normal	Enigmatical
Winning	Redeemed	Creative

With wing FOUR	FIVE	With wing SIX
Hopeless	Unredeemed	Distrustful
Delicate	Normal	Blocked
Inspired	Redeemed	Diligent

With wing FIVE	SIX	With wing SEVEN
Arrogant	Unredeemed	Panicky
Lawful	Normal	Morose
Expert	Redeemed	Warm-hearted

With wing SIX	SEVEN	With wing EIGHT
Addicted to acknowledgment	Unredeemed	Greedy
Defensive	Normal	• • • • • • •
Happy	Redeemed	Capable of leadership

With wing SEVEN	EIGHT	With wing NINE
Explosive	Unredeemed	Cold-blooded
Enterprising	Normal	Softly dominating
Magnanimous	Redeemed	Kind

With wing EIGHT	NINE	With wing ONE
Vindictive	Unredeemed	Arbitrary
Sensual	Normal	Self-contented
Soft *and* strong	Redeemed	Pure

Figure 18: The Wings

ONE). Since we are often blind to our main fault, it can happen that we first identify with these "neighboring sins."

The fact that the Enneagram circle continually changes has a further consequence. In order to reach a certain energy level that is not my direct neighbor, I must pass through the points in between. When I (*Andreas Ebert*) was beginning a year's sabbatical after eight years of work as a pastor, I, a TWO, unknowingly sought point NINE. In order to reach NINE, I had to pass through ONE. For me this was practical: I cleaned up, paid bills, and put my papers in order. Only after achieving order (ONE) did I find peace (NINE). At this same time, my relationship to some people who are NINEs intensified.

The dominance of one of the two wings can strongly influence the personality image: A SEVEN with a dominant SIX wing is strikingly different from a SEVEN whose EIGHT wing is more active.

There are also people who have identified with one of their wings for so long that they must first be redeemed at that level in order to take on their main energy.

In Figure 18, three key-words represent how a dominant wing can influence the respective personality image. They show one typical line of unredeemed, normal, and redeemed representatives of the wing types, and make no claim to completeness.[2]

The Arrows (False and True Consolation)

The Enneagram contains a third (double) continuum. It is marked by the connecting lines (arrows) that first link points 9-6-3-9 and second points 1-4-2-8-5-7-1.

The direction of the arrows marks the path of regression and disintegration. In situations of stress, people searching for relief and consolation move with the arrow to another type on the Enneagram that is the stress point. At this point, however, they find only false consolation, which eventually is destructive. The path opposite to the direction of the arrows shows integration.

In times of positive life-feelings, after satisfying peak experiences, and on the way to spiritual maturity, we find true consolation with the positive qualities of the energy that we reach if we move against the direction of the arrows to our "consolation point." For example, TWOs who are overburdened and at the end of their rope appear like unredeemed EIGHTs: they become authoritarian, aggressive, and in the worst case violent. Their false consolation is in the idealization of the EIGHT: "I am powerful." These same TWOs achieve consolation and integration when they simply go to FOUR. Their creative and aesthetic side lives

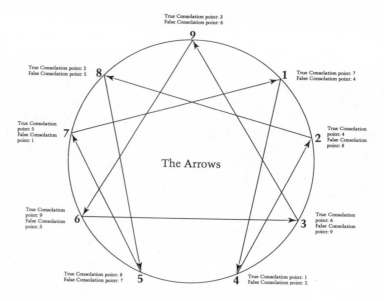

Figure 19: The Arrows

and they discover: "I am something special, even if once or twice I'm not there for others."

The "discernment of spirits" that Paul and Ignatius spoke of means developing a spiritual instinctive certainty for which of my impulses create life and which destroy it. According to Ignatius, false consolation expresses itself in spiritual confusion, tumult, and darkness, in restlessness and disgust or in doubt and selfishness. On the other hand, true consolation manifests itself through the experience of a spiritual fire, gratitude, peace, and power.[3]

The following explanations presuppose a knowledge of the personality descriptions and sometimes refer to examples that have already been explained.

ONE

False Consolation: ONE *goes to* FOUR. Unredeemed ONEs want to be right at all costs and to judge others. They are overzealous, impersonal, and full of suppressed anger. When ONEs are at the end of their rope, they direct their aggression against themselves and take on the subjective, melancholy, depressed, and self-destructive characteristics of an unredeemed FOUR (for example, Luther's self-castigation in the monastery). The self-image of the FOUR ("I'm something special") can also lead stressed-out ONEs to begin to flatter themselves. Paul, in his uncomfortable discussion with the community of Corinth, did not always escape this danger:

> Let no one think me foolish, but even if you do, accept me as a fool, so that I too may boast a little. . . . For you gladly bear with fools, being wise yourselves! But whatever anyone dares to boast of — I am speaking as a fool — I also dare to boast of that. Are they Hebrews? So am I. Are they Israelites? So am I. Are they descendants of Abraham? So am I. Are they servants of Christ? I am a better one — I am talking like a madman — with far greater labors, far more imprisonments, with countless beatings, and often near death. . . . Three times I have been shipwrecked, a night and a day I have been adrift at sea; on frequent journeys, in danger from rivers, danger from robbers, danger from my own people, danger from Gentiles, danger in the city, danger in the wilderness, danger at sea, danger from false brethren. In toil and hardship, through many a sleepless night, in hunger and thirst, often without food, in cold and exposure. (2 Cor. 11:16–27).

In the worst case, disintegrated ONEs end in complete resignation and are no longer prepared to do anything to improve their situation or that of the world.

True Consolation: ONE *goes to* SEVEN. The overstrained, controlled ONE must learn to relax, be happy, to settle for a "B." Redeemed ONEs still work hard, but have found a certain ease and inner peace. They can accept being on the way and not yet at the goal. One can sense a calm *joie de vivre* in Luther after his liberating experience in the tower: He is sociable, likes having guests at his table, makes music, and celebrates. His famous statement: "I sit there and drink my Wittenberg beer, as the Kingdom of God runs on and grows of its own accord, without anyone noticing it." Notes of joy sound in Paul too when he writes to the Philippians, who — as opposed to the Corinthians — always treated him with love and respect: "I thank my God when I think of you, and when I pray for you, I do so with joy. . . . Rejoice in the Lord always. Again I will say, Rejoice. . . . Have no anxiety about anything, but in everything by prayer and supplication with thanksgiving let your requests be made known to God" (Phil. 1:3–4; 4:4, 6).

TWO

False Consolation: TWO *goes to* EIGHT. Unredeemed TWOs make themselves irreplaceable and want others to love them. Much unredeemed anger boils inside them because their fellow human beings (and God) are so ungrateful. Normally TWOs are kind in order not to suffer the loss of love. But when they have been discouraged for too long, feel rejected or used, they lash out and resemble unredeemed EIGHTs ("I am powerful!"). At such times TWOs are ruled by a darkness that extinguishes their ability to love. The hatred and bitterness toward others who did not return their love adequately can be boundless. It manifests itself mainly in passive-aggressive behaviors, but can also in exceptional cases become violent. We have already described how Martha, ready to serve, attacked her sister Mary, as well as her guest Jesus, because she had the feeling she was being used and was not getting a fair deal. We have also already seen the aggressive side of the favored disciple John. He would have liked to destroy the village in which Jesus and his followers were turned away.

True Consolation: TWO *goes to* FOUR. TWOs on the way to integration give up the desire to make everything right and to save the world. Also, their unrealistic self-image — "I am Love personified!" — can finally be relativized. FOURs imagine the darker side of their own soul, instead of — like EIGHTs — seeking the guilt of others. Insight into their own brokenness and sinning breaks the pride of TWOs and opens their eyes to the fact that they too are in need of redemption and live on the grace of God. The experience of the love of God leads to true self-acceptance ("I am something special!"), which manifests itself above all in the way TWOs make friends with themselves, can deal with being alone, discover their needs, and let their creative side develop for its own sake and not just to do good. Most TWOs experience a desire and need to do something creative/artistic when they are doing well. TWOs at point FOUR are able to be grateful and to enjoy life. The love of an integrated TWO is no longer oppressive and selfish, but rather allows the loved one his or her own development. "Healed" TWOs can take pleasure in small signs of giving and do not overtax themselves and others with unreasonable expectations. When TWOs do good, they have in view above all the people who need help, not the thanks they expect.

THREE

False Consolation: THREE *goes to* NINE. On account of the many roles they play, THREEs find it very difficult to get in touch with their feelings.

At stresspoint NINE, they are drawn into the undertow of doubt; they lose interest in themselves and can no longer uphold their image, which their identity has not yet attained. This occurs above all when there is no recognition. The roles no longer function, but there is no motivation or power to concern oneself with the "true self." The life of a disintegrated THREE appears empty and senseless. At stresspoint NINE, all of the hate and hostility that they had developed for competitors is directed against themselves.

Extremely unredeemed THREEs whose game is discovered or no longer functions are in danger of suicide. Death as the final sleep is the only remaining escape route. It can also happen that disintegrated THREEs let go, neglect themselves, or give in to an addiction. THREEs need people who love them and can help them to discover worthwhile, "honorable" values and goals in life, and to develop new visions for life so that they can find their way out of this hole.

True Consolation: THREE *goes to* SIX. THREEs have problems with faithfulness, dependency, and trust. Faithfulness means to go through thick and thin with another. For marriage this means, for example, to stay together in good and bad times alike. THREEs, however, tend to break off projects when they are threatened with failure. Commitment also means that my roles and masks will eventually be seen through and so lose their effect. The fear of THREEs that apart from these many masks they have no actual self can manifest itself in anxiety about commitment. In reality, however, commitment is the only possible way for THREEs to overcome role fixation and to grow internally. It is especially helpful if the partner or group allows the THREE's underdeveloped and needy inner side to show. Point SIX ("I am loyal") helps THREEs further to place their gifts at the service of something bigger than themselves, instead of just needing these gifts for their own career. "By recognizing the existence of values beyond themselves, integrating THREEs develop their consciences. They recognize limits on their behavior and limits on what they can expect from themselves, from others, and from life."[4] Without connection and subordination, THREEs are in danger of falling prey to their own ambition.

FOUR

False Consolation: FOUR *goes to* TWO. Unredeemed FOURs are depressed, confused, and alienated, and they doubt themselves. When FOURs are at the end of their rope, then they try to reestablish contact with reality in a way that makes it unbearable for others ("I'm helping!"). Like caricatures of TWOs they try in their way to obtain their own identity through the love and attention of others. The difficulties that FOURs have right from the start with binding relationships worsen, however, when they are deserted. In such a situation they are completely incapable of really coming to terms with another person and want only sympathy and support. At the same time they begin to hate the people upon whom they are dependent. At this rate, every relationship must sooner or later break down.

We see this dynamic in the love relationship of the twenty-four-year-old Søren Kierkegaard with Regine Olsen, a fifteen-year-old girl. He is completely in love and wants to marry her. But the thought that marriage obligates one to absolute openness scares him. He finally makes himself offensive in the hope that she will repudiate him, break off the engagement, but remain caught up in the relationship for the rest of her life. The fact that she does not remain dependent upon him, but rather goes with another, is particularly unbearable for him. His whole behavior corresponds to the problems with distance and intimacy that characterize the program of the unredeemed TWO.

True Consolation: FOUR *goes to* ONE. ONE's world of values, clarity, and conscience is a healing balance for the chaos of emotion, the self-doubt, and the subjectivism of FOUR. The idealization of ONE ("I am right!") helps the FOUR to a healthy self-acceptance. For ONEs values are more important than feelings, diligence more important than genius, reason more important than symbolism. The sobriety of ONEs helps FOURs to get some distance from themselves and develop the ability to evaluate critically their own fantasy world. Artists who are FOURs need the diligence and perfectionism of ONEs in order to convert their original ideas into concrete work. The "raw material" that the soul of the FOUR constantly produces requires refining through the "form" of the ONE. To go to ONE means for the FOUR to allow objective criticism without being crushed as a person by it. The natural openness of ONEs helps the FOURs get in touch with their own naturalness and originality. As a ONE, I can say that more FOURs approach me for spiritual direction than any others. They intuitively know that I have what they need. This has been one of the great confirmations of the truth of the Enneagram for me personally.

For the growth of a Thomas Merton, it was vitally important that he submit to the discipline of a strict monastery. The fight with his abbot, who again and again rejected the subjectivism of this brilliant monk, was a hard but necessary lesson. It probably contributed to the refinement and formation of Merton's subjective experiences, to their broad validity, and to the fact that they continue to be a source of inspiration for many.

FIVE

False Consolation: FIVE *goes to* SEVEN. Unredeemed FIVEs take on nihilistic, schizoid, and autistic traits. They threaten to lose all contact with
reality and live in illusory mind games. In order to unburden themselves,
unredeemed FIVEs become selfish, seek diversion and pleasure, and retreat into any thought pattern that says "I'm O.K." Instead of becoming
active in a purposeful way, stressed FIVEs lose themselves in pointless
activism or cultivate silly behavior. In this stage they may attempt to
find solace in sensual pleasures. FIVEs thus betray their own strengths:
depth of reflection, contemplation, and sober wisdom. Moreover, they
stay in the realm of the head instead of noticing their own emotions and
daring to take the step from thinking to doing. The decadent English
dandy exemplifies this condition of FIVEs.

True Consolation: FIVE *goes to* EIGHT. The thinking of FIVEs tends to hinder action. A FIVE that goes to EIGHT is ready to convert knowledge —
no matter how incomplete or provisional it may seem — into practice.
That's the expression of a healthy audacity. Mature FIVEs are confident
that they needn't always take, but they have something original and
indispensable to give, something that can enrich or change the world.
Such is the case when Hildegard of Bingen shares her visions with the
outside world and through her insights actively intervenes in the tangled
ecclesiastical and secular politics of her time. It can also lead to someone
like Dietrich Bonhoeffer becoming a conspirator, even being ready to get
his hands dirty and personally murder the tyrant. The venture of action
at point EIGHT consists in converting prior and provisional knowledge
and trusting in it, believing that new experience will reveal new findings that can't be had at one's writing desk. The step into action means
that the FIVE initiates physical contact with reality and that head and
stomach connect.

SIX

False Consolation: SIX *goes to* THREE. Unredeemed SIXes are authoritarian and pathologically mistrustful. Because they have no self-esteem,
they betake themselves to dependency on any kind of "greater power."
Fascism is the historical illustration of what can happen when a SIX
system goes to THREE and becomes success-oriented. At point THREE,
SIXes don't attain competence and efficiency; they just fall into the hidden hostility of THREEs. Sadists are molded from masochists, who then
direct their pent-up anger at others and compensate for their feelings of

inferiority through a superiority complex. Frightened rabbits turn into frightening wolves.

In the early and medieval Catholic Church, people believed that one of the rewards for earthly renunciation and suffering would be that one could look out from paradise and gloat over the suffering of the godless. These are the success fantasies of people who basically feel like losers.

At this stage the SIXes no longer pay attention to their inner warning system and are capable of lies, betrayal, and unfaithfulness in order to save their own skin — and finally to lose it. The moment Peter falls into the THREE sin and repeatedly denies his Lord is the absolute low point of his life.

True Consolation: SIX *goes to* NINE. The calm and composure of NINE is the best medicine for SIX's fear. In the story of the calming of the storm, Jesus sleeps on a pillow at the bow of the boat while high waves crash against the boat. The disciples wake the master; he scolds them for their lack of faith and calms the sea with a word (Matt. 8:23–27). In another story, Jesus walks on the water and beckons the fearful Peter to leave the boat and come to him. As long as Peter looks at Jesus, everything goes well. As soon as he sees the waves and realizes his own fear, he sinks (Matt. 14:22–23). Oscar Romero is the prime example of how trust in God can make a functionary of the system into a free and courageous person. Integrating SIXes "attain not only security but the ability to trust."[5]

SEVEN

False Consolation: SEVEN *goes to* ONE. The inhibitive mechanism of an unredeemed SEVEN no longer functions; therefore the fear of coming into contact with pain and darkness is intensified. The mere thought of counseling or therapy arouses horrible images. All of this strengthens the hectic activism of SEVENs and/or their tendency to excessive pleasure. The step to stresspoint ONE can be the attempt to regain control over one's own emotional world. At point ONE SEVENs can take over a "waterproof" ideological system that they aggressively defend. Disintegrating SEVENs can damn everything that stands in the way of their need for a positive view of the world. We can observe this peculiar mixture of cheerfulness and intolerance in parts of the charismatic movement. As with the TWO that goes to EIGHT, the motto of this constellation is: "And if you don't want to be my brother, then I'll beat your head in!" In the worst case, such people (still smiling, and in the name of goodness) are capable of doing permanent harm to others, and ultimately to themselves.

True Consolation: SEVEN *goes to* FIVE. The optimism of SEVENs originates in their fear of depth, for pain lurks in the depths. The "voyage within" means giving up some of the false comforts of the outer world. After his repentance, Francis of Assisi withdrew into solitude and prayed constantly: "Lord, who are you — and who am I?" He chose prayers of extraordinary beauty in order to reach his own inner depths. Surprisingly, he found within himself not a brutal abyss, but rather the source of true, deep joy. When SEVENs go to FIVE, they stop suppressing the pain and trust that their fundamental joyfulness and gratefulness for life will be enough to bear a thorough confrontation with all of life. At point FIVE, SEVENs are more composed and more reasonable. They no longer consume the world, but rather learn to take responsibility for its preservation.

EIGHT

False Consolation: EIGHT *goes to* FIVE. The energy of an unredeemed EIGHT is hostile and violent. At point FIVE ("I am wise!"), the EIGHT begins to brood, to doubt, and to ponder. Fears arise, above all the fear of losing power. Very few EIGHTs willingly retreat into silence. Often their silence is the result of sickness or physical weakness; in the case of violent criminals it can be the involuntary solitude of a jail cell. In a state of enforced silence, EIGHTs sometimes experience for the first time a profound powerlessness, which they had never before tolerated. The fear that others could take advantage of their weakness and avenge previous humiliations gets the upper hand. Feelings of guilt arise. The EIGHTs' sense of justice suddenly allows them to see their own crimes, which demand punishment and retribution. Finally, EIGHTs direct their aggressions against themselves. Unredeemed EIGHTs without power, without a sphere of action, without objectives, and without dependents are in extreme danger of committing suicide. I have seen many unredeemed EIGHTs use the facts and information of FIVEs as ammunition and power against others.

True Consolation: EIGHT *goes to* TWO. TWOs defuse the power instinct of EIGHTs and encourage their "soft" side, which wants to help, nourish, and protect. EIGHTs that go to TWO no longer want just to rule, but also to heal; they leave their self-imposed isolation, become more affable, placid, and vulnerable. Martin Luther King, Jr., is an example of an integrated EIGHT, who put his leadership abilities at the service of both justice and love. Integrated EIGHTs are capable of bringing about a revolution of love. King learned Jesus' lesson of voluntarily foregoing rule by force and instead being simultaneously master and servant. To be weak, vulnerable, and loving is the greatest heroic deed that an EIGHT can achieve. Redeemed EIGHTs, in touch with the little child within, begin to trust and nurture the "little children" without.

NINE

False Consolation: NINE *goes to* SIX. Unredeemed NINEs can lose all contact with life. Their lifelong task has been to suppress all impulses, whether positive or negative. Now the only defense mechanism that they have falls apart: retreat. All fears of the world overwhelm the NINE; disorientation is no longer bearable. Even the tendency of the SIX to self-punishment can be activated. Because NINEs have no real defense mechanism, their inclination toward narcotics can also gain the upper hand, or even death — as the "final sleep" — can become attractive. We see this with the prophet Jonah, as each time he is in a crisis he wants to die, or is at least prepared to die. Another possibility is that the NINEs at this point — like unredeemed SIXes — will become masochistically dependent on others ("authorities"), who are to do their living and decision-making for them, and who are supposed to restore their peace of mind. An unredeemed NINE is paralyzed and unable or unwilling to act.

True Consolation: NINE *goes to* THREE. THREEs supply NINEs with what they need to learn: goal-directed and constructive action. At point THREE, NINEs conquer their Jonah syndrome, stop selling themselves short, and begin to discover and employ their talents. The NINEs who go to THREE become autonomous and self-assured and no longer define themselves by the expectations and impulses of others. They take the initiative and are surprised to find that others feel enriched by it. Integrating NINEs can change the world. Jonah stopped the destruction of Nineveh when he took on the role of prophet. John XXIII changed the nature of the Catholic Church. People gladly trust integrating NINEs, because they can sense that NINEs are using their gifts out of love, never to serve themselves.

I (*Andreas Ebert*) have a friend and colleague who is a healthy NINE. His position as a minister is only half-time, because he needs time "for life." His few but well-directed actions are set up so that lay people take on a lot of responsibility. Delegation is an unburdening for him. Recently, in a series of sermons on the seven deadly sins, he used the theme "unchastity and idleness" to hold a service on the theme "AIDS and the sin of the Church."

I have seldom heard a bolder sermon. Yet my friend presented everything in such a calm, conversational tone that it didn't stir up aggression, but stimulated reflection. After his sermon, an HIV-infected AIDS patient spoke and had the opportunity to articulate his disillusionment with the Church. Even very conservative churchgoers expressed their thanks at the end of the service. This friend does not attempt much. But what he does works. From all this there emanates a great peace and calm — which he says he often doesn't even notice.

It follows from what has been said that the confrontation with the individual points of regression and integration makes an important contribution to personal growth. We must learn to be sensitive to what really builds us up and heals, and to what destroys us.

Helen Palmer was certainly right to warn against thinking that we can stay at our point of healing and suppress the stresspoint.

It can happen, for example, that I as a TWO identify with the positive energy of the FOUR and try to become a kind of FOUR. But I thereby take on the negative aspects of the FOUR as well, become melancholy, narcissistic, and oversensitive. Suddenly I think that, through my healing point FOUR, I as a TWO should have a right to be "something special." In this way I nourish my root sin, pride.

On the other hand when I avoid EIGHT, then its destructive energy can work unhindered in my unconscious and someday break through violently. Moreover, the energy, clarity, and determination of the redeemed EIGHT are just the gift that the "soft" TWO needs (for example, to learn how to say no). "Cultivating the healing possibilities in the so-called stress point is implicit in techniques such as Gestalt therapy ... in which negative emotions are deliberately cultivated and engaged. The intention behind moving toward stress is to skillfully raise our passions to the overflow point and to release the compulsion of a negative habit by experiencing it fully and completely."[6] As C. G. Jung has taught so many of us, we cannot and should not avoid our shadow side. It has much to teach us that is necessary and good, as long as we are also free to call it "shadow" and reorganize its potential for evil.

GROWING WITH THE ENNEAGRAM

One can work with the Enneagram on very different levels and in the most varied contexts. The following suggestions are indications of how the Enneagram has already been successfully put into action or how it might possibly be used.

Self-study

This book can be helpful as an aid to self-understanding. The Enneagram is first of all a key to self-knowledge. It is not that I analyze others or have myself analyzed by others, but rather that I ask myself who I am, what dangers and possibilities there are within me, and how I can find my "true self," which God put inside me. Finally, only I can identify myself with a certain type or life program of the Enneagram. This process may move very quickly, or it may take a long time. I determine the tempo. Even those who don't immediately figure out their type can observe their own life story in the mirror of the new type description and thereby make progress. It will be helpful for some — if they are stimulated by the Enneagram — to write down key episodes from their own biographies and to reflect on them alone or discuss them with others (for example, with a counselor).

Partnership

One of the drawbacks of this book is that it was written by two bachelors. From our circle of friends, however, we know that the Enneagram can be excellent for opening up discussion between partners. Couples report that many conflicts that burden a relationship, but that previously could not be formulated, appear in a new light. The Enneagram helps people to view their partner's peculiarities more compassionately and their own peculiarities more critically. A woman who had been working rather intensively with the Enneagram said recently: "The more I study the nine types, the more I feel that we must love them all!"

The game of "who matches whom" that followers of astrology so love to play does not work with the Enneagram. There are no "super partners" who automatically make a good match. The only pattern that I have seen is that numbers right next to one another (e.g., 1–2, 5–6, 8–9) often have long and creative marriages. They seem to be enough alike and just enough different to sustain fascination. The Enneagram certainly helps people to understand better the specific dynamics at work in a given relationship. It would go beyond the limits of this book and of our previous range of experience if we tried to give a full account of this for all types. Therefore we offer here only a few basic possibilities.

"Birds of a feather . . . ": Experience shows that this doesn't hold for partnerships. There are very few people who marry the same Enneagram type. Such a relationship holds three specific dangers: (1) The one-sided energy of that particular type is doubled and dominates the entire relationship. (2) Because both partners are "playing the same game," they can challenge and complement each other very little. (3) If they discover their own mechanisms in the partner, it might be highly exasperating (shadow-projection). This final danger also contains a specific opportunity: Partners of the same type understand each other "through and through," and in the long run cannot put anything over on the other.

"Wing types as partners": Neighboring types often understand each other well. They are different enough not to be boring for each other, but they're also similar enough to get along well. Such partners can help each other to integrate their wings and hence to live up to their potential more fully.

"Arrow types as partners": Types who are connected in the Enneagram by arrows participate in a special dynamic. The problem is that in these relationships Partner A represents the stresspoint of Partner B, while Partner B is the point of consolation for Partner A. Classic example: an EIGHT man and a TWO woman. She suffers under his severity, unapproachability, and irascible manner; he finds warmth and protection with her. This relationship contains more subjective suffering for her than for him. But both can be enriched by this constellation: he by discovering and accepting his own tender and gentle side through her; she by being challenged by him to come to terms with her own aggression and demands for power, to find a clear standpoint, and to formulate her own needs and limits.

"Opposites attract": Many people unconsciously seek partners who are "completely different." Such relationships are never boring; both partners of course have to fight the problem that they sometimes feel as if they were living on two different planets, that they don't directly understand each other, and that they remain strangers at heart. On the other hand, they challenge each other to tolerance and to the difficult life task of opening up to the "totally other," the not-I. In the dynamic of the Enneagram such people meet each other only indirectly: through their wings or arrows. Two examples to illustrate this:

TWO and NINE: They are not of course directly connected, but have a threefold indirect connection: (1) ONE is their common wing; they can meet for example in political action for bettering the world or for reform within the family or in a larger community and are probably both tuned to the "progressive" side. (2) EIGHT is the stresspoint of TWO and also a wing of NINE. NINEs can understand and accept TWOs directly when the TWOs come to their stresspoint. The energy of EIGHTs does not scare the NINEs; in such moments they can find acceptance from the

TWOs. (3) THREE is the point of consolation for NINE and also a wing of TWO. The TWO can motivate the NINE to work purposefully and with concentration and to strive for success. A further point can be effective in the TWO/NINE constellation: TWOs often live for others, but long for unconditional acceptance. The NINEs oblige: They are probably the only type that can fully provide this acceptance for the TWOs; at the same time, the TWOs fulfill the wish of the NINEs to be stimulated and motivated by others.

THREE and SEVEN: These two types meet indirectly only at one point: SIX is the wing of SEVEN and also the point of consolation of THREE. The THREE's search for security and the tendency of the SEVEN to defend the family meet at this point. Both types are optimists, hard workers, and "growth-oriented." They must take care that the tendencies to superficiality and concern for the external that exist in both types are not strengthened from both sides. A good opportunity for this is provided by FIVE, which lies between the two types. SEVENs find in FIVEs their point of consolation; they can pull themselves together here and concentrate on the important things. THREEs come to FIVEs by way of their wing, FOUR: outer harmony and inner balance help the THREEs express their feelings. The move toward FIVE promotes the distancing ability of the THREEs, slows down their hyperactivity, and helps them to understand themselves critically. At point FIVE, SEVEN and THREE can together dare to look into the depths. A common *Weltanschauung*, or belief system, stabilizes this relationship, which can creatively bind inventiveness and energy.

It would be very helpful to bring the Enneagram into pastoral work with married couples and to use it for the understanding and resolution of marital conflicts. As of this writing, we know of no formal attempts in this area. I use it in my own marriage preparation of couples.

The relational dynamic that is at work, for example, between superiors and subordinates, but also between parents and children or teachers and pupils, can be better understood and worked at with the help of the Enneagram. The Enneagram produces interesting perspectives for family therapy. When you draw up a family tree, you can determine that certain Enneagram types appear frequently within a family, while others appear seldom or not at all.

Religious Exercises and Spiritual Guidance

The Enneagram has been used for several years now in spiritual exercises. "Exercises" are retreats of several days that offer spiritual assistance through lectures, meditations, quiet hours of solitude, pastoral counseling, and religious services. Exercises encourage individuals to come closer to themselves and to God, to dare to take concrete steps on the "spiritual path." Meditation and prayer play a central role in this, because the Enneagram cannot be mastered on a purely intellectual level, not even by a FIVE. It is an experiential method in which through a kind of "inner listening" I find out what "voices" are at work within me. The "discernment of spirits" is that instinctive spiritual certainty that helps me to realize which of these voices will free me for an "abundant life" (John 10:10) and which will lead me to jail and to death.

Discussion Groups

We suggest that discussion groups be organized to study the Enneagram for a certain period of time, for example, by spending an evening working on each of the nine types. Bible study groups and prayer groups could start with the nine faces of Jesus and the corresponding biblical texts, which we have presented in the following chapter.

Perhaps one day there will even be "self-help groups" for each of the types. We know from experience that exchanges with people who have similar problems and who function on the same wave length can be a great relief and a real liberation.

JESUS AND THE ENNEAGRAM

Some call the Enneagram "the face of God" because they see the nine energies manifested in the nine personality types as nine attributes of God (nine refractions of the divine light). Christians see in Jesus Christ the face of God, the God become man, the revealer and the revelation of divine love:

> He is the image of the invisible God, the first-born of all creation. In him all things were created, in heaven and on earth, visible and invisible, whether thrones or dominions or principalities or authorities — all things were created through him and for him. He is before all things, and in him all things hold together. . . . In him all the fullness of God was pleased to dwell, and through him to reconcile to himself all things. (Col. 1:15–17, 19–20).

Christ represents God and hence the essence of the world, its true being. He was also, however, a real person who suffered through the conditions of existence with all of its menaces, temptations, and abysses:

"For we have not a high priest who is unable to sympathize with our weaknesses, but one who in every respect has been tempted as we are, yet without sin" (Heb. 4:15).

In the following passages, when we describe the Enneagram as the icon of the face of Christ, we interpret this as at once "the face of God" and "the face of the (true) man."

The Sufis saw Jesus as a "redeemed TWO" and understood Christianity first of all as a TWO religion. Without denying this aspect, we want to go a step further and make a statement of faith: Jesus realized "true personhood" in a manner that explodes the possibility of pinning him down to one personality type. In fact there are indications in the Gospels that he understood all nine temptations and — in various situations — brought forth all nine "fruits" of the Enneagram. He is the perfect image of a person who has heard the invitation of God and who had the freedom to answer it. Otherwise, certain types in their specific situations would not be able to orient themselves to Christ.[7]

In the following passages we want to demonstrate to what extent each of the nine types of the Enneagram may be securely connected to Jesus Christ. Meditation on the biblical passages cited for each type can help us to recognize our own temptations in the mirror of his person and in prayer and to develop an eye for the talents that have been placed within us.

ONE: Teaching, Tolerance, Patience

Jesus was a practicing Jew who wanted not to abolish Jewish law (the Torah), but to fulfill it (Matt. 5:17). His preaching calls us to turn back from the intellectual and spiritual dead-ends of this world. This is not a matter of "moral rearmament." But Jesus doesn't just want the law to be fulfilled formally and outwardly, since this could easily turn into a religious superstructure on one's own egoism. And so in the Sermon on the Mount he calls for righteousness exceeding that of the Pharisees (Matt. 5:20) and "good works" that come from a reconciled heart, not from compliance with duty.

The Sermon on the Mount contains a much-discussed phrase: "Be perfect, as your Father in Heaven is perfect" (Matt. 5:48). He also calls the rich young man to perfection (Matt. 19:21). The path to Christian morality always runs across the collapse of our own moral efforts and invented ideals. First the experience of God's unconditional love leads to the realization of our own sins, brings about repentance, and makes conversion possible. For ONEs, a key paradox of the Gospels is that we become perfect by accepting our own imperfection. We must recognize that it is part of the process of growth, that we make many mistakes.[8]

Jesus did not suppress his anger or hide it behind a friendly façade. In the story of the healing of the man with the withered hand (Mark 3:1–6) he looks at his accusers with "anger and grief " because they want to lure him into a trap and have hidden their motives. When his disciples don't manage to free a possessed boy from his suffering, he shows obvious signs of impatience: "O faithless generation! How long must I bear with you?" (Mark 9:19).

Jesus had no double morality. Whatever he preached, he lived and translated into reality. He gave himself nothing, and the last three years of his life required an enormous physical and psychic effort.

Jesus was a gifted teacher. Parables, allegories, and not least of all the model he provided made his circle of disciples into a spiritual school of life. Despite their slowness, he never withdrew his love from them and constantly made new attempts to illustrate his message in more and more graphic terms.

Unlike the Pharisees, Jesus never condemns sinners and "fallen" people, but accepts them. He combines unconditional acceptance with a clear challenge. He never tolerates the condemnation of one person by another; but neither will he tolerate any objectively destructive behavior by which people ruin themselves. Forgiveness and atonement are his keys to repentance and a new start: When he saved the woman about to be stoned by her persecutors for adultery, he said to her: "I do not condemn you. Go now and do not sin again!" (John 8:10).

Jesus' parables about growth are an invitation to all perfectionists not to be always in a state of panic, but rather to trust in the evolution of God's Reign. Patience with oneself, patience with one's fellow human beings, and patience with God make angry improvers of the world into effective reformers and visionary teachers of truth and justice.

TWO: Care, Compassion, Solidarity

The name "Jesus" means "Yahweh helps" or "Yahweh saves." We are all familiar with the pictures of the Savior that show him seeing and relieving the physical and spiritual suffering of people — when as shepherd he seeks out the lost sheep, when he embraces and blesses the children. It is no coincidence that one could take Jesus to be a TWO. Jesus considered himself to be a servant of humankind and said: "I have come not to be served, but to serve" (Matt. 20:28). His death on the cross is the last act of his mission.

In the story of the healing of the ten lepers (Luke 17:11–18) we experience his disappointment that of the ten who were healed only one, and a Samaritan to boot, returned to give thanks. Even Jesus expected thanks. But he is capable of directly expressing his disappointment, and that seems to settle the issue.

Despite his caring and solidarity, Jesus was no "helpless helper." It is obvious that the main motive of his giving was compassion and friendship and not the hidden need to manipulate others or to "buy" God's love and human recognition.

Jesus perceived and lived his own needs. After he had been with people for some time, he withdrew by himself to collect fresh energy through dialogue with God. Before he washed the feet of his disciples (John 13:1–20), he allowed a woman to anoint his feet with expensive perfume and to wipe them with her hair (John 12:1–8). In this passage he harshly rejected the TWO argument that the perfume could have been sold and the money given to the poor.

In the garden of Gethsemane, he expected his disciples to watch with him and to share the burden of his spiritual struggles. He shared his fears with them and was sad that they took refuge in sleep when he needed them most.

Jesus could let go. People who prematurely and overzealously wanted to attach themselves to him were sent back home. After only three years of life together, he trusted his disciples to continue the work without his physical presence.

The invitation to the TWO is the call to freedom. It is the freedom to commit oneself and to liberate others, the freedom to help and to let oneself be helped, the freedom to be alone and to be in the company of others. TWOs find in Jesus the model of a person who loves without losing freedom and without abusing the freedom of others.

THREE: Ambition, Energy, Vision

Jesus wanted to achieve something. He had the vision of the Reign of God and he did his utmost to preach and pursue this vision at the risk of losing his life. He accepted the role of Savior that God intended for him and identified himself with it. With his "maiden sermon" in the synagogue of his home city of Nazareth he made a ringing presentation of his program. He cited a passage from the book of Isaiah: "The spirit of the Lord is upon me, because he has anointed me to preach good news to the poor. He has sent me to proclaim release to the captives and recovering of sight to the blind, to set at liberty those who are oppressed, to proclaim the acceptable year of the Lord." Then he began his sermon with the statement: "Today this scripture has been fulfilled in your hearing" (Luke 4:16–21). The Sermon on the Mount (Matt. 5–7) can be understood as the Magna Carta of the Reign of God.

Because Jesus was completely focussed on his role and mission, he was threatened at this point by the greatest temptation, the only temptation of Jesus of which the Gospels speak directly. After forty days of fasting in the desert the "tempter" challenges him to make bread from stone to ease his hunger. Jesus answers him with the words: "Be gone, Satan! You shall worship the Lord your God and him only shall you serve!" (Matt. 4:1–11). When the people want to make Jesus king after his miracle of the multiplication of the loaves of bread, he retreats from them. That is not his way. Jesus withstood the temptation of the THREE: to seek success without frustration and disappointment, the miracle as cheap public relations show, triumph without the cross, life without death. That's why he calls Peter "Satan" for not accepting the fact that the way of his master leads to the cross (Mark 8:33).

Jesus had leadership qualities. He sought out his fellow campaigners and enabled them to act responsibly for themselves. He delegated his activity as a preacher and healer to his disciples while he was still alive; and through his teaching and his example, he provided them with the "know-how" of the Reign of God that they would need later to carry on his work. Jesus certainly did not leave them in doubt that they would one day share his fate: rejection, arrest, murder. Jesus put his cards on the table and made no promises that wouldn't be fulfilled later.

His powers of communication were amazing. He could reach the masses, and in every situation he found the right words to bring his message to the people. He could hold discussions with scholars and move the hearts of simple, uneducated country people.

Jesus was not indifferent to failure. After the entry into Jerusalem he weeps over the city that did not realize what makes for peace (Luke 19:41–42). He accuses the city: "Jerusalem, Jerusalem. . . . How often would I have gathered your children together as a hen gathers her brood under her wing; but you did not want it!" (Matt. 23:37).

And yet Jesus knew that the victory he sought to achieve was a victory won consistently through the paradox of defeat. He chose a path that appeared to be a failure. He was able to do this only because his hope in his Father, who can create life from death, was greater than his fear of failure. Only this hope can prevent THREEs from resting on their laurels and clinging to the "security" of status and money, thereby missing the much greater possibilities of the Reign of God.

FOUR: Creativity, Sensitivity, Simplicity

Jesus was sensitive to his environment and had a rich emotional life. He could be "sky high" (his cry of joy in Matt. 11:25–27) and be deeply depressed: He wept, trembled, shook, and sweated blood and water when in the Garden of Gethsemane he prepared for his final battle (Matt. 26:36–46). The Gospels tell of his crying several times. When he heard of the death of his friend Lazarus, "he began to weep" (John 11:34). The desperate situation of his people moved him to have compassion for them (Matt. 9:36; 15:32). He admitted this sadness and was not ashamed of his tears.

Jesus had an eye for beauty in nature. Flora and fauna inspired him: the lilies of the field, which are arrayed more splendidly than Solomon (Matt. 6:28–29) or the sparrow that doesn't fall to the ground without the will of God (Matt. 10:29).

Nor can we deny that Jesus had a special feeling for symbols and dramatic effects. The water in the well, the housewife's search for a lost coin, day laborers arguing about their pay — everything that Jesus sees inspires him to create images and parables, which catch onto simple and incidental things in order to illustrate universally valid divine mysteries and truths. Everything can become part of God's code. The Gospel of John understands Jesus' miracles as "signs" that point beyond Christ himself. Some gestures, such as when Jesus anoints the eyes of a man blind from birth with a salve of spittle and clay, have a particularly dramatic effect (John 9:6). When Jesus enters the holy city of Jerusalem on an ass, even this apparently accidental scene has the effect of a carefully thought-out plan (Matt. 21:1–9). Every Jew knew about the promise of the messianic king who was to arrive one day riding an ass (Zech. 9:9) and would have immediately realized the connection between this "entrance" and the scriptures. Shortly thereafter Jesus made a fig tree wither because he found no fruit on it (Matt. 21:18–22). This is reminiscent of the symbolic acts performed by the prophets of the Hebrew Bible. At the Last Supper with his disciples, Jesus finally connects his "mystical" future presence with the bread and wine. After the resurrection, Jesus waits for the disciples at the Sea of Tiberias. On the shore he has arranged a breakfast; a charcoal fire burns — just as on the night when Peter had denied Jesus by the side of a charcoal fire. At this fire, Jesus asks the disciples a question three times: "Do you love me?" (John 21:1–17). The scene strikes us as an anticipation of the modern psychological technique of psychodrama.

Despite all the dramatic effects, Jesus' way of living and speaking was unaffected and natural. Like all FOURs, he didn't allow the world to be divided into "sacred" and "profane" realms. For him the whole world was holy and belonged to God. The holiest thing in the world was for him the most natural too.

The calling of Jesus' inner circle at first gives the impression that he was interested in assembling an elite or esoteric group around himself (the elite consciousness of the FOUR!). But on closer inspection it seems that this was far from his purpose. The gathering of the disciples lacks all the elitist criteria. The disciples were mostly simple fishermen; there were no "special" people. When the disciples are fighting over their position, Jesus calls a child to come to him, and says, "Whoever humbles himself like this child, he is the greatest in the kingdom of heaven" (Matt. 18:4).

In spite of being rejected by his family, his village, and the powerful elite of Israel, in spite of the fact that even his own disciples do not understand him, Jesus does not fall into melancholy self-pity. Despite all his fears of failure he doesn't leave the path he has to follow. He puts his subjective fears and needs at the service of God and of people and thus raises them into the realm of universal validity.

FIVE: Distance, Sobriety, Wisdom

Jesus was able to distance himself like a FIVE, to withdraw, to claim undisturbed space for himself, and to repel the invading demands of his family and his surroundings.

The story of the visit of the twelve-year-old Jesus to the temple portrays the boy as a talented and precociously independent scholar of the scriptures. His parents take him for the first time to the feast of Passover in Jerusalem. On the way home they realize that their son is missing. They return and, after three days of looking for him, they find him in the temple, where he is sitting "among the teachers," listening, asking questions, and astounding everyone with his intelligence. He has no sympathy for his mother's protests: "Why were you looking for me?" he asks. "Did you not know I must be in my Father's house?" The evangelist Luke frames this story by twice mentioning the extraordinary wisdom of Jesus as a child (Luke 2:40–52).

He cut himself off even more frequently from demands made by his family. While Jesus is preaching one day to the people, his mother and his brothers let him know that they are there and wish to speak with him. He turns them away: "Who is my mother, and who are my brothers?" and stretches his hand toward his disciples: "Here are my mother and my brothers! For whoever does the will of my Father in heaven is my brother, and sister, and mother" (Matt. 12: 46–50).

Jesus turned people away and sent them home when they wanted to cling to him with fanatical enthusiasm (e.g., Luke 9:57–62). He demands of all who would follow him that they calmly consider the "costs" of this undertaking: "For which of you, desiring to build a tower, does not first sit down and count the cost, whether he has enough to complete it? Otherwise, it can happen that the foundation has been laid, but the building cannot be completed" (Luke 14: 25–30). In the Sermon on the Mount he admonishes his disciples to be "wise" and not build their lives on sand, but rather on solid rock, so that it can withstand catastrophe (Matt. 7:24–29).

The teaching of Jesus was carefully thought out — and lived out. He was able to captivate people, because they felt that he knew what he was talking about. At the end of the Sermon on the Mount, Matthew reports: "And when Jesus finished these sayings, the crowds were astonished at his teaching, for he taught them as one who had authority, and not as their scribes" (Matt. 7:28–29).

Again and again, Jesus retreated into silence to put his thoughts in order and to find his center through prayer. This retreat was not an end in itself. It served to restore and prepare him for his active work for people. Jesus did not give in to the temptation to remain an indifferent spectator or observer of the world. The Christian teaching of the incarnation of God in Christ reveals a God who seeks close contact with people and lets himself be drawn into the dirt and the "low points" of history. The "word" does not remain word, thought, philosophical explanation of the world or metaphysical idea, but becomes "flesh" and world-changing act.

Christ is no esoteric thinker! He renounces intellectual arrogance and does not refuse to share his understanding with others. In his farewell talk he promises his disciples that he will send his spirit, which will "lead them to all the truth" (John 16:13).

SIX: Fidelity, Obedience, Trust

Jesus had "inner authority," which grew out of the trusting relationship to his heavenly father. This inner authority freed him from outer authorities and norms: He had the freedom to obey laws, rules, and traditions, as long as they weren't taken to be "the real thing." Thus he regularly attended the religious services in the synagogue (Luke 4:16). But he could also reject the rules when they enslaved people instead of serving them. This is particularly apparent with his treatment of the Sabbath. He especially liked to heal the sick on the Jewish holy day of rest, in order to show that the Sabbath was established by God so that creation could regenerate and recover. His healings served this purpose and are signs that God wants to reestablish the original wholeness: "The Sabbath is there for the people, not the people for the Sabbath" (Mark 2:27).

While Jesus argued with the religious leaders about the correct interpretation of the law, he had little use for worldly power structures. He calls King Herod a "fox" (Luke 13:32). When they try to entrap him with the question of whether to pay taxes, he answers enigmatically: He asks for a coin with the likeness of Caesar on it, and says: "Render to Caesar the things that are Caesar's, and to God the things that are God's" (Mark 12:17). This passage, which is so often misused to legitimize the subjection of Christians, in reality contains a great relativization of the authority of the state. The coin that bears the image of Caesar may belong to Caesar. But the person who bears and is the image of God belongs to God, as his opponents understood very well. Jesus' position on the question of taxes leads to one of the accusations at his trial: "He forbids to pay taxes to Caesar" (Luke 23:2).

Jesus was obedient in the strict sense of the word only to God and to his own calling. In the letter to the Philippians Paul interprets the life of Jesus as an act of obedience as he echoes a hymn to Christ from the early Christian community: "He was in the form of God, but he did not count equality with God a thing to be grasped, but emptied himself, taking the form of a servant, being born in the likeness of men. And being found in human form he humbled himself and became obedient unto death, even death on a cross" (Phil. 2:6–8).

Again and again Jesus invited people to overcome their fear and to trust in God: "Do not fear, only believe" (Mark 5:36) or "In the world you have fear; but be of good cheer, I have overcome the world" (John 16:33). He overcame his own fear of death with the trust that while God's way may seem incomprehensible, it will nevertheless prove to be right and good: "Abba, Father, all things are possible for thee. Take this cup from me. Yet not what I will, but what thou wilt, shall come to pass" (Mark 14:36).

Jesus did not want any hierarchy in the circle of his disciples: "You know that the rulers of the Gentiles lord it over them, and their great men exercise authority over them. It shall not be so among you; but whoever would be great among you must be your servant, and whoever would be first among you must be your slave" (Matt. 20:25–27). It is almost incomprehensible that the Church that was to follow Jesus Christ has, over the course of history, placed so much value on power, hierarchy, and norms. Church leaders cannot invoke their founder on this point.

SEVEN: Festivity, Light-heartedness, Pain

Jesus was no child of sadness; he was also no ascetic. His movement differed from John the Baptist's circle of disciples in that, among other things, the followers of Jesus did not fast. When John's disciples ask him about this, he says: "Can the wedding guests mourn so long as the bridegroom is with them?" (Matt. 9:15). His message about the coming Reign of God is good news. He prefers to describe this Reign using the image of a wedding celebration.

The enjoyment of life's pleasures that Jesus and his disciples exhibited were so conspicuous that he was accused of being a "glutton and a drunkard" (Matt. 11:19). In fact he did enjoy being invited to dinner, and it made no difference to him whether the invitation came from law-abiding Pharisees, a leper, or a politically suspect tax-collector.

At the wedding in Cana (John 2:1–11) he supplied the guests at the celebration with a tremendous amount of wine (about six hundred liters!). The story of the miracle of the loaves of bread (e.g., John 6:1–15) shows that Jesus cared about the physical as well as the spiritual well-being of others.

The message of Jesus can be summed up in one sentence: God wants people to rejoice. Even at his birth, the angel tells the shepherds of "great joy which will come to all people" (Luke 2:10). In his farewell discourse he tells them that their "sorrow will turn into joy" and their "joy will be full" (John 16:20; 15:11).

But Jesus also warns against a false and superficial joy. In the original version of the Beatitudes found in the Sermon in the Field in the Gospel of Luke, there are four "woe" phrases: "Woe to you who are rich, for you will have no more consolation. Woe to you that are full now, for you shall hunger. Woe to you that laugh now, for you shall mourn and weep. Woe to you, when all men speak well of you, for so their fathers did to the false prophets" (Luke 6: 24–26). It is clear what kind of light-heartedness is being condemned here: boundless pleasure at the cost of the poor. It is the guilt that we rich Christians in the West bear with respect to the "poor Lazarus" at the fringes of our society and in the Third World. The joy that Jesus promises goes through the eye of the needle of giving and brotherly-sisterly sharing.

The joy of Easter meant for the world is impossible without the cross. Christ's death on the cross is no "representative suffering" in the sense that we are now free from crosses and suffering and can directly enter heaven, bypassing fear, pain, and failure. The Greek Orthodox theologian Kallistos Ware aptly says that "Jesus does not show us a path around life, but rather all the way through life, which means not substitution for our suffering but saving leadership."[9]

Matthew reports that shortly before his death Jesus refused to drink the narcotic used at that time, a mixture of gall and wine. He suffered physical and spiritual pain and at the end endured the deep pain of distance from God: "My God, why have you forsaken me? (Matt. 27:34, 46). This low point that Jesus lived and suffered through is the gateway to Easter joy.

EIGHT: Confrontation, Clarity, Authority

Jesus knew what he wanted. He defended his position without compromise and steadfastly bore the consequences of his words and actions. He never beat around the bush. He asked his disciples, "Let what you say be simply 'Yes' or 'No' " (Matt. 5:37), and he practiced the same himself. Paul put it this way: "The Son of God was not Yes and No together" (2 Cor. 1:19).

The decisiveness of Jesus was very threatening to the ruling class. The people felt his inner authority; above all the simple people, who suffered most under the social and religious injustices, followed him in the greatest crowds. Again and again people tried to lure Jesus into traps with trick questions. He usually turned the tables in such situations so that the hypocritical questioner was the one who was unmasked and disgraced in the end.

Jesus conceded nothing to his opponents and confronted them, in the tradition of the prophets, with the uncompromising demands of God. Shortly before his arrest, his provocative actions reach a critical point. He rides like the promised messiah into Jerusalem on an ass. He brandishes a whip in the temple, driving the money-changers out of the house of God, and releases the sacrificial doves. He tells a series of parables that affront the leaders of Israel. He makes statements such as: "Tax-collectors and prostitutes go into the kingdom of God before you" or "The kingdom of God will be taken away from you and given to a nation producing the fruits of it." Of the scribes and Pharisees he said, "They do all their deeds to be seen by men"; "You hypocrites! You shut the kingdom of heaven against other men. You yourselves will not enter, nor will you allow those who would enter to go in"; "Woe to you, you are blind leading the blind" (Matt. 21–23). No wonder Jesus was arrested. The picture of the soft and "sweet" Savior Jesus is in any case one-sided. He could be very sharp in both word and deed.

Is there a contradiction in the Sermon on the Mount, then, when

Jesus seems to call us to passivity and to nonresistance of evil? He asks his listeners to turn the left cheek if someone strikes them on the right; to go a second mile, if they are forced by a soldier in the army of occupation to carry his pack one mile; to give a person their shirt, if that person sues them for their coat (Matt. 5: 39–41). Walter Wink has pointed out that these requests are not concerned with passivity but rather with the most subversive form of nonviolent resistance. Wink compares them with the activities developed by the American civil rights activist Saul Alinsky. Through such surprising behavior, the "victim" prevents the perpetrator from determining the standard of behavior, wins back his or her own dignity, and offers the perpetrator the chance to change voluntarily without losing face. Jesus himself didn't quietly "turn the other cheek" when he was struck during his trial (John 18:23).[10] In the Sermon on the Mount he praises those "blessed ones" who "hunger and thirst for justice" (Matt. 5:6).

Jesus stands on the side of the weak and takes up their cause. He may treat the rulers roughly, but he is tender with the weak and those in need of help (see the blessing of children in Mark 10, and the "adulteress" in John 8).

Jesus was strong but not invulnerable. He resisted the temptation to use the power that was available to him. He did not bid "legions of angels" (Matt. 26:53) to come to his aid. His Church was often struck down by the temptation of violence, power politics, and militarism. Jesus, however, chose the power of powerlessness, in order to unmask the powerlessness of power: "He disarmed the principalities and powers and made a public example of them, triumphing over them in him" (Col. 2:15). EIGHTs like Martin Luther King, Jr., followed his example to the final consequence.

NINE: Composure, Peaceableness, Love

Despite his untiring creative power, Jesus radiated calm and peace. In his "Savior's call" he calls upon the people: "Come to me, all who labor and are heavily burdened. I will give you rest. Take up my yoke and learn from me. For I am meek and humble of heart. And you will find rest for your soul. For my yoke is easy, and my burden is light" (Matt. 11:28–30). In the most difficult situations Jesus was calmness itself. In the middle of a storm he lay on a cushion in the bow of the fishing boat and slept. This calmness is an expression of a deep inner peace and of his trust in God. When his disciples are alarmed and frightened, he tells them they are "of little faith" (Mark 4:35–41).

Even in the Hebrew Bible sleep is seen as a gift of God: "I lie down and sleep in peace, for thou alone, O Lord, makest me dwell in safety" prays a psalmist (Ps. 4:9); "he gives to his beloved sleep, " says another (Ps. 127:2).

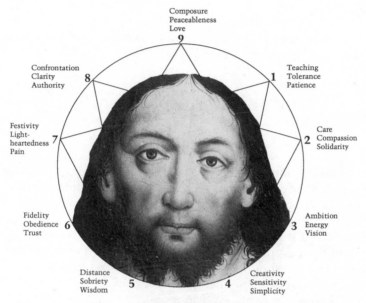

Composure
Peaceableness
Love
9

Confrontation
Clarity   **8**
Authority

Teaching
1 Tolerance
Patience

Festivity
Light-   **7**
heartedness
Pain

Care
2 Compassion
Solidarity

Fidelity
Obedience **6**
Trust

Ambition
3 Energy
Vision

Distance
Sobriety   **5**
Wisdom

Creativity
4 Sensitivity
Simplicity

Figure 20: The Christ-Enneagram

But the other side of sleep is also well known: Sleep is branded in the Bible as a sign of indifference or as a place of hiding, where people can avoid decisions and responsibility. In Gethsemane the disciples escape into sleep, because they don't feel up to the conflict (Matt. 26:40–45). "Watch and pray, so that you do not enter into temptation," Jesus tells them. This idea is similarly expressed later in the letter to the Ephesians: "Awake, O sleeper, and arise from the dead, and Christ will give you light" (Eph. 5:14). For Jesus peace was anything but idleness. Love activated him. He was decisive and conscious of his goal. Jesus was passive only insofar as he always passed on what he had already received from his Father.

His love did not judge and excluded no one. In this respect Jesus was a good NINE. His life work was the reconciliation of people with God and the reconciliation of people with each other. Paul discusses the matter: "God reconciled us to himself through Christ and gave us the ministry of reconciliation. . . . So we are ambassadors for Christ . . . and on his behalf we beseech you: be reconciled to God" (2 Cor. 5:18–20);

"Christ made peace and reconciled both (Jews and non-Jews) to God in one body through the cross, thereby bringing hostility to an end. And he came and preached peace to those who were far from God, and to those who were near to God" (Eph. 2:15–17).

NINEs love community and need it in order to be motivated and inspired. Christ lived community and expected his disciples to become active. Every person was dear to him; he even noticed the NINEs, who are otherwise so easily overlooked.

THE ENNEAGRAM AND PRAYER

Three Kinds of Prayer

In all world religions there are three basic types of prayer and meditation: (1) *From the outside in:* Something from the outside reaches me — a picture, a symbol, a text. Something happens in me because of this impulse that I accept into myself. (2) *From the inside out:* I sit down and let whatever is within me arise. I let my inner moods and images develop and then express them, for example, through words or painting. (3) *Emptiness:* The third way is the way of the Void, which involves letting the outer and inner impulses go, in order to get to complete stillness. The "object-less" way of Zen belongs here too.

These three ways can be correlated to the three centers of the Enneagram.[11] *Heart types* want to express themselves from the inside out. *Gut types* seek emptiness. *Head types* seek input from outside. The "natural" approach to meditation and prayer is determined by the center that has primary control. Therefore it makes sense to begin with what seems easy to me.

Of course, this can become a pitfall in the long run. Heart types who only express themselves must, on their way to integration and redemption, leave this realm and allow themselves to enter other realms that are further away from them (for example, forms of meditation that help them to recollect and reflect upon themselves). For growth, we all need to move beyond our own natural space, eventually incorporating the challenges of the other two styles.

The Enneagram's Our Father

J. G. Bennett, a follower of Gurdjieff, has coordinated the Our Father with the dynamic of the Enneagram.[12] This appears at first glance to be arbitrary game-playing. But it's amazing how accurately the elements of this prayer correspond to the particular types.

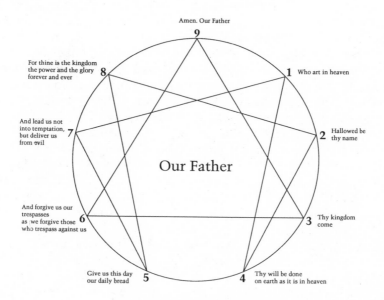

Figure 21: The Our Father

NINE: *Our Father*. Point NINE is the beginning and end-point of the Enneagram, and it represents the sum of all the types. God, the Father of all people, is the creator and purpose of the universe. Biblical hope proceeds from the belief that God will be "everything to every one" at the end of time (1 Cor. 15:28). God is not only "my" father, but the father "of us all." Just as NINEs put themselves in perspective and recognize themselves as a part of the whole, so we cannot imperialistically claim God for our own or pocket God for our own purposes. We must rather "share" God with everyone and everything.

ONE: *Who art in heaven*. Heaven is symbolic of the perfection and completion that has not yet been achieved. At the same time it is — according to the teaching of Jesus — "in the midst of us" or "in us" (Luke 17:21; both translations are possible). Jesus describes the "kingdom of heaven" as something that continually grows toward its completion.

TWO: *Hallowed be thy name*. TWOs tends to use their "good deeds" to make a name for themselves and to establish themselves in the name of God (saint and martyr complex). This request in the Our Father reminds TWOs critically to examine their motives again and again and not to abuse the name of God (cf. the second commandment: "Thou shalt not take the name of the Lord your God in vain").

THREE: *Thy kingdom come*. THREEs are overly concerned with building their own kingdom and seeking their own fame. The request for the kingdom of God puts all human kingdoms in their place and releases us from the law of "production." It points out further that this kingdom is an event and a gift that comes to us and can be neither forced nor manipulated. Keeping the Sabbath holy (third commandment) reminds the THREE that the meaning of life does not consist in action alone.

FOUR: *Thy will be done*. FOURs are enticed by their subjectivism into making elitist demands and going their own way. The recommitment to the will of God helps FOURs to put their uniqueness and narcissistic demands in their place and to subject them to a higher will.

FIVE: *Give us this day our daily bread*. This request has to do with receiving today what we need today. In the Old Testament story of Israel's wandering through the wilderness, God fed the people daily with manna. The food spoiled if one tried to keep it overnight (Exod. 16). This request protects FIVEs from their impulse to hoard whatever they take to be vitally important. Anyone who prays in this way trusts in God's daily care and lets go of the need to collect securities.

SIX: *And forgive us our trespasses, as we forgive those who trespass against us.* SIXes tend to be law-abiding and to make themselves and other lawbreakers pay. Forgiveness means freedom from the compulsion of the law: "Christ is the end of the law" (Rom. 10:4). This request points out that forgiveness is not a one-way street. Reconciliation with God and reconciliation with other people are inextricably linked with one another.

SEVEN: *And lead us not into temptation, but deliver us from evil.* SEVENs, more than all other types, are endangered by immediate sensual temptations. They tend to cover up the experience of pain and evil with pleasure and optimism. This request in the Our Father invites SEVENs to leave the deliverance from evil to God, instead of constantly seeking their own illusory deliverances.

EIGHT: *For thine is the kingdom and the power and the glory forever and ever.* "Strength," "power," and "glory" are themes of life for EIGHTs. The last phrase of the Our Father relativizes the false self-confidence that one stands alone, relying on one's own strength, power, and glory. Thus it invites powerful and unbending EIGHTs to bend before One more powerful and to understand their own strengths as "on temporary loan."

NINE: *Amen* (So be it!). With the Amen, we return to the beginning. The circle is complete, the cycle is repeated. The old custom of repeating the Our Father several times intuitively grasped this dynamic and put it into practice.

Finally, the Kabbala says that there are ten attributes of God. Without much effort it is possible to recognize the nine Enneagram reflections of the "face of God." The first attribute is the "wholeness and yet nothingness of God" which is the entire circle and all its truths. From there we could reasonably plot the attributes as producing these qualities in people:

> The Wisdom of God produces "Pathfinders" (ONEs)
> The Understanding of God produces "Partners" (TWOs)
> The Love of God produces "Motivators" (THREEs)
> The Beauty of God produces "Potentiators" (FOURs)
> The Foundation of God produces "Explainers" (FIVEs)
> The Endurance of God produces "Stabilizers" (SIXes)
> The Majesty of God produces "Celebrators" (SEVENs)
> The Power of God produces "Revolutionaries" (EIGHTs)
> The Presence of God produces "Reconcilers" (NINEs)

The End of Determinism

The Enneagram tells it "like it is." As a "mirror for the confessional," it makes us aware of blocks and abysses that enslave us. All religions sense the human need for enslavement and redemption. Hinduism and Buddhism speak of *karma*, which must be worked out as many reincarnations run their course until we can finally enter the condition of having no desires or passions (*nirvana*). Even atheistic Marxism proceeds from the economically caused alienation of people, which is to be overcome in the course of history, so that in the end there will be paradise on earth, the "classless society." Christianity calls the unredeemed condition the "dominion of the law."

Paul describes people "under the law":

I do not understand my own actions. For I do not do what I want, but I do the very thing I hate. I can will what is right, but I cannot do it. So I find it to be a law that when I want to do right, evil lies close at hand. For I delight in the law of God, in my inmost self, but I see in my members another law at war with the law of my mind and making me captive to the law of sin which dwells in my members. (Rom. 7:15–23)

At the end Paul (representing all of us) moans: "Wretched man that I am! Who will deliver me . . . ?"

The New Testament tells us that God took on this dilemma. In Jesus Christ God ventured "under the law" and was laid open to the compulsions, temptations and penalties of this law, " . . . in order to redeem those who were under the law" (Gal 4:4).

Christ is the prototype of the new, free person. "Faith" in him, a living, personal, and trusting relation of friendship, leads us out of the compulsions of the inflexible law. We can honestly look at our failures and defense mechanisms and then surrender step by step because the death and resurrection of Christ tells us: "The war is over! You can throw your weapons on the scrap heap! God is not your enemy, but your friend. You no longer need all of these safety devices."

If we trust Christ, we no longer need to understand ourselves solely as slaves of the law, as products of our parents, as victims of our circumstances, and as determined cogs in the machinery of the world. All of that is true in a sense, of course, but it's not the final truth. We are no longer slaves, we are free: sons and daughters of God. As children of God we can call God "Father" (Jesus affectionately said Abba, which is about the same as "Papa" or "Daddy"), without having to be afraid that this father figure will belittle us, browbeat us, punish us, or confine us. "Because you are now children of God, God has sent the spirit of his son into our hearts, crying, 'Abba! Father!' " (Gal. 4:5).

In the Gospel of John, the story is told how a Pharisee comes to talk to Jesus one night:

> Now there was a man of the Pharisees, named Nicodemus, a ruler of the Jews. This man came to Jesus by night and said to him, "Rabbi, we know that you are a teacher come from God; for no one can do these signs that you do, unless God is with him." Jesus answered him. "Truly, truly, I say to you, unless one is born anew, he cannot see the kingdom of God." Nicodemus said to him, "How can a man be born when he is old? Can he enter a second time into his mother's womb and be born?" Jesus answered, "Truly, truly, I say to you, unless one is born of water and the Spirit, he cannot enter the kingdom of God. That which is born of the flesh is flesh, and that which is born of the Spirit is spirit. Do not marvel that I said to you, 'You must be born anew.' The wind blows where it wills, and you hear the sound of it, but you do not know whence it comes or whither it goes; so it is with every one who is born of the Spirit." (John 3:1–8)

Nicodemus is on a search. He is a representative of the religious and public law, a Pharisee and a councilor. Apparently he is no longer satisfied with fulfilling laws and norms. His secret longing for more brings him "by night" to Jesus. He begins by giving the master compliments ("we know ... "), with which most of his colleagues certainly would not have agreed. But Jesus gets right to the point. He shows the way out of the prison of the law into freedom, and he calls the way "new birth" or "birth from above," as it can also be translated. He does not take this new birth in the literal sense as reincarnation (return to one's mother's womb), but as the work of the Spirit, which is possible at any time. Baptism with water is the outer sign that the "old person" has died; the experience of the Spirit is the inner confirmation and empowerment of the new, liberated person.

Jesus compares the life of this new person with the blowing of the wind. The direction of the wind can be determined only vaguely and for a short time; then it can suddenly change: "You do not know whence it comes and whither it goes." So long as we are under the rule of the law, we ourselves as well as others know, rather quickly, "which way the wind is blowing with us." We live like machines (Gurdjieff) and follow compulsions and programs that we have been chained to and to which we have chained ourselves. Those who are filled with the Spirit, on the contrary, are ready for surprises. They can find that they are capable of things that were not "sung to them when they were in the cradle."

Those who are filled with the spirit also remain children of the forces that have shaped them. The new and the old person stand in a continuum. Renewal is a life-long process that has moments of stagnation and regression. Luther said that a person is always both a sinner and a just person (*simul justus et peccator*). But the old laws no longer rule my identity. My "true self" is free: "Now the Lord is the Spirit, and where the Spirit of the Lord is, there is freedom" (2 Cor. 3:17).

The Enneagram too is part of the realm that the Bible calls "law." It conceals what is. It is not freedom itself but it can become a signpost, once we have the goal itself before our eyes, the goal that is described in many images and colors in the Bible: as the city of God, as a gorgeous celebration, as the harvest of life.

Notes

Preface: A Mirror of the Soul

1. See Richard Rohr, *The Enneagram: Naming Our Illusions* (six audio cassettes), Credence Cassettes, P.O. Box 419491, Kansas City, MO 64141.
2. Teresa of Avila, *The Interior Castle*, trans. Kieran Kavanaugh and Otilio Rodriguez (New York, 1979), p. 36.
3. By "baptism" I mean that someone or something is released from its original context, is oriented to Christ, and placed at his service. Christianity does not have its own language. All attempts to create one lead to that dreadful and often caricatured "language of Canaan," which outsiders find repugnant. Christianity does not have its own "material." A picture does not, for example, become "Christian" by the painter's using different colors, but rather by what he *represents* with these colors. So too many scientific findings or religious experiences are not "in themselves" Christian or un-Christian; they become so through the way we handle them.
4. Ole Hallesby, *Dein Typ ist gefragt: Unsere Veranlagungen und was wir daraus machen können* (Wuppertal, 1986).

PART I: THE SLEEPING GIANT

1. Bibliography (a selection): Ernst Kretschmer, *Physique and Character: An Investigation of the Nature of the Constitution and of the Theory of Temperament*, trans. W. A. Sprott (New York, 1970); Carl Gustav Jung, *Psychological Types*, Collected Works, vol. 6 (Princeton, 1970); Isabel Briggs Myers, *Introduction to Type* (Gainsville, 1976); also *Gifts Differing* (Palo Alto, 1980); Karen Horney, *Our Inner Conflicts* (New York, 1966); also, *Neurosis and Human Growth* (New York, 1970); also, *The Neurotic Personality of Our Time* (New York, 1964); Fritz Riemann, *Grundformen der Angst*, 14th ed. (Munich, 1979). Axel Denecke has linked Horney with Riemann and investigated how, in the case of women ministers, being a certain type influences the way one preaches: *Persönlich predigen* (Gütersloh, 1979), pp. 62–67.
2. See Idries Shah, *The Sufis* (Garden City, N.Y., 1964), pp. 286ff.
3. Annemarie Schimmel, *Gärten der Erkenntnis: Das Buch der vierzig Sufi-Meister* (Düsseldorf and Cologne, 1982), p. 21.
4. The standard work on the Sufis is Annemarie Schimmel, *Mystical Dimensions of Islam* (Chapel Hill, N.C., 1975). For an introduction: Idries Shah, *The Sufis*.

5. Quoted in P. D. Ouspensky, *In Search of the Miraculous* (New York, 1949), p. 294.

6. For a description of the method of Oscar Ichazo, see Sam Keen, "Oscar Ichazo and the Arica Institute," *Psychology Today*, July 1973, 66–72.

7. *Andreas Ebert:* During my sabbatical year in Munich, when I joined a (Catholic) church choir and introduced myself as a theologian to the choir director, his first reaction was: "I've had bad experiences with theologians. People who are so concerned with their piety usually have no time left to care about developing a normal, decent character." This "greeting" struck me greatly and gave me pause.

8. See Christian Wulf, "Lebensentscheidung — Entscheidung zum Leben: Exerzitien des Ignatius als Herausforderung und Weg," in *Korrespondenz zur Spiritualität der Exerzitien*, nr. 53, 38, 1988, pp. 84ff.

9. Dietrich Bonhoeffer, the theologian and resistance fighter against Hitler, wrote the poem "Who am I?" in his prison cell in Tegel in 1944. He was concerned with the question: Am I more the person whom others see in me, "calm, cheerful and firm," "free and friendly and clear," "equable, smiling and proud" — or am I that person whom I experience when I am alone, "restless, longing, sick, like a bird in a cage, struggling for breath . . . yearning for colors, for flowers, for the voices of birds, thirsting for words of kindness, for neighborliness, trembling . . . , fearful . . . , tired and empty . . . ?" At the end he comes to the conclusion that neither others nor he himself can define his identity, but only God: "Who am I? They mock me, these lonely questions. Whoever I am, thou knowest, O God, I am thine" (Dietrich Bonhoeffer, *Letters and Papers from Prison* [New York, 1971], p. 347).

10. See Richard Rohr, *Letting Go: A Spirituality of Subtraction* (eight audio cassettes), St. Anthony Messenger Press, 1615 Republic Street, Cincinnati, OH 45210).

11. See Richard Rohr, *Breathing Under Water: Spirituality and the Twelve Steps* (two audio cassettes), St. Anthony Messenger Press, Cincinnati.

12. Etty Hillesum, *An Interrupted Life* (New York, 1982), p. 48.

13. The American pastoral theologian Donald Capps linked the traditional Catholic teaching of the seven deadly sins with the psychological development theory of Erik Erikson and came to the conclusion that in every stage of development in a person a specific mistaken attitude or block can set in. Conversely, in every stage a very specific "virtue" can also develop (Donald Capps, *Deadly Sins and Saving Virtues* [Philadelphia, 1987]).

14. For the seven gifts of the spirit see Jürg Splett, *Zur Antwort berufen* (Frankfurt/Main, 1984), pp. 94–110. Splett coordinates (with Bonaventure) the seven traditional gifts of the spirit with the seven deadly sins, which results in the seven traditional virtues. Each petition of the Our Father serves this process. Moreover one of the Beatitudes of Jesus from Matthew 5 is coordinated with each group. Thus the following seven series of five arise: fear of God, pride, temperance, hallowed be thy name, poverty; piety, envy, justice, thy kingdom come, meekness; knowledge, anger, prudence, thy will be done, mourning; strength, laziness,

fortitude, our daily bread, hunger and thirst; counsel, greed, hope, forgive us our sins, compassion; insight, intemperance, faith, lead us not into temptation, purity in spirit; wisdom, unchastity, love, deliver us from evil, peacemaking.

15. This very strongly reflects the teaching of the medieval Church. At the same time, however, in Chaucer's *Canterbury Tales* there are clear reminiscences of Sufi texts, above all of the Parliament of the Birds by the Sufi Master Attar. See the synopsis of the Parson's Tale in Geoffrey Chaucer, *The Canterbury Tales* (Harmondsworth, 1977), pp. 505–6; Idries Shah, *The Sufis*, p. 104.

16. Karen Horney, *Unsere Inneren Konflikte* (Frankfurt/Main, 1984), p. 15 (ET: *Our Inner Conflicts* [New York, 1966]). In her book *Neurosis and Human Growth* (New York, 1970), especially pp. 187–290, she speaks of "expansive solutions" (gut), "self-effacement as solution" (heart), and "resignation" (head).

17. See Palmer, p. 48.

18. The expositions of the three centers are based in part on an unpublished manuscript (December 1988) by Hildegard Ehrtmann, used with the kind permission of the author.

19. Dietrich Bonhoeffer, *Life Together*, trans. John Doberstein (New York, 1954), p. 77.

20. See Dietrich Bonhoeffer's poem "Who am I," in note 9 above. Bonhoeffer was a "head person."

21. *Life Together*, p. 78.

PART II: THE NINE TYPES

Type ONE

1. Parts of the "Overview" are based on unpublished materials from the Institute for Spiritual Leadership (Chicago, 1984) in the treatment by Hildegard Ehrtmann (1987).

2. Alice Miller, *The Drama of the Gifted Child* (New York, 1981).

3. See Riso, p. 326.

4. Palmer, p. 91.

5. *Andreas Ebert:* A woman I knew, who determined that she is a ONE and her husband a TWO (the root sin of the TWO is pride), told me that in their many years of marriage, the following happened again and again when they had an argument: She criticized him for his anger; he criticized her for her pride. This example shows how difficult it is for us to perceive our own sins, while we discover immediately those of other people.

6. *Andreas Ebert:* My grandmother, a ONE, was a bookseller. She threw herself completely into her work. Cleanliness, propriety, and order were her life. The disorder that we caused as children was abominable to her. Shortly before her death she said: "I always did everything right, I was never to blame!" Yet this apparent conformist risked her life under the Third Reich by hiding a Jewish

acquaintance. On this point her value system and her sense of "propriety" were so touched that she was capable of a courageous act.

7. *Andreas Ebert:* A friend of mine (SEVEN), married to a ONE woman, recently complained: "When we fight, the biggest problem is that she is *always* right. What she says is solid as a rock, while my arguments are impulsive and usually built on sand. I know it myself. But I would like to be right at least *once.*"

8. Robert L. Short, *The Gospel According to Peanuts* (New York, 1964), pp. 15–16.

9. Erik M. Erikson, *Young Man Luther* (New York, 1958), p. 58.

10. Ibid., p. 65.

11. Ibid., p. 158.

12. Ibid., pp. 205–6.

13. Each of the nine types has its own peculiar "integration energy" and "regression energy." These connections are marked by the lines and arrows that connect the numbers of the Enneagram with one another. The integration energy of the ONE is the SEVEN, the regression energy is the FOUR. This "arrow theory" is explained in detail in the third part of the book.

14. Thomas Merton, *Conjectures of a Guilty Bystander* (Garden City, N.Y., 1968), pp. 11–12.

Type TWO

1. See Dan Greenburg, *How to Be a Jewish Mother* (Los Angeles, 1964). The author stresses that "you don't have to be either Jewish or a mother to be a Jewish mother. An Irish waitress or an Italian barber could also be a Jewish mother"; quoted in Paul Watzlawick, *The Situation Is Hopeless but Not Serious: The Pursuit of Unhappiness* (New York, 1983), p. 16.

2. Wolfgang Schmidbauer, *Die hilflosen Helfer: Über die seelische Problematik der helfenden Berufe* (Reinbek, 1977).

3. Quoted in the Bavarian edition of the Evangelical Church songbook, p. 469.

4. Robin Norwood, *Women Who Love Too Much* (Los Angeles, 1985).

5. See Nogosek, *Nine Portraits of Jesus.* In the third part of our book, a separate section is devoted to the relationship between Jesus and the Enneagram.

6. *Andreas Ebert:* In her spare time a woman I know, who is obviously a TWO, models over and over again the image of a curled-up cat. She knows that in doing this she is depicting herself.

7. Heinrich E. Benedikt, *Die Kabbala als jüdisch-christlicher Einweihungsweg,* vol. 1: *Farbe, Zahl, Ton und Wort als Tore zu Seele und Geist* (Freiburg im Breisgau, 1985), p. 98.

8. On this point see the arrow theory in the third part of the book, especially p. 202.

9. The question of who composed the Gospel of John can not be discussed here. Even if it was not John himself, it is generally accepted that it goes back to

his followers, who looked at Jesus *with the eyes of John.* Of course our practice of putting together personality profiles from the often meager details about certain biblical persons is not, as a rule, historically solid. These character sketches, therefore, do not claim to match the "historical" form correctly. What we have here is rather those characteristic features that the authors of the Bible attached to certain figures. In this regard see too note 8 for type THREE.

10. From Hitler's speech of January 30, 1939, quoted in *Die Zeit,* January 27, 1989, p. 41.

11. Peter Schellenbaum, *Das Nein in der Liebe: Abgrenzung und Hingabe in der erotischen Beziehung* (Stuttgart, 1985.)

12. Barbro Bronsberg and Nina Vestlund, *Ausgebrannt: Die egoistische Aufopferung* (Munich, 1988).

13. Christian Feldmann, *Träume beginnen zu leben: Grosse Christen unseres Jahrhunderts* (Freiburg-Basel-Vienna, 1983), p. 76. Hereafter cited as Feldmann, *Träume).*

14. Ibid., pp. 78–79.

15. Ibid., p. 81.

16. Ibid., p. 86.

17. Ibid., p. 88.

18. Ibid., p. 94.

Type THREE

1. There seems to be a connection between bodily constitution and character type, as Ernst Kretschmer said in the 1920s. It would be worthwhile to pursue this conjecture systematically with respect to the Enneagram, something which has not yet been done.

2. The prototype of the unsuccessful THREE is Donald Duck. His value system is oriented to glory and success, but something always gets in the way: either his cousin, Gaston, a lucky devil who achieves success without striving for it — or his three nephews Huey, Louie, and Dewey, who are successful and competent young THREEs, must help him out of his mess.

3. Dante was influenced by the work of the Sufi master Ibn El-Arabi. According to Miguel Asin Palacios (*Islam and the Divine Comedy* [New York, 1926]) he "took over Ibn El-Arabi's literary work and crystallized it within a frame of reference that was acceptable to his age. In so doing, he robbed Ibn El-Arabi's message of its Sufi validity, and left only . . . an embalmed example of what to the modern mind almost amounts to piracy" (quoted from Idries Shah, *The Sufis* [Garden City, N.Y., 1964], p. 140) However that may be, it is in any case striking that the *Inferno, Purgatorio,* and *Paradiso* were each arranged into nine (!) stages by Dante. Dante himself explains his work as the troublesome path of a lost soul to salvation. The question of whether *The Divine Comedy* does not finally represent a literary version of the Enneagram would be worth a thorough investigation, which might also throw light on the future of the Enneagram.

4. M. Scott Peck, *People of the Lie: The Hope for Healing a Evil* (New York, 1983).

5. Heinrich E. Benedikt, *Die Kabbala als jüdisch-christlicher Einweihungsweg,* vol. 1: *Farbe, Zahl, Ton und Wort als Tore zu Seele und Geist* (Freiburg im Breisgau, 1985), p. 101.

6. Johannes Itten, *Kunst der Farbe* (Ravensburg, 1961/1970), p. 85.

7. In the view of the Old Testament, the life power that the "Shalom" brings: Health, long life, prosperity, happiness, success — everything, in other words, that the heart of a THREE desires.

8. The story of Jacob grew over the course of time out of many elements, in part very archaic. I take as my point of departure the final form of the story that was ultimately canonized. In his book *Geist und Materie* (Munich, 1988), pp. 226–32, Walter Hollenweger impressively traces the process of how the story of Jacob's wrestling by the Jabbok evolved. Hollenweger shows that even within the Bible the story was continually reinterpreted. Walter Wink correctly stresses: "It would be psychologizing to develop from the Jacob saga in Genesis a personality profile of the man Jacob. We simply cannot know to what extent legend and folk memory have colored or even created the traditions. We can legitimately inquire, however, into the psychological dynamics of the story *as we find it.* Here we are asking, not about Jacob, but the intentions of the storytellers: what they intend their hearers to understand, and how the story is designed to move the hearers" (Walter Wink, *Transforming Bible Study: A Leader's Guide* [Nashville, 1980], p. 163).

9. Isaac B. Singer, *Der Büsser* (Munich and Vienna, 1987), p. 8 (ET: *The Penitent* [New York, 1983]).

10. Ibid., p. 7.

11. Feldmann, *Träume,* p. 138.

12. Ibid., p. 139.

13. Ibid., p. 144.

14. Ibid., p. 151.

Type FOUR

1. See Idries Shah, *The Sufis* (Garden City, N.Y., 1964), pp. 99–100.

2. Novalis, "Heinrich von Ofterdingen," in *Gedichte, Romane* (Zurich, 1968), pp. 164–65. Novalis internalized the search for life fulfillment: "The secret path goes *inward.* Eternity with its worlds, the past and future, is in us or nowhere."

3. Palmer, p. 191.

4. Throughout his entire life the poet August Graf von Platen was in search of "salvation through form" and hence on the path from the Romantic to the Classic. The famous poem "Tristan" (1825) is stylistically completely classical; in this way the "romantic" theme of unfulfilled yearning is further heightened.

5. Especially instructive is his "Dairy of a Seducer" in *Either/Or* (Garden City, N.Y., 1959), pp. 297–440.

6. See Palmer, p. 177.

7. See ibid., p. 178.

8. Elisabeth Kübler-Ross, in *On Death and Dying* (New York, 1969) developed five phases of dying: denial, anger, bargaining, depression, and acceptance. The process that is necessary for the working through of early childhood privations can be described in the same five phases, as has been shown impressively by the American Jesuits Matthew and Dennis Linn in their book *Healing Life's Hurts: Healing Memories through the Five Stages of Forgiveness* (Mahwah, N.J., 1978). Letting traumatic memories die can lead to inner healing.

9. See David Dalton, *James Dean: The Mutant King* (New York, 1974).

10. Ernesto Cardenal and Dorothée Sölle, *Gebet für Marilyn Monroe: Meditations* (Wuppertal, 1984).

11. *Andreas Ebert:* A FOUR told me that as a child she was perfectly calm in the air-raid cellar while everyone else fell into fear and panic. She was able to flee from the real danger into a beautiful and safe dreamworld.

12. Benedikt, *Kabbala*, pp. 123, 126.

13. The FOUR belongs to those types that have a special intuitive gift. FOURs often feel safer in the world of dream images and symbols than in the real world.

14. Christian Feldmann, *Träume*, p. 277.

15. Ibid., p. 294.

Type FIVE

1. Wilhelm Weischedel, *Die philosophische Hintertreppe* (Munich, 1975), p. 70. Most of the information about the philosophers mentioned and cited in the course of this chapter comes from this excellent book, which is an introduction to the life and thought of thirty-four great philosophers in a bright yet serious way. A third to a half of them would in my opinion be considered FIVEs.

2. See ibid., pp. 90 ff.

3. Ibid., p. 116.

4. Ibid., p. 117.

5. Cited in ibid., p. 238.

6. Ibid., p. 274.

7. *Wörterbuch der Religionen*, Kröner's paperback edition, 3rd ed., 1976.

8. Wehr, *Wörterbuch der Esoterik*, p. 100.

9. See Weischedel, pp. 291 ff.

10. Abraham H. Maslow, *Psychologie des Seins* (Munich, 1973), p. 125 (ET: *Toward a Psychology of Being*, 2nd ed. [New York, 1968].

11. Friedrich Dürrenmatt, *Die Physiker* (Frankfurt, 1962.)

12. Palmer, p. 227.

13. Quoted in Ingrid Riedel, *Farben in Religion, Gesellschaft, Kunst, und Psychotherapie* (Stuttgart, 1983), p. 53.

Type SIX

1. Riso, p. 163.
2. See Palmer, pp. 255–57.
3. Karl Ledergerber has described three forms of the flight from fear: (1) *Forward flight* or *aggression* (as an example he cites Senator Joseph McCarthy, who in the 1950s "spread an atmosphere of fear, since he saw a disguised communist swearing fealty to Moscow in every other politician, intellectual, diplomat, and official"); (2) *Backward flight* or *renunciation of life* (e.g., animals that play dead; in this context Ledergerber speaks of "voluntary" stupefaction, regression, and depression); (3) *Flight to the sidelines* or *substitute actions* (compulsive acts, addictions, fear of purpose). All three forms of flight from fear are found in SIXes. Karl Ledergerber, *Keine Angst: vor der Angst — Ihre Überwindung durch Einsicht und Vertrauen* (Freiburg im Breisgau, 1978), pp. 102–15.
4. See Paul Watzlawick, *Anleitung zum Unglücklichsein* (Munich, 1983), pp. 37–38.
5. Horst-Eberhard Richter, "Fortschrittsmythos und Unsterblichkeitswahn," in Helmut A. Müller, ed., *Naturwissenschaft und Glaube* (Bern-Munich-Vienna, 1988), pp. 302–15.
6. Thomas Meyer, *Fundamentalismus: Aufstand gegen die Moderne* (Reinbek, 1989).
7. Walter Wink has explored the interaction between "projection" and "introjection" that leads to the emergence of hostile images. On the one hand we project our own unacknowledged and unaccepted "shadows" onto others. But at the same time in direct confrontation we also absorb the negative energies of others: Without noticing it, we transform ourselves into what we are fighting against. We become what we hate (Walter Wink, *Violence and Nonviolence in South Africa: Jesus' Third Way* (Philadelphia, 1987), p. 64.
8. Fyodor Michailovich Dostoyevsky, *The Brothers Karamazov*, trans. Constance Garnet (New York, 1950), p. 298.
9. Umberto Eco, *The Name of the Rose*, trans. William Weaver (New York, 1983), p. 474.
10. Tilmann Moser, *Gottesvergiftung* (Frankfurt, 1976), pp. 15–38.
11. Raymond Franz, a former member of the executive board of the Jehovah's Witnesses in New York, left this "theocratic organization" because he couldn't go along with the irregularities at the top, which contradicted its claims to infallibility. With a care and precision that only SIXes have at their disposal, he collected the incriminating evidence and documented the charges in a watertight case. His book has the significant title, *Crisis of Conscience: The Struggle Between Loyalty to God and Loyalty to One's Religion* (Atlanta, 1983).
12. From Luise Rinser's piece in *Reden über das eigene Land: Deutschland*, vol. 5 (Munich, 1987), pp. 90–91.
13. See Benedikt, *Kabbala*, p. 146.
14. See the Grimm brothers' story of Rumpelstiltskin, where as soon as the king's daughter learns the name of the goblin, he can no longer destroy her life.

15. Studies have shown that the left half of the brain, which governs the right side of the body, is in charge of analytic and abstract thought, while the right half of the brain "thinks" in images and symbols instead, and is "synthetically" oriented. Western society, in its schools, for example, gives much more encouragement to the left side of the brain, so that the right side gets stunted — at least, it has been charged, among Germans. A good introduction to this "split brain theory" and its consequences for the interpretation of the Bible can be found in Walter Wink, *Transforming Bible Study*.

16. Christian Feldmann, *Träume*, p. 29.

17. Ibid., p. 35.

18. Ibid., p. 39.

Type SEVEN

1. The refusal of many men to grow up is the target of Dan De Kiley's book, *The Peter Pan Syndrome* (New York, 1984).

2. In a critical confrontation with Western consumerist society and in connection with the Francsican tradition, Richard Rohr has sketched out a "spirituality of subtraction." In a culture that equates a "good life" with "always getting more" the call "to let go" is a necessary challenge. Rohr invites his listeners to "subtract" everything that keeps us from standing by the side of the cosmic Christ in a hungry and suffering world. In so doing he points both to our jammed "interior world" as well as to our material prosperity: *Letting Go: A Spirituality of Subtraction* (eight audiocassettes, St. Anthony Messenger Press, 1615 Republic Street, Cincinnati, OH 45210).

3. "I always stop only when I've had too much. At meals I'm really not satisfied until I'm overstuffed — and actually *dis*-satisfied with this feeling of fullness." A SEVEN.

4. Fifth maxim of the "catechism" in Epicurus, *Von der Überwindung der Furcht* (Munich, 1983), p. 59. On Epicurus see Wilhelm Weischedel, *Die philosophische Hintertreppe* (Munich, 1975), pp. 60–66.

5. Quoted in Weischedel, *Hintertreppe*, p. 64.

6. See Norman Vincent Peale's *The Power of Positive Thinking*. This approach assumes that our thoughts have a substantial influence on our whole condition. By deliberately thinking "positive thoughts" I have the potential of becoming happy, content, and successful. A whole wave of books based on this approach has swept over the market in recent years.

7. Palmer, p. 276.

8. Eric Carle's delightful children's book *The Very Hungry Caterpillar* describes the process that SEVENs go through, from their unredeemed insatiability until they actually achieve "ease of being." For seven (!) days the caterpillar eats its way through enormous amounts of tasty things without getting full. Every day it has to have more. The result is a bellyache. Only after a time of com-

plete rest in the ugly cocoon does it become metamorphosed into a wonderfully beautiful butterfly.

9. Quoted from Stefan Siegert and Niels Frédéric Hoffmann, *Mozart: Die einzige Bilderbiographie* (Hamburg, 1988), p. 48. This biography, with its splendid anecdotes and caricatures of Mozart, is a "must" for SEVENs who want to be informed about their musical patron saint. The authors themselves must be SEVENs.

10. Ibid., p. 152.

11. Karl Barth, *Der reiche Jüngling*, edited and introduced by Peter Eicher (Munich, 1986), p. 13.

12. Ibid., pp. 17–18.

Type EIGHT

1. Kenneth Walker, quoted in Palmer, p. 14. On Gurdjieff see Palmer, pp. 10–24.

2. See Ruth C. Cohn and Alfred Fahrau, *Gelebte Geschichte der Psychotherapie* (Stuttgart, 1984), pp. 300–304.

3. Frings Keyes, p. 65.

4. Ibid.

5. For example, *Death in the Afternoon* (New York, 1932) and *The Dangerous Summer* (New York, 1985).

6. See Walter H. Nelson, *Ernest Hemingway: 100 Blitzlichter aus seinem Leben* (Munich and Esslingen, 1971), p. 23.

7. Ibid., p. 56.

8. Ibid., p. 78.

9. Ibid., p. 109.

10. Kenneth S. Lynn, *Hemingway* (New York, 1988).

11. Frings Keyes, p. 64.

12. A series of Latin American liberation theologians has recently taken up the theme of machismo and begun to give it a psychological and theological elaboration. See Elsa Tamez, ed., *Against Machismo* (Bloomington, Ind., 1987).

13. The following ideas are based on an article by Johanna Haberer, "Befreiung braucht Poesie: Auf den Spuren der Sprachgewalt biblischer Frauen," Sunday paper of the Lutheran Church in Bavaria, March 26, 1989, pp. 16–17.

14. The Hebrew Bible calls "Judges" those figures who before the founding of the kingdom of Israel are called by Yahweh in emergencies to lead the people into battle. After the victory, which comes about through divine intervention, they generally retire to private life.

15. Gerhard von Rad, *Old Testament Theology*, 1:333.

16. Frings Keyes, p. 66. In the following section see the discussion of King David as an EIGHT. Two great novels about David illustrate David's EIGHT energy and the power politics of his reign: Stefan Heym, *Der König David Bericht*, 10th ed. (Frankfurt, 1987), and Joseph Heller, *God Knows* (New York, 1984).

17. Frings Keyes, ibid.

18. Quoted in Christian Feldmann, *Träume*, p. 110.

19. Ibid., p. 115.

20. Ibid., p. 119.

21. On the theory and practice of nonviolent resistance in the spirit of Martin Luther King see Walter Wink, *Violence and Nonviolence in South Africa.*

Type NINE

1. *Der Papalagi: Die Reden des Südseehäuptlings Tuiavii aus Tiavea* (Munich, 1977), pp. 64–65.

2. *Andreas Ebert:* A NINE who is a friend of mine describes the tragicomic side of this situation: "Sometimes it takes me hours to fall asleep at night, because I struggle with the pillow and the coverlet until I find the right position. Sometimes I fall asleep then simply from exhaustion."

3. Evagrius Ponticus, *Capita practica ad Anatolium,* quoted from Anselm Grün, *Der Umgang mit dem Böse* (Münsterschwarzach, 1979), pp. 37–38.

4. See Palmer, p. 360.

5. Ivan A. Goncharov, *Oblomow,* trans. from the Russian by Joseph Hahn, Afterword by Rudolf Neuhäuser (Munich, 1980).

6. Rudolf Neuhäser in the Afterword, ibid., p. 665.

7. Ibid., p. 668.

8. Tatiana Goricheva, *Die Kraft christlicher Torheit: Meine Erfahrungen* (Freiburg-Basel-Vienna, 1985), p. 97.

9. Ibid., p. 98.

10. Franz Xaver Kroetz, *Oblomow* (Munich, 1989). The weary applause and the faces of many theatergoers on opening night in Munich suggest that they rediscovered themselves in the "successful" upwardly-mobile characters Stolz and Olga.

11. Heathcote Williams, *Kontinent der Wale* (Frankfurt/Main, 1988.)

12. Ibid., p. 55.

13. Ibid., p. 50.

14. The Book of Jonah is not a historical account, but a theological parable about the mission of the people of Israel to proclaim God's salvific will to all nations.

15. Palmer, p. 377.

16. This is the heading in Christian Feldmann, *Träume*, p. 186.

17. Quoted in ibid., p. 209.

18. Ibid., pp. 197, 200.

PART III: INNER DIMENSIONS

1. Wagner, p. 104.

2. A considerably more detailed presentation can be found in Riso in connection with his description of each of the types. In contrast to us, however, Riso works from the assumption that every type has only *one* wing.

3. See Beesing, Nogosek, and O'Leary, pp. 199–210.

4. Riso, p. 101.

5. Ibid., p. 185.

6. Palmer, pp. 44–45.

7. Robert J. Nogosek, C.S.C., has found that the different sides of Jesus can be discovered with the Enneagram. He has devoted a whole book to this subject, *Nine Portraits of Jesus* (Denville, N.J., 1987). We are indebted to this book for a series of insights and biblical references that have not been individually annotated.

8. Ibid., p. 39.

9. Kallistos Ware, *Aufstieg zu Gott: Glaube und geistliches Leben nach ostkirchlicher Überlieferung* (Freiburg, 1986).

10. See Walter Wink, *Violence and Nonviolence in South Africa.*

11. See the detailed presentation in Metz and Burchill, *Enneagram and Prayer.*

12. Bennett, p. 132.

Index

TYPE	SELF-IMAGE	AVOIDANCE	TEMPTATION	QUALITIES OF CHRIST	OUR FATHER
ONE	I AM RIGHT	VEXATION	PERFECTION	TEACHING, TOLERANCE, PATIENCE	WHO ART IN HEAVEN
TWO	I HELP	SUPPRESSING NEEDS	HELPING OTHERS	CARE, COMPASSION SOLIDARITY	HALLOWED BE THY NAME
THREE	I AM SUCCESSFUL	FAILURE	EFFICIENCY	AMBITION, ENERGY, VISION	THY KINGDOM COME
FOUR	I AM DIFFERENT	ORDINARINESS	AUTHENTICITY	CREATIVITY, SENSITIVITY, SIMPLICITY	THY WILL BE DONE ON EARTH AS IT IS IN HEAVEN
FIVE	I SEE THROUGH	EMPTINESS	KNOWLEDGE	DISTANCE, SOBRIETY, WISDOM	GIVE US THIS DAY OUR DAILY BREAD
SIX	I DO MY DUTY	DOUBT	STRIVING FOR SECURITY	FIDELITY, OBEDIENCE, TRUST	AND FORGIVE US OUR TRESPASSES AS WE FORGIVE OUR THOSE WHO TRESPASS AGAINST US
SEVEN	I AM HAPPY	PAIN	IDEALISM	FESTIVTY, LIGHT-HEARTEDNESS, PAIN	AND LEAD US NOT INTO TEMPTATION, BUT DELIVER US FROM EVIL
EIGHT	I AM STRONG	HELPLESSNESS WEAKNESS SUBORDINATION	JUSTICE	CONFRONTATION, CLARITY, AUTHORITY	FOR THINE IS THE KINGDOM AND THE POWER AND THE GLORY FOREVER AND EVER
NINE	I AM CONTENT	CONFLICT	SELF-DEPRECATION	COMPOSURE, PEACEABLENESS, LOVE	AMEN. OUR FATHER

253

TYPE	ANIMALS	COUNTRY	COLOR	DEFENSE MECHANISM	PITFALL	ROOT SIN
ONE	TERRIER, ANT, BEE	RUSSIA	SILVER	REACTION FORMATION	OVER-CRITICALNESS	ANGER
TWO	DONKEY, CAT, PUPPY	ITALY	RED	REPRESSION	OBLIGINGNESS (FLATTERY)	PRIDE
THREE	CHAMELEON, PEACOCK, EAGLE	U. S. A.	YELLOW	IDENTIFICATION	VANITY (SUPERFICIALITY)	UNTRUTH (DECEIT)
FOUR	BASSET HOUND, DOVE, OYSTER, BLACK HORSE	FRANCE	BRIGHT VIOLET	ARTIFICIAL SUBLIMATION	DEPRESSION (MELANCHOLY)	ENVY
FIVE	OWL, FOX, HAMSTER	GREAT BRITAIN	BLUE	WITHDRAWAL (SEGMENTATION)	AVARICE	GREED
SIX	HARE, DEER, MOUSE, WOLF, GERMAN SHEPHERD	GERMANY	BEIGE	PROJECTION	COWARDICE/ RECKLESSNESS	FEAR (ANXIETY)
SEVEN	MONKEY, BUTTERFLY	IRELAND, BRAZIL	GREEN	RATIONALIZATION	SCHEMING	INTEMPERANCE (GLUTTONY)
EIGHT	RHINOCEROS, RATTLESNAKE, TIGER, BULL	SPAIN, OPPRESSED NATIONS	BLACK & WHITE	DENIAL	REVENGE	SHAMELESSNESS (LUST)
NINE	SLOTH, ELEPHANT, DOLPHIN, WHALE	MEXICO	GOLD	NARCOSIS (ADDICTION)	LAZINESS (COMFORT)	LAZINESS

254

TYPE	INVITATION	FRUIT OF THE SPIRIT	STYLE OF SPEAKING	SEXUAL SUBTYPE	SOCIAL SUBTYPE	SELF-PRESERVING SUBTYPE
ONE	GROWTH	CHEERFUL TRANQUILLITY (PATIENCE)	TEACHING MORALIZING	JEALOUSY	NON-ADAPTABILITY	ANXIETY
TWO	FREEDOM (GRACE)	HUMILITY	FLATTERING ADVISING	SEDUCTION/ASSAULT	AMBITION	PRIVILEGE
THREE	HOPE (GOD'S WILL)	TRUTHFULNESS (HONESTY)	WOOING INSPIRING	MASCULINITY/FEMININITY	PRESTIGE	SECURITY
FOUR	ORIGINALITY (UNION WITH GOD)	HARMONY	LYRICAL LAMENTING	COMPETITION	SHAME	RESISTANCE
FIVE	WISDOM (GOD'S DISPENSATION)	OBJECTIVITY	EXPLAINING SYSTEMATIZING	CONFIDENCE	TOTEMS	RETREAT
SIX	FAITH (TRUST)	COURAGE	WARNING LIMITING	STRENGTH/BEAUTY	DUTY	WARMTH
SEVEN	COOPERATION WITH GOD	SOBER JOY	GARRULOUS STORY-TELLING	SUSCEPTIBILITY	UNSELFISHNESS	DEFENSE
EIGHT	MERCY	INNOCENCE	CHALLENGING UNMASKING	STRIVING FOR POSSESSION/DEVOTION	FRIENDSHIPS	SATISFACTORY SURVIVAL
NINE	UNCONDITIONAL LOVE	ACTION	MONOTONOUS RAMBLING	UNION	PARTICIPATION	APPETITE